Chess: The Art of Logical Thinking

From the First Move to the Last

Neil McDonald

First published in the United Kingdom in 2004 by
Batsford
10 Southcombe Street
London W14 0RA

An imprint of Anova Books Company Ltd

ISBN 9780713488944

A CIP catalogue record for this book is available from the
British Library.

15 14 13 12
10 9 8 7 6 5

Printed by Bell & Bain Ltd., Glasgow

This book can be ordered direct from the publisher at the website:
www.anovabooks.com, or try your local bookshop

Distributed in the United States and Canada by Sterling Publishing
Co., 387 Park Avenue South, New York, NY 10016, USA

Contents

Introduction

*Chess is the art that expresses the
science of logic.*

Mikhail Botvinnik

When you sit down to play a
game of chess you are in command
of exactly the same eight pieces and
eight pawns that Capablanca,
Fischer and Kasparov have used to
create masterpieces of grand
strategy and tactical precision. Their
pieces didn't have heightened
powers nor more fertile soil on
which to work their stratagems: just
the same 64 squares, 32 white and
32 black.

The conclusion is obvious: there
is a dynamic potential concealed in
your pieces that could be released if
only you had the right skill and
insight. This book will help you
acquire the necessary mastery by
guiding you through thirty of the
greatest games of the modern age.

Because every single move of
every single game is annotated you
get to see both sides of the picture.
This is absolutely vital if you wish
to understand what really happened.
Take Game 23 for example. Karpov
builds up his positional advantage,
step by step, and wins: yes, the
evidence is all there. But what was
Kasparov doing in the meantime?
Why did he let it happen to him?

Chess annotations, like history in
general, are normally written from
the winner's point of view. The
unrealized hopes and dreams of the
loser are allowed to vanish forever.
But this is to miss half of the story
as a big part of chess success is
based on restraint and prevention of
the opponent's plans. Therefore it is
vital to consider what didn't happen
as well as what did occur.

So what then is the key to
mastering chess strategy? First of
all, it cannot be an infallible formula
or some other secret known only to
great players, as otherwise
Kasparov, Anand and Korchnoi
wouldn't figure on the losing side of
games in this book!

If you pressed me to name the
three most important things that a
chess strategy should provide, it
would be a secure king, a sound
pawn structure and an efficient
co-ordination of the pieces.
Inextricably linked with these is
control of the centre squares – d4,
d5, e4 and e5. If a player has control
of the centre it means his pieces are
more active than his opponent's,
and this gives him the initiative –
the ability to attack.

As well as this psychological
factors should be considered. There
is an eternal dilemma when
choosing a move: should you seek
safety or adventure; play solidly
or creatively; grasp a fleeting

opportunity or remain in security? When there is no obvious right or wrong, the character of the player has a major impact on the decision taken. This can be for both good and bad as the games of even the greatest players are frequently won and lost by impulsive or inspired decisions. Sometimes the urge to win fills a player with fabulous creativity; at other times it over-rides his capacity to find moves that suit the position rather than his irrational hopes and he suffers disaster.

Nevertheless, whatever your temperament and style, you cannot fail to improve your understanding and results if you familiarize yourself with the strategy and tactics of top class players.

I hope you enjoy playing through the games in this book, which have been chosen for their beauty as well as their instructional value.

Neil McDonald
Gravesend,
February 2004

How to read the moves in this book

It takes just a few minutes to learn algebraic notation and then you can play through any recorded game in a chess book or magazine. You can even write down your own masterpieces!

Every piece is given its own letter (or figurine): the rook is R (♖), the knight N (♘), the bishop B (♗), the queen Q (♕) and the king K (♔). By this logic, the letter for pawn should be P (♙) but in fact no shorthand is used for the pawn: if a move has no letter in front of it, you should just assume it is a pawn move. It certainly saves having to write down P or ♙ a lot of times.

As well as every piece, every square on the board has a unique name, which consists of a letter and a number.

8	a8	b8	c8	d8	e8	f8	g8	h8
7	a7	b7	c7	d7	e7	f7	g7	h7
6	a6	b6	c6	d6	e6	f6	g6	h6
5	a5	b5	c5	d5	e5	f5	g5	h5
4	a4	b4	c4	d4	e4	f4	g4	h4
3	a3	b3	c3	d3	e3	f3	g3	h3
2	a2	b2	c2	d2	e2	f2	g2	h2
1	a1	b1	c1	d1	e1	f1	g1	h1
	a	b	c	d	e	f	g	h

The numbers rise from 1 to 8 as you go up the board counting from the starting position of the white pieces. The letters meanwhile go across the board left to right from a-h. So White's rooks begin the game in the corner squares a1 and h1, Black's rooks in the corner squares a8 and h8.

Thus the square e4 is where the number 4 rising up the board intersects with the letter e running across the board. It is on the fourth row up the board, and five rows from the left hand side of the board. Therefore the shorthand 1 e4 means that on his first move, White moves the pawn in front of his king two squares up the board, from e2 to e4; similarly 1...e5 indicates that Black on his first move has moved the pawn in front of his king two squares forward, from e7 to e5. Then 2 ♘f3 signifies that on the second move White moves his knight to the third row, from g1 to f3, and so on.

Remember that the counting is from White's starting side of the board: so the white queen begins the game on d1 and the black queen on d8.

Sometimes for the sake of clarity it is necessary to indicate the square the piece came from. Thus if White has knights on c3 and g1, which can both go to e2, it isn't enough to say White played ♘e2: you have to write ♘ge2 to indicate that White's knight, which was on the g file, went to e2 (Or ♘ce2 if he moved the other knight there).

If a piece captures an enemy piece or pawn the sign x is used, for example ♗xe5 indicates the bishop captures whatever piece or pawn is on e5. If a move gives a check, the sign + is used; and castles kingside is indicated by 0-0, while castles queenside is 0-0-0.

If Black resigns the game the shorthand is 1-0 (symbolic of one point to White, nothing to Black); while if White resigns it is 0-1. A draw is ½-½ – both players get half a point each.

A good move is given an exclamation mark: ! A bad move is a question mark: ? A brilliant move is !! and a terrible move is ?? A dubious move is ?! and an interesting move is !? Some annotators become twisted in their thoughts and indulge in oddities such as ?!? or !! (?)

Now you are fully prepared to read the book!

1 Classical Chess Thinking: 1 e4 e5

The d and e pawns are the only ones to be moved in the early part of the game.

Steinitz

Bring all your pieces out! Give them scope! Occupy the centre squares!

Tarrasch

The quotations above, from two of the greatest chess minds of the 19th century, exemplify the *classical* approach to chess strategy. In the opening phase this dictates that no time is to be wasted: every move has either to develop a piece or clear a line for the development of a piece. In fact, no piece is to be moved more than once in the opening if it can be at all helped.

The emphasis is on controlling the centre by occupying it with pawns, ideally on d4 and e4 if you are White, or on e5 and d5 if Black.

Meanwhile the king is to be castled on the kingside as quickly as possible.

This is all excellent advice! It is by no means the whole story: in fact we soon realize that it is not only possible but necessary at times to break the laws of classical chess. They represent an idealized view of the nature of the chess struggle that often proves impractical in a real game.

Nevertheless, anything that warns us against wasting time with frivolous pawn moves or aimless excursions with the pieces is to be applauded. It also puts the emphasis on the centre – those four magical squares right in the centre of the board. If material is equal and you control the squares d4, d5, e4 and e5 you will most likely have a winning advantage. That is as true nowadays as it was in 1880, and will be for as long as chess is played.

Classical chess thinking is revealed most clearly in games that begin 1 e4 e5 – the most ancient way to open a game of chess, and still one of the best. Let's begin by seeing how Anatoly Karpov, the 12th World Champion, applies the rules of classical chess first postulated by Wilhelm Steinitz – the 1st World Champion. As will be seen, 'classical' doesn't mean 'dull', as soon Korchnoi is facing unstoppable checkmate!

Game One
A.Karpov - V.Korchnoi
World Championship,
Baguio City 1978
Ruy Lopez

1   e4

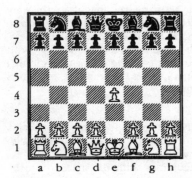

The most active move on the board. In a battle it is good to have control of the high ground, so that you can pour down fire on the heads of those attacking you. In chess the high ground is the centre, and by advancing this pawn White takes control of two important centre squares: d5 and f5.

Not only that, but White opens up a diagonal for both his queen and king's bishop. It is no wonder that 1 e4 has always been the favourite of those looking to play an aggressive, fighting game.

1   ...   e5

White's first move is so good that Black decides to copy it. Apart from the knights all the pieces are immobile at the start of a game, completely entombed behind a row of pawns, so in the opening there is a race going on to be the first player

to get out all his forces. If you lag too far behind you might find yourself seriously outnumbered when the battle begins.

2   ♘f3

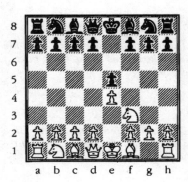

The best move on the board! White

♦ develops his knight to a safe, centre square

♦ attacks the pawn on e5

♦ is now one move nearer to castling his king into safety on the kingside.

2   ...   ♘c6

A very economical way to meet the threat to the e5 pawn. Black develops his queen's knight and so doesn't fall behind in development. This is a much more efficient approach than 2...f6 which not only fails to develop anything but weakens the kingside, or 2...♛e7, which shuts in the king's bishop and leaves the queen with a laborious defensive duty.

3   ♗b5

White continues his straight-forward, no-nonsense approach to development. He clears the way for castling and puts pressure on the knight which defends the e5 pawn.

3   ...   a6!

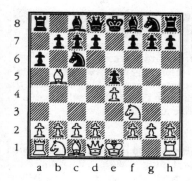

Black takes time out from developing to attack the white bishop. This is known as Morphy's Defence after the brilliant American player Paul Morphy who was the best player in the world in the 1850s.

4   ♗a4

White's attacking energy would be dissipated after 4 ♗xc6 dxc6 5 ♘xe5, when Black can regain the pawn with 5...♕d4! 6 ♘f3 ♕xe4+ and White will lose the right to castle after either 7 ♔f1 or 7 ♕e2 ♕xe2+ 8 ♔xe2. Therefore White retreats the bishop and keeps the idea of ♗xc6 as a long term threat. Here we see that Black hasn't lost time with 3...a6: on the contrary, he has given himself the extra option of b7-b5 if the pressure on c6 becomes too acute.

4   ...   ♘f6

Black brings out his other knight with an attack on e4.

5   0-0!

White could defend his e pawn with a move like 5 ♘c3 or 5 d3, but it is more attractive to keep his options open by castling immediately – after all, every plan he might choose requires him to castle kingside, but the development of his queenside can be amended for the better according to what Black plays on the next move.

Castling leaves the e4 pawn undefended, but such is White's pressure along the e file and against c6 that he is bound to regain the pawn sooner or later.

5   ...   ♘xe4

The Open Variation of the Ruy Lopez. Black has no intention of holding onto the pawn but instead hopes to gain activity for his minor pieces by getting rid of the pawn that controls the d5 and f5 squares.

6   d4!

The correct way for White to increase his initiative. There is no rush to regain the pawn; instead he would have given up his strong attacking light-squared bishop for no good reason after 6 ♖e1 ♘c5 7 ♗xc6 dxc6 8 ♖xe5+ ♗e7.

6   ...   b5

Black decides it is the right moment to block White's idea of ♗xc6. Snatching another pawn in his undeveloped state would be fraught with peril: 6...exd4 7 ♖e1 d5 8 ♘xd4 and White has the double threat of 9 ♘xc6 and 9 f3, winning material in either case.

7   ♗b3

The bishop has to retreat but it now has a good view of f7 – the weakest square in Black's position.

7   ...   d5!

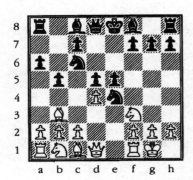

Black returns the pawn in order to:

♦ shut out the white bishop

♦ support the knight on e4

♦ open the diagonal for the queen's bishop.

8   dxe5

White regains his pawn and can be pleased at having emerged from the opening with a little space advantage: the pawn on e5 can be used as the spearhead for a kingside attack.

8   ...   ♗e6

The threat of 9 ♗xd5 had to be met, and if it can be done whilst developing a piece, then so much the better!

9   ♘bd2

White develops and challenges the black knight which is sitting on an excellent centre square. A horrible mistake would be 9 ♘c3? as after 9...♘xc3 10 bxc3 White's queenside pawns are inert and the bishop on b3 finds itself unable to move anywhere.

9   ...   ♘c5

Black could have continued developing with 9...♗c5, but preferred not to have his pawns broken up in the unclear variation 10 ♘xe4 dxe4 11 ♗xe6 fxe6 12 ♘g5. Therefore the knight retreats and keeps the tension in the centre.

10   c3

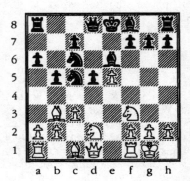

White contests the d4 square and prepares to retreat his bishop to c2 where it would enjoy an open diagonal.

It is a good moment to sum up the outcome of the opening phase.

Classical opening law dictates that you should:

♦ bring out the minor pieces as quickly as possible

♦ castle within the first five or so moves

♦ only move a piece once in the opening.

So far we have seen an exemplary display of classical chess by the World Champion.

White's play has been direct and forceful: every move has developed a piece or opened fresh lines of attack and put pressure on his opponent's defences. He has castled as quickly as possible and only moved one piece twice: the bishop when it was attacked on move three.

Meanwhile Korchnoi has brought out three of his minor pieces and strayed from rapid development only to take the e4 pawn and cause discomfort to the white bishop: no complaints can be made about this.

10   ...   g6?

This move however belongs more to the dynamic school of chess: in King's Indian style Black prepares ♗g7 to attack the e5 pawn. A very worthy idea, but it proves a dangerous loss of time. The solid, classical move was 10...♗e7 followed by 11...0-0 when Black has completed his development with a safe game.

Note that 10...♘xb3 isn't a good idea here, despite the fact that Black acquires the two bishops. The point is that the centre is congested with pawns, so that having the two bishops isn't an appreciable advantage; and even worse, after 11 ♘xb3 followed by 12 ♗e3 White

has a grip on the centre dark squares. Black has to be careful about handing over the c5 square to White as it represents a nasty hole in his pawn structure.

11   ♕e2

Karpov prepares an excellent pawn sacrifice to defeat Black's plan.

11   ...   ♗g7

Now Black only needs one more move to castle kingside and he will have a good position: his idea of putting the bishop on g7 would be justified.

12   ♘d4!

White offers the e pawn in order to clear the way for the f pawn to run at the black kingside and split it in half.

12   ...   ♘xe5

Korchnoi prefers to undergo a kingside attack rather than decline the offer with 12...♘xd4 13 cxd4 ♘xb3 14 ♘xb3. In that case White would have a clear winning plan: double the rooks on the c file, add in ♕c2 if necessary, and win the weakling on c7. But a better chance was 12...♛d7 holding firm in the centre.

13   f4

One of the good features of pawns is that they are cheap and disposable compared to the major pieces: therefore if they lunge at an opponent's piece it always has to give way. This makes them irresistible attacking weapons. Indeed, it could be said that hardly any attacking plan can succeed without the help of the pawns at some stage.

13   ...   ♞c4

The knight chooses a square where it blocks the white bishop on b3.

14   f5!

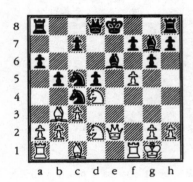

The battering ram finally strikes the black kingside and leaves it permanently splintered.

14   ...   gxf5

Eliminating the charging pawn is the only way to avoid immediate disaster.

15   ♞xf5

White's attack flows nicely as the white knight, supported by the queen and rook, makes a formidable replacement for the pawn.

15   ...   ♖g8

Korchnoi concedes that the kingside will never be a safe retreat for his king from the perils of the centre. He therefore makes a virtue out of necessity by defending the bishop with his rook: if White's onslaught falters he may begin a strong attack of his own down the g file.

16   ♞xc4

In response Karpov clears the way to bring reinforcements into the battle with gain of time by exchanging off knights.

16   ...   dxc4

When there is a choice of recaptures with a pawn, classical thinking dictates that you should retake towards the centre, which here indicates 16...bxc4. However, Korchnoi has a definite plan in mind: he wants the d file to be open so that his queen supports the knight next move when it goes to d3. He also hopes that in the future he might be able to play ♗d5 when the bishop would join in a counterattack against g2.

17 &c2

The bishop has to retreat but now has a useful role in fighting for the important d3 square.

17 ... ♘d3

Black's counterplay begins to look impressive: his knight enjoys a beautiful centre post and all his other minor pieces are fairly active, as is the rook on g8; but the logic of the position is against him as he cannot easily bring his queen's rook into the game, and his king is still sitting uneasily in the centre. With his next move Karpov speeds up his development.

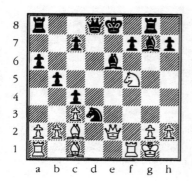

18 &h6!

Now strategically speaking 18...&xh6 19 ♘xh6 would be a lucrative transaction for White: he exchanges off a bishop that was doing nothing for one that was guarding the dark squares around the black king. And from a tactical point of view the exchange would leave Black struggling to find a good move as besides the obvious 20 ♘xg8 he would be facing 20 ♘xf7! breaking up the black king's cover.

18 ... &f8

The bishop retreats, so that after 19 &xf8 ♔xf8 the black king would at least be out of the firing line of the white queen and the bishop on e6 consequently freed from the pin.

19 ♖ad1!

A methodical move which brings into play White's last undeveloped piece.

Black cannot return the compliment as the rook on a8 isn't easy to activate. Therefore it is no surprise that White will have a marked advantage in firepower when the tactical combat begins.

19 ... ♛d5

A strong entrance by the black queen, who is evidently dreaming of mate on g2.

20 &xd3!

An essential exchange: if White paused for even a move then 20...0-0-0! follows when suddenly Black has an excellent game – his problem rook on a8 is strongly centralized in support of the wonder knight on d3.

20 ... cxd3

Black recaptures with a heavy heart, as the opening of the d file will mean that his king will be forever cut off from the safety of the queenside.

21   ♖xd3

At last White has regained his pawn and in doing so has maintained all his attacking chances.

21   ...   ♕c6

The queen must retreat as if 21...♖xg2+? 22 ♕xg2 ♕xd3 loses a rook to 23 ♕xa8+.

22   ♗xf8

Now the defender of Black's dark square holes on e7, f8 and g7 is put to death.

22   ...   ♕b6+

A necessary check as Black would lose a piece after 22...♔xf8 23 ♘d4 ♕b6 24 ♕xe6.

23   ♔h1

The white king can sit in perfect safety on this square and watch gleefully the suffering of his opposite number.

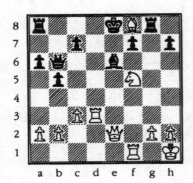

23   ...   ♔xf8

After 23...♖xf8 a clean kill is 24 ♕f3! – hitting the rook on a8 – 24...♖d8 25 ♘g7+ ♔e7 26 ♕f6 mate.

24   ♕f3!

As in the variation above White exploits the undefended rook on a8 to decisively strengthen his attack along the f file.

24   ...   ♖e8

All the black pieces are now clustered around their king, but they cannot prevent disaster as the dark squares are riddled with holes.

25   ♘h6

The attack on the rook on g8 wins time to put lethal pressure on the f7 square.

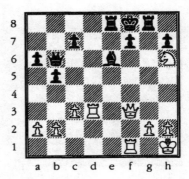

25   ...   ♖g7

If Black prefers 25...♖g6 then White can reply 26 ♘xf7, but much stronger is 26 ♕xf7+!! ♗xf7 27 ♖xf7, when the rook and knight have combined to force a neat mate.

After the game move Black has added another defender to f7. The question is, does White have a way to alter the ratio of forces attacking/defending f7 in his favour?

Every White piece is on an optimum attacking square and the target is clear: to mate the black king. But the final breakthrough will require some imagination and attacking finesse.

26 ⟶d7!!

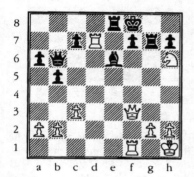

The star move.

26 ... ⟶b8

After this f7 collapses, but on 26...♗xd7 27 ♕xf7+ ⟶xf7 28 ⟶xf7 is a mate that is familiar from the variation above.

27 ♘xf7!

The triumph of White's strategy.

27 ... ♗xd7

If 27...♗xf7 28 ⟶xf7+ ♔g8 29 ⟶f8+ ⟶xf8 30 ♕xf8 mate.

28 ♘d8+! 1-0

Wherever Black moves his king, it is mate with 29 ♕f8 next move.

Game Two
R.Hubner - L.Portisch
Brussels 1986
Ruy Lopez

Among top players of the latter half of the 20th century the German

Grandmaster Robert Hubner has a strict, logical style that is an embodiment of the classical chess precepts popularized by his compatriot Tarrasch. Here he outplays Lajos Portisch, a Hungarian Grandmaster himself famed for his depth of positional understanding.

1 e4

Just as Dracula would be helpless if he were unable to escape from his coffin, or a butterfly could never emerge unless it discarded its caterpillar husk, so too the pieces cannot at all perform unless the pawns are first moved out of the way. By this reasoning 1 e4 is an excellent move: both the queen and bishop see daylight. The same effect could be achieved with 1 e3, but by moving the pawn two squares White gives himself more space behind which he can amass his forces. And more space = more activity = more chances to attack = more chances to mate!

1 ... e5

Imitation is the highest form of flattery. Black makes no attempt to imbalance the game with 1...c5, or indulge in trench warfare with 1...e6: he is happy to copy White, knowing that no other first move offers his pieces so much freedom.

2 ♘f3

A sound developing move that contains a threat is the epitome of good opening play. Now Black must think about guarding the e5 pawn.

2 ... ♘c6

This meets the threat without breaking his stride towards a harmonious opening set up.

3   &b5

White completes his kingside development and at the same time harasses the knight which is the guardian of the e5 pawn.

3   ...   a6

Sometimes the best answer to a threat is to ignore it! Black positively encourages White to take on c6 as he has seen that after 4 &xc6 dxc6 5 ♘xe5 ♛d4! the double attack on the knight and e4 pawn will mean that he regains his pawn with a highly comfortable position after 6 ♘f3 ♛xe4+.

4   &a4

Does it mean that White's opening plan has failed as he is forced to retreat the bishop? Not at all! Although the immediate 4 &xc6 doesn't work, sooner or later it is going to become a real threat and then Black is going to have to waste time or weaken his position slightly to prevent it.

4   ...   ♘f6

Having made some moves on the queenside to safeguard the e5 pawn, Black now turns his mind to the mobilization of his own kingside.

5   0-0

White isn't to be diverted from rapid development by the threat to his e4 pawn. If now 5...♘xe4 6 d4! will ensure White regains his pawn whilst keeping a space advantage. We have seen an example of this in the game Karpov-Korchnoi.

5   ...   &e7

This is a sensible developing move which ensures Black will be able to castle kingside.

6   ♖e1

White defends his e4 pawn as he still gets no advantage from 6 &xc6 dxc6 7 ♘xe5 after 7...♘xe4 8 ♖e1 ♘f6. Now however 7 &xc6 followed by 8 ♘xe5 is a real threat.

6   ...   b5

Now we see the value of the interpolation 3...a6: Black is able to shut out the white bishop from the attack on c6 and so meet the threat to his e5 pawn. At the same time he gains space on the queenside.

7   &b3

The bishop has to retreat, but it is by no means all bad news for White. On the contrary, by provoking 6...b5 he has made Black weaken his queenside pawns somewhat. These can be undermined by a subsequent a2-a4.

7   ...   d6

Black fortifies his hold on the e5 point and opens the diagonal for his queen's bishop.

8   c3

The obvious developing move was 8 ♘c3, but White knows when to bend the rules of classical development to meet the true needs of the specific position. He prefers the game move because:

♦ he wants to build a pawn centre with d2-d4. Therefore by playing 8 c3 he readies himself to answer e5xd4 with c3xd4, when he maintains two pawns abreast in the centre.

♦ he makes an escape hatch on c2 for his bishop, so that if Black tries ♘a5 at any point to gain the two bishops he can play ♗c2.

Note that White 'bends' the rules of classical development rather than 'breaks' them. After all, classical precepts point out that White does well to play 1 e4 and 2 d4 on his first two moves if possible, as having two pawns side by side in the centre gives his pieces a lot of space; with 8 c3 White is belatedly trying to build such a centre with pawns on e4 and d4, without allowing Black to break them up with e5xd4. Classical thinking also argues that two bishops are better than two knights, so preventing Black gaining the two bishops with ♘a5 and ♘xb3 is also in accordance with such thinking.

8   ...   0-0

After only eight moves, both Grandmasters have attended to setting up a solid base in the centre and secured their king's safety by castling. White has developed a rook and two minor pieces, whilst Black has developed three minor pieces.

Don't mess about in the opening – get your pieces out and your king castled as soon as possible.

9   h3!

Every pawn move without a clear purpose is to be criticized said the great World Champion Emanuel Lasker: so why does White make a little pawn move on the h file when he could have played 9 d4 immediately, which seizes space in the centre?

Harmonious opening play is as much about preventing your opponent from playing good moves as playing good moves yourself! Here 9 d4 would allow Black to respond 9...♗g4! when the black bishop is excellently placed: it pins the knight that is a vital support of the white centre.

Therefore White prefers to take time out to prevent the pin. His thoughts are very much focused on the centre, even when he makes a move on the rim.

9   ...   ♗b7

The bishop has been frustrated on one diagonal, but finds another perfectly reasonable post on another where it may become involved in an attack on the important e4 point. In fact, all Black's minor pieces have found decent squares where they influence the centre and it has only taken nine moves.

10   d4

At last all White's preparations are complete and he seizes a slight, but enduring, space advantage.

10   ...   ♖e8

Black both centralizes the rook and clears the f8 square for his bishop in order to improve the strategic disposition of his pieces.

11   ♘bd2

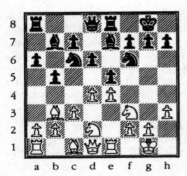

As c3 is blocked the knight goes to the only other available centre square. From d2 it can be manoeuvred via f1 to g3 where it helps defend e4 and has influence on the centre without getting in the way of the other pieces. Alternatively the knight could be redeployed to e3 in order to control both d5 and f5, but this would be more double edged as the knight might obstruct both the bishop on c1 and the rook on e1 and so leave the e4 pawn more vulnerable. Yes, it is by no means easy to keep all your pieces happy!

11   ...   ♝f8

A useful retreat as the bishop can now be activated with g7-g6 and ♝g7 if desired. At the same time White's knight manoeuvre

described above is hindered, for if 12 ♘f1 then he has to reckon with 12...exd4 uncovering a double attack on the e4 pawn.

12   a4

Why suddenly a move with the rook's pawn?

So far Hubner has played good, sensible developing moves which are primarily aimed at controlling the centre – or at least gaining a slight upper hand there as befits the player who has the right to move first. But now a more specific plan begins to take shape in his mind. White hopes to profit from the slight breach in Black's pawn structure created by 6...b5, either through magnifying the weakness of the pawn itself or by using it as a hook to force open lines for his pieces on the queenside. The game move fits the requirements of both these closely linked plans.

12   ...   ♛d7

Instead 12...bxa4? 13 ♝xa4 would play into White's hands. Not only would Black be left with a weak pawn on a6 but he would also be faced with the awkward threat of 14 d5, pinning the knight against the rook. Alternatively 12...b4 causes less damage to the black queenside, but would leave the c4 square at White's disposal. So Portisch stands his ground and moves his queen forwards, so that she is available to protect the b5 pawn once the knight moves away from c6. Black has also connected his rooks, which means they can now work in unison – this is normally the sign of a healthy position, as it suggests that the queen and all the minor pieces have been moved off the back rank and the player has succeeded in castling.

13   d5

In the Ruy Lopez White often has to choose whether to block the centre or maintain the tension by keeping the pawn on d4. Sometimes it is a matter of very subtle judgment: here the advance to d5 blocks in White's own bishop on b3 and removes flexibility from his pawn structure, which can now be undermined by an eventual c7-c6. On the other hand, White seizes space and drives the black knight from its useful post on c6 and furthermore prevents a sudden discovered attack on his e4 pawn by e5xd4.

No doubt what guided Hubner in this instance was his wish for the situation to stay quiet in the centre, so that he could focus all his attention on his plan of queenside pressure without being disturbed by any possible counterattack.

13   ...   ♘e7

The knight retreats but stays in the centre. If instead 13...♘a5 14 ♗c2 leaves Black facing the annoying threat of 15 b4 ♘c4 16 ♘xc4 bxc4 17 ♕e2, when he loses a pawn.

14   c4

All according to plan: the pressure on b5 is intensified. If now 14...b4 15 c5! threatens 16 c6 winning a piece and if 15...dxe5 16 ♘xe5 leaves Black's pawns in ruins. Also inadequate for Black is 14...bxc4 15 ♘xc4 when the knight is well placed on c4, the bishop on c1 is freed and White has a clear plan of attack down the c file, which includes ♘a5 hitting the bishop on b7 and aiming at the hole on c6.

14   ...   ♘g6

Portisch refuses to be bullied into a queenside concession. He stands his ground and defends the e5 pawn, so that b5-b4 becomes an option as it doesn't allow the break c4-c5 by White given in the previous note.

15   ♗c2

A quiet retreat which prepares to answer 15...b4 with 16 ♘b3 – heading for a5 to cause disruption – 16...a5 17 ♗e3, when White will continue his queenside initiative with c4-c5.

15   ...   c6

A vigilant response: Portisch bolsters the b5 pawn and prepares to answer 16 ♘b3? with 16...dxc4, dismantling the white pawn structure.

16   b3

White feels compelled to solidify his centre, even though this means he no longer has the option of ♘b3.

16   ...   b4

Only now: Black blocks the queenside at precisely the right moment. White maintains his space advantage, but his plan of exerting pressure on the queenside hasn't produced any immediate results.

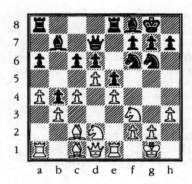

17   ♘h2

A horse is only 'dim on the rim' if it isn't on its way to greener pastures. For now Hubner is concerned with increasing the efficiency of his knights: f3 was a good square for the knight, but g4 is better, and in time d5 might prove better still!

In quiet positions with a fixed pawn centre strategical regroupings lasting three or more moves are not uncommon.

A key idea for White is to exchange with d5xc6 in order to open a line of attack against the d6 pawn, which is especially weak as it is a so-called backward pawn – no other pawn can offer it any assistance. However, 17 dxc6 would be double edged as the d5 pawn is doing a sterling job in preserving White's space advantage: in particular once it disappears Black's light-squared bishop has more scope and can harass the e4 pawn. As is so often the case in chess the threat is stronger than the execution as the maintenance of the idea of d5xc6 soon provokes a blunder from Portisch.

17   ...   ♛c7

A semi-waiting move which introduces the possibility of ♘d7 and ♘c5, when the knight is delighted to be placed on a centre square where it cannot be driven back by an enemy pawn.

18   ♘g4

White reactivates his knight and prepares to answer 18...♘xg4 with 19 hxg4 when he has a grip on the f5 square which can be tightened with a second knight manoeuvre: ♘f1, ♘e3 and then ♘f5. This could be combined with an attack along the h file involving g2-g3, ♔g2 and ♖h1, etc.

18   ...   ♗e7

Portisch wisely avoids the capture on g4. He could have carried out the little strategical operation 18...♘d7 and then 19...♘c5, but he decides that overall it is preferable to stop the white knight reaching d5 after the response 19 dxc6 ♗xc6 20 ♘e3.

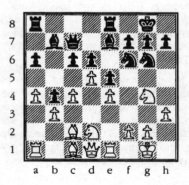

19   ♘f1

Now the other white knight has aspirations to find an ideal centre post. It aims for e3 where it can spring to f5 or, after d5xc6, the d5 square.

19   ...   cxd5?

White's knight manoeuvres have unnerved Portisch. He is keen to deny them the d5 square, but this is a disastrous way of going about things as Hubner will be able to exploit the resulting open file. Instead 19...c5, followed by ♗c8 to reactivate the bishop, would leave Black solidly placed, though White can continue to probe for weaknesses with ♘fe3, etc.

20   cxd5

After a phase of cat and mouse manoeuvring, White is presented with a clear strategical plan: seize control of the c file with the rooks.

20   ...   ♘xg4

In a cramped position every exchange usually helps the defender by lessening the force of any impending onslaught and also increasing the space available for the remaining pieces.

21   hxg4

White must recapture with the pawn or else the bishop on c2 drops. Nevertheless, he isn't complaining as he has gained a pincer-like hold on the f5 square.

21   ...   ♗c8

The bishop was doing nothing on b7 except stare at the d5 pawn, so it makes sense to redeploy it, especially as Black now has a threat: 22...♗xg4 23 ♕xg4 ♕xc2.

22   ♘e3

The knight completes the next stage of its journey.

22   ...   ♗g5

Meanwhile Portisch continues with the sensible policy of swapping

off pieces, but the drawback is that White can use the exchanging sequence to obtain control of the c file.

23   ♘f5!

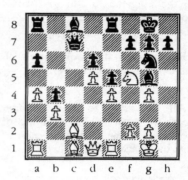

Such is the power of Hubner's accurate and patient play that with his first incursion into enemy territory since 3 ♗b5 he gains a strategically winning position.

23   ...   ♗xc1

The only consistent move, even though it develops White's rook for him.

24   ♖xc1

Finally a white rook reaches the c file. This wouldn't cause Black much trouble if the rest of his game was in good order – but here he has to worry about his vulnerable pawns on b4 and d6.

24   ...   ♕d8

The black queen steps out of the firing line.

25   ♗d3

Already there is the threat of 25 ♖c6, attacking d6, when Black would be obliged to play 25...♗xf5

26 gxf5 ♘e7, but then a pawn drops anyway to 27 ♖xa6.

Generally speaking Black is reluctant to play ♗xf5 as after g4xf5 White's pawns are strengthened and he gains attacking chances on the kingside to add to Black's woes on the queenside.

25   ...   ♘e7

Black keeps the rook out of c6 and challenges the white knight.

26   ♕d2!

All according to plan. Hubner clears the way for the doubling of the rooks on the c file with gain of time by attacking b4.

26   ...   ♖b8

It is uneconomical for the black rook to be tied to the defence of the b4 pawn: we would expect it to be fighting for control of the c file. But the pawn on b4 must be defended, and how else can it be done?

Firstly, if 26...♕b6 then 27 a5! dislodges the black queen – she must either retreat passively to b8 or allow White a strong passed pawn after 27...♕xa5 28 ♘xd6.

Secondly if 26...a5 27 ♗b5! when the bishop seizes the newly created

outpost square on b5. Black couldn't then challenge the bishop with 27...♗d7 as 28 ♘xd6 ♗xb5 29 ♘xb5 leaves White a pawn up.

Therefore by logical reasoning we see that using the black rook to defend the pawn is the lesser evil.

27   ♖c2

Note that if 27 ♖c4, which on the face of it appears even stronger as it attacks the pawn on b4, Black can reply 27...a5 when White can't respond 28 ♗b5. Black would then gain time for his development with 28...♗a6.

27   ...   ♘xf5

Black cannot tolerate the knight on f5 any longer. He prefers this to 27...♗xf5 as his bishop is better equipped to fight for the light squares on the queenside – which will soon include b5 as well as a6 and c6.

28   gxf5

Now White has a bind that stretches across the whole board.

28   ...   f6

You might wonder why Black plays this quiet pawn move when

things are getting hot on the queenside. Well all eyes are focused on the c file, but here is how Black could be mated if he plays the immediate 28...♖e7 to defend c7: 29 f6! ♖c7 30 ♖xc7 ♕xc7 31 ♕g5 g6 32 ♕h6 and mate follows on g7.

Or 29 f6 gxf6 30 ♕h6 ♖c7 31 ♖e3 ♖xc2 32 ♖g3+ ♔h8 33 ♕g7 mate.

These snap mating attacks are possible because of the superior mobility of the white rooks. Therefore Portisch has to take time out to safeguard his kingside before thinking about fighting for the c file.

29   ♖ec1

'When you double rooks you double their power' said Chernev.

The triumph of White's strategy. Rooks thrive on open lines: there is only one open file on the whole board and White's rooks have control of it.

29   ...   ♖e7

Portisch defends his second rank, but he will be undone by his pawn weaknesses on a6, b4 and d6.

30   ♖c6!

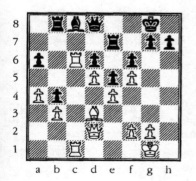

It looks as if this intrusion can be met by 30...♗b7, driving back the rook, but Hubner has prepared the sacrifice 31 ♗xa6 ♗xc6 32 dxc6 with a crushing position: White can follow up with ♕d5+ and ♗b7 and a4-a5, when the passed pawns swamp the defending rooks.

30   ...   ♖a7

Therefore Black has no choice but to tolerate the invasion on c6.

31   ♕e2

Another weakness please! The threat of 32 ♗xa6 forces Black to give away the b5 square.

31   ...   a5

Normally it is a good sign when a player's pawns are on the opposite coloured squares to his bishop, as is the case here; but the bishop on c8 is nonetheless a miserable piece with little scope.

32   ♗b5

In contrast, the white bishop cannot be dislodged from this commanding post.

32   ...   ♗b7

Portisch tries to extricate himself by forcing simplification, even at the cost of letting a white rook get to the seventh rank.

33   ♖c7

Rooks have had a love affair with the seventh rank since the dawn of chess history.

33   ...   ♖c8

White cannot possibly be allowed to play 34 ♖d7 and 35 ♖cd7 with two rooks on the seventh rank!

34   ♕c4

White supports his rook and is by no means adverse to the exchanging sequence 34...♖xc7 35 ♕xc7 ♕xc7 36 ♖xc7 as it leaves Black defenceless against 37 ♗c6 exploiting the pin on the black bishop to win at once.

34   ...   ♖aa8

Portisch however fights hard. He has expertly reorganised his pieces in their cramped surroundings to hold the white pieces at bay.

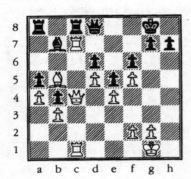

35   f3!!

The beginning of an absolutely brilliant idea. White could force an endgame with a rook on the seventh rank immediately with 35 ♗d7. But Hubner sees that Black can do nothing: so why not centralize the king so that it will be better placed for the endgame?

35   ...   ♔f8

In anticipation of the endgame the black king also moves a square towards the centre, but compared to the white king's bold advance it is a feeble gesture.

36   ♔f2!

The white king strolls to the centre of the board as if to inspect the siege works on the c file.

36   ...   ♖ab8

Of course the black pieces would love to strike a blow against the wandering white king, but they are confined in their dungeon on the first rank.

37   ♔e3

Now every white piece is superior to its opposite number in the black camp.

37   ...   g6

A desperate move, but if Black did nothing then White would play 38 ♗d7 in any case and force a winning endgame – assuming of course that Hubner hadn't intended to send his king on another little promenade.

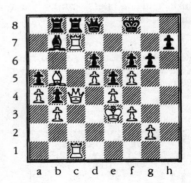

38   ♗d7

With every piece on its optimum square White decides it is time to cash in on his advantage.

38   ...   ♖xc7

Black gets rid of one powerful enemy...

39 ♕xc7

...but another one immediately takes its place.

39 ... ♕xc7

Black has to exchange or else d6 drops.

40 ♖xc7

'Take first and philosophize later' said GM Savielly Tartakower about such positions.

40 ... ♗a6

At last the bishop has an open diagonal but it is far too late.

41 ♗e6

Calmly does it: the black pawns are all at the mercy of the white rook, so Hubner has no need to hurry.

41 ... ♖b7

Black cannot allow his pawns to be massacred with 42 ♖xh7, etc.

42 ♖c6

Of course Black can only dream of the exchange of rooks.

42 ... ♗f1

Black tries one last trick as 42...♖a7 43 ♖xd6 is clearly hopeless.

43 ♖xd6

All White's positional pressure is finally converted into material gain.

43 ... ♗c4!?

This is Black's last gasp idea. If now 44 bxc4 b3 and unbelievably the white pieces are unable to stop the passed pawn queening!

44 ♖d8+ 1-0

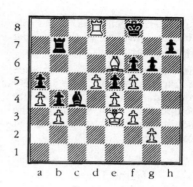

But this check persuaded Portisch that his opponent wasn't going to fall for any tricks.

If 44...♔e7 45 ♖h8! and Black has no time to take on b3 as 46 ♖xh7+ picks up the rook with a skewer. Therefore he would have to retreat with 45...♗a6 when 46 ♖xh7+ wins even more pawns. Alternatively after 44...♔g7 45 d6 White's bishop suddenly defends b3 through the black bishop. If then 45...♗xe6 46 fxe6 and the passed pawns win easily.

A great player is a master of all styles, or to put it more precisely, is a master of all situations. He may seek complicated, fighting games or delight in the exploitation of a tiny advantage in quiet surroundings; but whatever his preferences – which will be indulged to some extent by his choice of openings – he will always treat the position in front of him in the correct manner. If it requires direct, aggressive action he will not hesitate; if placid manoeuvring is called for he will be patient. Thus in Game One we saw Anatoly Karpov, who is famed for his wonderful technique, in the role of fearless attacker, as that is what the position demanded.

Here in Game Three we shall see that Garry Kasparov, who strongly favours dynamic play, is equally accomplished at handling the tranquil positions so typical of classical chess.

Game Three
G.Kasparov - E.Bacrot
Sarajevo 2000
Scotch Opening

1   e4

Garry Kasparov, the 13th World Champion, is in full agreement with Paul Morphy, the chess genius of the 1850s, that 1 e4 is a great way to begin a game.

1   ...   e5

The decks are cleared: Black keeps the status quo by copying his opponent.

2   ♘f3

Direct, powerful and best: it is White's task to preserve the advantage of the first move for as long as possible, and this can best be done by rapid development with concrete threats.

2   ...   ♘c6

The cavalry arrives to defend the e5 pawn.

3   d4

This is much more forceful than 3 ♗b5 as White provokes an immediate crisis in the centre by challenging the e5 pawn.

3   ...   exd4

Black cannot stand his ground with 3...d6 as 4 dxe5 dxe5 5 ♕xd8+ forces him to give up castling with 5...♔xd8 because 5...♘xd8 drops a pawn to 6 ♘xe5.

4   ♘xd4

White now has a small space advantage as the enemy pawn on e5 has been eliminated whilst his own pawn still stands on e4 controlling d5 and f5.

4   ...   ♘f6

A sensible move that both develops and targets the e4 pawn.

A fundamental mistake would be the exchange 4...♘xd4, as after 5 ♕xd4 the white queen is well placed in the centre and can only be driven away by 5...c5, which would be a seriously weakening move.

5   ♘xc6

White prepares to advance the e pawn to get it out of range of the knight on f6. If instead 5 ♘c3 then 5...♗b4, renewing the threat of ♘xe4, gives Black an active game.

5   ...   bxc6

The correct recapture as 5...dxc6 6 ♕xd8+ costs the right to castle.

Black now has doubled pawns but he hopes that they will be of value in guarding the d5 square and also in opening a gap to develop the queen's bishop via b7.

6 e5

The idea behind the exchange on c6: the pawn advance gains more space and aims to drive the black knight from its beloved post on f6.

6 ... ♕e7

The hunter hunted: Black pins the pawn which must now be defended.

7 ♕e2

White responds in kind as after 7 f4 d6 the white centre is crumbling. Now both queens are blocking in their king's bishop, which creates mutual problems with development.

7 ... ♘d5

The knight is forced to move but at least stays active as 7...♘g8 would be unbearably painful.

8 c4

Kasparov is determined not to allow the knight to remain undisturbed on a centre square.

8 ... ♗a6

...but rather than retreat the knight Bacrot pins the pawn and develops another piece.

9 b3

This solidifies the barrier against the black bishop as White wants to prove that it is badly placed on a6 rather than developed to a good square.

9 ... g6

Since the way out via e7 has been blocked, Black prepares the

alternative development of the bishop on g7. This is especially attractive as White has weakened the long diagonal a1-h8 with his last move.

10 f4

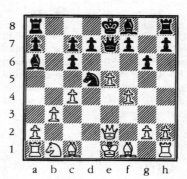

White adds support to his centre spearhead.

Ten moves have gone by, and White has only his queen developed; indeed, he has made a succession of pawn moves. So much for everything that has been said about the need for rapid development!

Nevertheless, White is only taking unacceptable liberties if in the meantime his opponent has been developing in good classical style. And looking closely we see that Black's piece deployment has been far from spotless.

We are entitled to ask: is the bishop on a6 really well developed, or is 'entombed' a better way to describe its situation? And what about the knight on d5 – is it well centralized or is it hanging precariously on an unsuitable square?

Assuming the centre remains blocked and Black doesn't find a tactical blow to get the bishop and knight working together then White will reap the benefits of his superior pawn structure, which confers a space advantage upon him.

10   ...   ♕b4+

Because of his lead in development Black tries to play dynamically. He reroutes his queen to b6 where she enjoys an excellent diagonal with gain of time. If instead 10...♘b4? then 11 a3 would win the knight.

11   ♗d2

And not 11 ♘d2? allowing 11...♘xf4.

11   ...   ♕b6

Now it is Black's turn to avoid a trap as if 11...♘xf4? 12 ♕e4 wins a piece.

12   ♕e4!

Kasparov prevents 12...♕d4, which would have won the rook in the corner, and threatens 12 cxd5.

12   ...   f5!

It is worth offering a pawn to keep up the momentum of Black's initiative for if now 13 exf6+ ♔f7 clears the way for 14...♖e8, winning the queen, which means that White has no time to capture the knight.

13   ♕f3

As White is behind in development it is essential to keep the position closed.

13   ...   ♕d4

A tempting move, but the attack eventually runs out of steam. Instead 13...♘b4 – intending a fork

on c2 – 14 ♔d1 ♗b7 – making an escape route for the knight on a6 should White play 15 a3 – was the way to keep the dynamism in Black's set up.

14   ♘c3

The only good way to meet the threat to the rook.

14   ...   ♘xc3

So Black has avoided losing time by retreating his knight, but on the other hand every exchange clarifies White's structural advantage as there will be fewer black pieces to generate counterplay.

15   ♗xc3

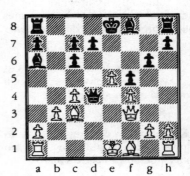

White regains his piece and is ready to answer a queen move with 16 e6! hitting the rook on h8 and so winning time to break up Black's centre with 17 exf7+.

15   ...   ♗b4

A pretty little trick to develop and meet the threat to the queen. Of course the bishop is taboo because of the loss of the rook on a1.

16   ♖c1

Another necessary move, though White isn't too upset at being obliged to develop his queenside pieces to good squares.

16 ... ♝xc3+

Yet again a piece vanishes from the board that might have caused White problems in exploiting his better pawn structure.

17 ♖xc3

He must retake this way or else f4 would drop.

17 ... 0-0-0

Black castles queenside so that the rook is developed immediately to d8 where it can support the advance d7-d5 or d7-d6 to open lines before White can deploy all his pieces.

18 c5!

The pressure on d6 is increased to impair the strength of a d7-d5 break out.

18 ... ♝b7

Black has no wish to help White's development with 18...♝xf1 19 ♖xf1 when the rook can be activated with ♖f2 and ♖d2, etc.

19 ♕e3

It is necessary to challenge Black's queen in order to clear the way for ♝e2 and 0-0.

19 ... ♕xe3+

Much too obliging. Bacrot doesn't want to lose time by moving his queen around but 19...♕b4! keeping the queens on the board would have preserved counterplay after 20 ♝e2 d6.

20 ♖xe3

A crucial moment has been reached. Either Black will succeed in breaking free from his cramped

position and neutralise White's space advantage; or else he will spend the rest of the game being tortured in a prospectless endgame.

20 ... d6

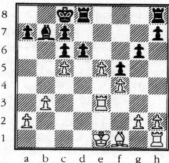

Now after 21 cxd6 cxd6 22 exd6 ♖xd6 23 ♝e2 ♖hd8, intending 24...♖d2, Black's fully mobilized army would compensate for the weakness on c6.

21 ♝c4!

This crosses Black's plans. White can ignore the threat to c5 as after 21...dxc5 Black may have an extra pawn, but the tripled pawns would be hideous. Furthermore the dominance of the white pawn on e5 would be uncontested and the black bishop on b7 shut out of the game.

21 ... ♚d7

The black king rushes to the centre as 21...♖he8 22 0-0 dxe5 23 fxe5 leaves White with a passed pawn which can be supported by the bishop, whilst the black bishop might as well be off the board.

22 h4

A move that is both aggressive and defensive. White rules out any flank attack on the f4 pawn that supports e5 with h7-h6 and g6-g5 and also prepares to undermine g6 with h4-h5 at an appropriate moment.

22   ...   d5

A major concession as White's pawn on e5 is left unchallenged as a protected passed pawn. Nevertheless, Bacrot feels it is necessary to stabilize his pawn structure to counter White's projected thrusts with his pawns.

23   ♗d3

Now a strategical menace is h4-h5, combined with g2-g4, to bludgeon the black pawns out of the way and so create connected passed pawns on the e and f files.

23   ...   h5

Black stops the plan outlined above, but at a huge cost: a backward pawn on g6 that is open to attack.

24   ♖g3

Here a careless move such as 24 g3?? would prevent White's attacking plan in the game. A pawn move should never be played on whim, as it can never be reversed.

24   ...   ♖h6

Black defends the pawn in such a way as to avoid being pinned on the g file. After 24...♖hg8 Kasparov intended the following clever breakthrough: 25 ♖g5 ♔e6 26 g4! hxg4 27 h5 gxh5 28 ♗xf5+ followed by 29 ♖hxh5 and White wins.

25   b4

Having tied a black rook down to g6 White turns his attention to the queenside, which should prove under-defended.

25   ...   ♔e6

Black hurries to get his king over to the kingside, but the last chance of gaining any freedom for his pieces was with the counter attack 25...a5! even though after 26 b5 cxb5 27 ♗xb5+ ♗c6 28 ♖b3 White can try to exploit the open b file as the challenge with 28...♖b8? loses material to 29 ♗xc6+.

26   ♔d2

As it is the endgame the king needs to be given an active role in any strategical plan. It would be quite absurd to try to shelter him with 26 0-0?.

26   ...   ♖a8

At last there is an attempt to break out with 27...a5, but Kasparov is ready.

27   ♖b1!

Now 27...a5 28 b5 doesn't help Black.

27   ...   a6

Sooner or later White can put enough pressure on a7 with ♗e2, ♖a3, ♖a5, ♖b3 and ♖ba3 to make this move necessary, so Bacrot bites the bullet and plays it straightaway.

28 ♖b3

The rook heads for a3, when all Black's pieces will be tied down on both sides of the board. Note that White has avoided the routine pawn move a2-a3, just as he has refrained from g2-g3 on the kingside. The squares a3 and g3 are vital avenues of attack for the rooks and must be kept unblocked.

28 ... ♔f7

The black king reaches f7 and offers its support to the beleaguered pawn. Nevertheless, this is a feeble task compared to the active role of the white king, which can saunter to the excellent square d4 where it surveys the whole board.

29 ♖a3

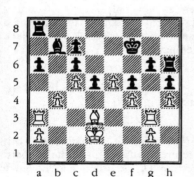

Now Black has to reckon with two schemes of attack:

on the queenside: ♖a5, ♗e2 and ♖ga3

on the kingside: ♖g5, ♗e2 and ♖ag3

Kasparov however is in no hurry. He sees that Bacrot cannot improve

his position and so quietly probes for the next few moves without committing himself to any definite plan.

29 ... ♖hh8

All Black can do is mark time and hope that his defences hold firm.

30 ♖g5

White hopes that there will be an immediate collapse after 30...♖hb8 31 g4!! hxg4 32 h5 gxh5 33 ♖xf5+ ♔e7 – going to g6 would walk into a discovered check – 34 ♖xh5 when the connected passed pawns easily decide the game.

30 ... ♖h6

The rook feels obliged to return to the defence of g6.

31 ♔c3

The white king eases forwards towards the d4 square. It will be seen that the Black's bishop is a useless piece except in a local defensive role on the queenside as all but one of the black pawns are on light squares. In contrast White's pawns are on dark squares and so don't impede his bishop, which can attack a6, f5 and, as will be seen, h5. The fact that White's pawns are on dark squares also means that the black bishop would have nothing to attack even if it did somehow escape from its prison on b7.

31 ... ♖b8

Black hopes against hope that White will fall for 32 ♗xa6? ♖a8 when he loses the exchange. But of course Kasparov is never going to miss such a simple tactic.

32 ♖a5

Now the rook is defended and so 33 ♗xa6 really is a threat.

32   ...   ♖a8

The rook has no choice but to return to its miserable defensive role.

33   ♔d4

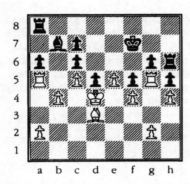

Total domination: Black hasn't the slightest glimmer of counter-play. His pieces are all tied down to defending pawns whereas White's pieces are mobile and can attack on either wing as they please.

33   ...   ♖hh8

Although Black has a protected passed pawn in the centre it is of no value, whereas the white pawn on e5 still has potential to advance thanks to the dynamism of the pieces that can support it. Kasparov builds this factor into his winning plan.

34   ♗c2

The bishop clears the third rank so that White's rooks can co-ordinate their action.

34   ...   ♖ab8

Black makes a feint to attack b4...

35   ♗d3

...which persuades White that he wants the bishop on e2 rather than c2, where it ties down the black rook by attacking a6.

35   ...   ♖a8

The position has been repeated, so why did Kasparov play 34 ♗c2, as he is obviously not interested in a draw? Perhaps he was short of time and wanted to use up a move before the time control at move 40. Or perhaps it was psychological: he wanted to demonstrate to Black that he has all the time in the world to press home his attack. Or finally, Kasparov might have used the repetition to clarify his thoughts about some aspect of his plan.

36   ♗e2

Whatever the reason for the repetition, White is now back on track towards the win. This bishop retreat not only keeps a6 under threat but introduces the idea of a sacrifice on h5 to break up the black defences.

36   ...   ♖hb8

A most frustrating life for a self-respecting rook!

37   ♖a3

The winning breakthrough will require the use of all White's assets: both rooks, the bishop and the pawn on e6.

37   ...   ♖h8

It is normal for rooks to show their prowess at a later stage of the game, but here despite the diminution of material the black rooks can only wander backwards and forwards from their starting squares.

38   ♖ag3

The final preparatory move: the pressure on g6 is about to become lethal. With the black bishop absent from the struggle it is inevitable that something has to give on the kingside.

38 ... &ag8

Black has to defend the g6 square but now a little combination finishes off the game.

39 &xh5! 1-0

As Grandmaster Tartakower once remarked, no one ever won a game by resigning, but not surprisingly Bacrot has had enough. If 39...gxh5 (the pawn also barges through after 39...&xh5 40 &xh5 gxh5 41 e6+! &f8 42 e7+ and Black has to give up his rook) 40 e6+! and the pawn inevitably deflects the black king from the defence of the rook or queens: 40...&f8 41 e7+ &xe7 42 &xg8 &xg8 43 &xg8. Then White is not only the exchange up but is ready to trap the bishop with 44 &b8.

2 Sicilan Defence: Dynamic Chess Strategy

Chess is imagination.

D.Bronstein

In the first chapter we saw the value of classical chess thinking. Nonetheless it has severe limitations. Here are some reasons why classical chess rules might have to be broken in a given situation:

1) It might be better to spend two moves developing a piece to a good square, rather than rushing it out as quickly as possible to a merely reasonable square.

2) In certain set ups, there is a 'star' piece on which a successful strategy can be based. It is often worth spending time to exchange off this piece if it belongs to the opponent, or preserving it from exchange if it is one of your own.

3) By delaying rapid kingside castling, you might get the chance to castle queenside and start an attack with the pawns against the opponent's kingside.

4) Some positions, especially those with a fixed or blocked pawn centre are naturally resistant to attack; therefore development can be delayed in favour of a more strategically appropriate move.

Modern thinking in chess tries to combine a knowledge of the fundamental classical laws with a sensitivity to the needs of any specific position.

This chapter is concerned with that most fighting and double-edged of chess openings: the Sicilian Defence. Here 'natural' moves are frequently avoided in favour of a move that really suits the position. Of course it doesn't always work, and this means that at times Black's blood gets spilt.

I guess this is all rather abstract, so let's look at some games – in some classical principles come out on top, in others dynamism is triumphant. It is this tension that leads to such fascinating fights in the Sicilian.

Game Four
V.Anand - V.Ivanchuk
Linares 1991
Sicilian Defence

In the early 1990s Vasily Ivanchuk was widely regarded as the Crown Prince of Chess. He had a logical positional style, deep opening knowledge and a quirky tactical fantasy which many thought would make him the natural challenger to Kasparov.

Alas he never quite made it through the candidates matches, perhaps due to his excessive nervousness, and with the arrival of Kramnik on the elite scene around 1994 he ceased to be regarded as the most promising player in the world. Nevertheless, his interest in the world title was by no means over and in 2002 he was runner up to his countryman Ponomariov in the FIDE World Championship.

At Linares in 1991 Ivanchuk crushed the World Champion, Gary Kasparov, in the Sicilian Defence with the white pieces. In another game he defeated Anand in the Sicilian with Black. Here is the second of these games.

1   e4

Throughout its long history there have been many schools of chess thought, each with its own champions and views to defend; but never has the value of gaining space in the centre been doubted.

1   ...   c5

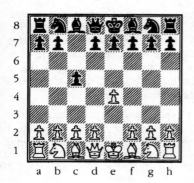

The Sicilian Defence is the most exciting response to 1 e4. Black isn't interested in copying White with 1...e5, or playing a defensive game with 1...e6 or 1...c6. Instead

he tries to imbalance things by gaining influence over the d4 square.

2   ♘f3

First blood to classical chess: 'Develop knights before bishops!' say the books. And rightly so: a knight normally knows from the outset where it wants to be placed, whereas a bishop likes to wait a couple of moves to see how the pawn structure is forming before it commits itself. Thus if White had played 2 ♗b5, the bishop could be attacked with 2...a6 – a useful move for Black who gains time for his queenside action. And if White then persisted with 3 ♗a4, the bishop is swallowed up by the black pawns after 3...b5 4 ♗b3 c4, when Black wins a piece! This trap is referred to as the Noah's Ark Trap: this is either because of the arc of pawns that trap the bishop or because it is such an old trap that it was known in the days of the Great Flood!

Another ineffective development is 2 ♗c4 when after 2...e6 Black is again ready to gain time by attacking the bishop with 3...d5. Finally 2 ♗d3 would block in the white queenside pieces by obstructing d2-d4, while 2 ♗e2 leaves the bishop on a non-attacking square.

So it is best to leave the bishop at home for a couple of moves. The knight doesn't need to see where Black is going to put his pieces to know that he has a safe, active square on f3.

2   ...   d6

Black wants to develop his own king's knight but if 2...♘f6 3 e5 might be awkward. So first of all he stabilizes his centre.

3   d4

White attacks the spearhead of Black's pawn formation in order to win control of d4 for his knight. At the same time he frees his queen's bishop. Now the threat is 3 dxc5 dxc5 4 ♕xd8+ ♔xd8, when the black king would be stuck in the centre. In this scenario the black king is unlikely to be mated, but he would be a target of time-gaining operations by the white pieces and get in the way of the active deployment of Black's rooks.

3   ...   cxd4

Here Black can counterattack against e4 with the immediate 3...♘f6 when White should reply 4 ♘c3 as the over-aggressive 4 e5 allows 4...dxe5 5 dxe5 ♕xd1+ 6 ♔xd1 ♘g4 when in contrast to the previous move White is the one to lose the right to castle.

Therefore Black concedes a space advantage to White in the centre, but it is by no means all bad news. Firstly, he has eliminated White's d pawn and so prevented him from setting up a broad centre. This means that he can play ♘c6 without worrying about being chased back by d4-d5. Also the c file is now half open and Black may be able to put pressure on c2 with his queen or one of the rooks in the future.

4   ♘xd4

Knights love centre squares where they are safe from attack by pawns. Here the white knight can be attacked by e7-e5, but this is problematical for Black as it would leave him with a backward pawn on d6 as well as a hole on d5 – a square that cannot be defended by a pawn. As a rule such holes should be avoided unless there are other strategical factors that outweigh the structural weakness.

4   ...   ♘f6

The most precise move order: Black begins his kingside development with gain of time by hitting the e4 pawn.

If instead 4...♘c6. White would have had the chance to increase his pawn control of the centre with 5 c4! when he has a firm grip on the d5 square. This c4/e4 pawn wedge is known as the Maroczy Bind after the Hungarian Grandmaster Geza Maroczy who used it to develop a stranglehold on the centre.

Good strategy depends as much as on preventing your opponent playing good moves as playing good moves yourself.

5   ♘c3

The natural response which guards e4 and deploys the knight on a centre square. On the other hand, White is now unable to play c2-c4.

5   ...   a6

Black prepares to expand on the queenside with b7-b5 and then play ♗b7, when the bishop is excellently placed attacking the e4 pawn. The attack on e4 would be exacerbated by the threat of b5-b4, driving the white knight from its defensive post.

You might be thinking 'this is all very well in the long term, but can Black afford to spend his time like this rather than develop his pieces?' This is the eternal question in the Sicilian!

6   ♗c4

White puts the emphasis on rapid development. He aims his bishop at the weakest square in Black's pawn phalanx – f7.

6   ...   e6

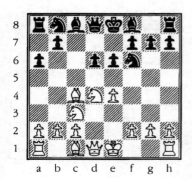

Black responds with a little move that is an essential part of his opening deployment. The pawn on e6 blocks the bishop's attack on f7 and at the same time gains control of two important centre squares: d5 and f5. In some circumstances Black might play d6-d5 to liquidate White's space advantage, but for the moment he is happy with his compact centre.

Black's set up is sometimes referred to as the 'hedgehog', a terminology which reflects both its solidity – the pawns on d6, e6 and a6 are like bristles that will spear any white pieces that fall upon them – and also its slight lack of space: if the juggernaut that crashes into it is heavy enough, the poor hedgehog will be squashed!

7   0-0

Again White meets his opponent's sophisticated and modern opening set up with good old fashioned development of his pieces.

7   ...   ♗e7

Black's game also unfolds nicely as the bishop clears the way for castling by slipping into the convenient gap left by his previous move.

8   ♗b3

White is wise to show respect for the Hedgehog System as the c4 square is by no means safe. The bishop steps backwards in order to avoid being harassed by b7-b5, which in conjunction with b5-b4 driving away the knight from c3, could put the e4 pawn in jeopardy. The bishop retreat is also a precaution against a possible d6-d5 or even a so-called 'Fork Trick' involving the temporary piece sacrifice ♘xe4 by Black when after White takes the knight with ♘xe4 he can regain the piece with d6-d5, having eliminated White's strong centre pawn.

8   ...   0-0

It is often a pleasant moment when you get to castle as Black, as it usually means you haven't suffered a quick catastrophe.

9 f4

After a straightforward, efficient developing phase Anand's plan begins to take shape. He wants to attack the e6 pawn with f4-f5 and try to make it advance to e5, when he wins control of the important d5 square.

9 ... b5

In contrast to classical methods of play, in which Black tries to meet White's plan headlong and defeat it, or at least prevent it, in the Sicilian the emphasis is on counterattack. White is allowed to play his desired advance...

10 f5?

...which at first glance appears to be a strong attacking move as it hits the vital e6 pawn...

10 ... b4!

... but Black has prepared this powerful counter-blow on the queenside. Now the white knight must evacuate the excellent c3 square where it defends the e4 pawn. Already White's last move is looking too impulsive. He might have tried attacking in a different manner with 10 e5!?.

11 ♘a4

The main point of 10 f5 was to win the d5 square for this knight, so it is a sad reflection on his strategy that the horse has become stranded offside on a4.

11 ... e5!

Black isn't afraid of the so-called 'hole' on d5 as it can be defended by his knight on f6 and a bishop stationed on b7.

12 ♘e2

Both white knights have now been obliged to vacate strong centre squares, which indicates that White's attempt to gain the initiative has failed.

12 ... ♗b7

The bishop assumes control of a fine diagonal where it has the e4 pawn in its sights and guards d5. Very foolish would have been 12...♘xe4? 13 ♗d5 and White wins a piece.

13 ♘g3

Again White has to use tactical means to support the pawn on e4, though this time the punishment isn't so obvious if Black snatches the pawn. Nonetheless White has attacking chances after 13...♘xe4 14 ♘xe4 ♗xe4 15 ♕g4 d5 16 ♗h6 ♗f6 17 ♗xg7! ♗xg7 18 f6 ♗g6 19 fxg7 etc.

13 ... ♘bd7!

Ivanchuk sees that simple development promises him the superior game as his pieces are better placed strategically. Therefore he quite rightly refuses to have anything to do with the complications that occur if he takes on e4. In fact, a player should only play for complications as the last resort if the position offers him no decent plan.

14 ♕e1

White's attacking aspirations have been replaced by the need to defend. Already his opponent has taken over the initiative, which is in White's possession at the start of a game due to his right to move first.

14 ... a5

This prevents 15 ♕xb4 and strengthens the cordon around the knight on a4. Now Ivanchuk is planning d6-d5, perhaps even immediately with 15...d5, to seize control of the centre.

15 c4

Anand obstructs the d6-d5 advance, as Black has no wish to let the knight back into the centre after 15...bxc3 16 ♘xc3.

15 ... ♕c7

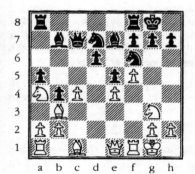

On the other hand, the pawn on c4 can be added to Ivanchuk's list of potential targets. His plan is to keep the knight immobilized on a4 and gradually build up pressure on the c4 and e4 pawns, or even the knight

itself – in the latter case this would include ♗c6 followed by ♕d7, once this square becomes free and after making sure there is no fork on b6 in reply.

But he must tread very carefully, especially against a genius of defence such as Anand. Therefore his first aim is to prevent White organizing a successful break out with ♗e3, ♖ac1 and c4-c5. This means rushing to put as much pressure on c4 and c5 as possible: first the queen, then a rook is pressed into this service.

16 ♕e2

Anand defends the pawns on c4 and e4 in anticipation of the coming onslaught and gets his queen off the first rank so that his rooks can work together.

16 ... ♖fc8

Black shows contempt for any dreams White may still have had of a successful kingside attack by moving his king's rook away to the c file. And rightly so: a direct assault cannot hope to succeed with a white knight trapped on the other wing and a bishop on b3 which has had its diagonal blunted by c2-c4.

17 ♗g5

The bishop vacates the c1 square so that the queen's rook can defend c4 and at the same time restrains Black by pinning the knight against the bishop.

17 ... ♘c5

After the game Ivanchuk suggested 17...h6 when if 18 ♗xf6 ♘xf6 gives him very good chances. The game move looks excellent, as 18...♘cxe4 is threatened, and if 18 ♘xc5 ♕xc5+ 19 ♗e3 ♕c6 is horrible for White – both 20...♘xe4 and 20...a4 followed by 21...♕xc4 after the bishop retreats from b3 are in the air.

18   ♖ac1!

Anand chooses this moment to demonstrate why he is a great defender. If now 18...♘fxe4 19 ♘xe4 White can hold his own in the complications after 19...♗xe4 20 ♗xe7 ♗d3, while if 19...♘xe4 the white knight on a4 has the last laugh: 20 ♗xe7 ♕xe7 21 ♘b6 with a deadly fork.

18   ...   h6

Before deciding his best course of action Ivanchuk first of all makes the white bishop decide what it is doing on g5.

19   ♗e3

Anand has no wish to hand over control of the dark squares to the enemy bishop after 19 ♗xf6 ♗xf6 followed by ♗g5.

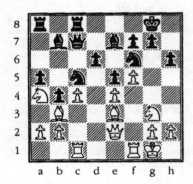

19   ...   ♘cd7!

A splendid retreat which is completely free of Ego – most players are too stubborn to admit they have chosen a wrong plan and

persist with it, often all the way to the destruction of their position. Here the pawn on e4 would prove poisoned after 19...♘fxe4? 20 ♘xe4 when 20...♘xe4 21 ♘b6 loses Black the exchange and 21...♗xe4 21 ♗xc5 costs him a piece.

Instead Ivanchuk realizes that going after the e4 pawn with ♘c5 is inaccurate and has the humility to revert to his original plan: proving the knight on a4 is badly placed. Certainly Black has gained nothing by playing ♘c5 and then putting the knight back on d7; but neither has the strategical layout of the pieces changed, which means that White is still hampered by his wretched knight on a4.

20   ♗f2

White has to retreat his bishop in order to defend e4.

20   ...   ♖a6!

A chess genius is aware of all the squares on the chess board. You might think that the a8 square is a backwater where no self-respecting queen would ever be found, but Ivanchuk has come up with a brilliant plan to increase the pressure on the e4 square.

Every square is important that can be used to influence the situation in the centre.

21   ♖c2

White has to take measures against an assault on c4 with ♖c6 and ♗a6. Therefore he frees c1 to make way for ♖fc1 if necessary.

21   ...   ♕b8!

Ivanchuk continues his inspired manoeuvre. By removing his best piece from the c file he also rules out any tricks based on c4-c5 followed by a discovered attack or pin on the queen.

22   ♖e1

Anand can only defend his weak points and hope for a tactical or positional oversight from his opponent.

22   ...   ♛a8

The pressure on the white centre dramatically increases now that the black queen has found her best square.

23   ♛d3?

After his careful defence Anand loses concentration for a move and allows Black to carry out a very advantageous exchange. Instead he should have continued to wait patiently with 23 h3.

23   ...   ♞g4!

White is solidly entrenched on the light squares, even though they are under siege; on the other hand his pawns aren't offering much protection to the dark squares. Therefore having to concede the exchange of his dark square bishop for a knight is a grievous loss for him.

24   ♞f1

Anand does his best by regrouping his knight to d2 in order to bolster e4 again.

24   ...   ♞df6

Black is in no hurry to take the bishop: first he attacks e4 again.

25   ♞d2

Now defence and attack are evenly balanced on the light squares...

25   ...   ♞xf2

...but White loses all resistance down the dark square diagonal a7-g1.

26   ♔xf2

The white king finds himself drawn unwittingly into the battle.

26   ...   ♝c6

Suddenly White has to reckon with the terrible threat of 27...♛a7+ followed by 28...♛d7, when the knight on a4 is trapped and lost!

27   ♖cc1

Anand clears the way to save the cornered knight with ♝d1 and b2-b3, but as we shall see in doing so his pieces become dangerously uncoordinated.

27   ...   ♛a7+

Meanwhile the black queen finds a great diagonal with gain of time by announcing check.

28   ♔e2

If 28 ♛e3 ♞g4+ ends the game, while after 28 ♔f1 28...♞g4 is still awkward – for example 29 ♛e2 – to stop mate on f2 – then 29...♞xh2 mate!

28   ...   ♖d8

The knight on a4 won't run away: therefore Black has no need to hurry to capture it. It isn't quite time for 28...♛d7 as White can save himself with 29 c5! uncovering an attack on the rook on a6 and at the same time threatening a fork with 30. ♘b6. If then 29...♝xa4 30 ♝xa4 ♛xa4 31 ♛xa6 leaves White the exchange up while 29...♝b5 30 ♝c4 ♝xc4 31 ♛xc4 also allows White to escape.

29   ♝d1

Like all great players, Ivanchuk knows when to change his plan. Up until now his aim has been to exploit the stricken knight on a4; but here he realizes there is a new and greater target: the white king. There is nothing inconsistent in this: the appropriate method of capitalizing on a positional advantage often changes according to the defensive plan the opponent adopts.

Here White aims to rescue his knight from the edge of the board with b2-b3 and ♘b2.

This slow, manoeuvring plan is acceptable as long as the position is closed. But should it become open then the white king will face a

whirlwind, as he is sitting right in the path of the storm, rather than sheltering on h1.

How can Black change the nature of the position from a closed one into an open fight? Is there a sacrifice? We look around the board for a breakthrough and notice to our joy that we can burst out with...

29   ...   d5!!

This pawn sacrifice is like a nuclear explosion that releases all the energy stored in the black position.

30   cxd5

White's only hope is to accept the material and hope that Black bungles the attack.

30   ...   ♘xd5!

The required follow up to Black's sacrifice. Now is no time to be fainthearted!

31   exd5

There's many a slip betwixt cup and lip ... as before, White's only chance is to take everything on offer and hope for a mishap in Black's attack. But Ivanchuk is absolutely relentless in finishing off the battle.

31   ...   ♖xd5

In return for the piece Black has all the facets of a decisive attack. Let's look at the attacking forces at his disposal. He has:

♦ Two bishops which can trap the white king in a deadly pincer movement from the flanks with ♗b5 and ♗g5

♦ A rook that attacks both the white queen and beyond it the knight on d2

♦ A queen aimed along an unprotected diagonal which runs right into the heart of White's defences.

Meanwhile White's king is leading his forces from the front in a bizarre manner: indeed he is obstructing the action of both his bishop on d1 and the rook on e1. When you consider that the knight on a4 is shut out of the battle, so that for all practical purposes Black isn't even a piece down, it is easy to conclude that it is all over for White.

32   ♕b3

The white queen has to give way and chooses a square where she at least keeps some semblance of control of the light squares. Instead she would be lost if she tried to stay in the centre: 32 ♕c4 ♗b5 or 32. ♕f3 ♖xd2+! while if 32 ♕e3 then simply 32...♕xe3+ 33 ♔xe3 ♗g5+ 34 ♔e2 ♖xd2+ is crushing.

Now Black has sacrificed a piece, so he must get every piece involved if he is to carry the day.

32   ...   ♗g5!

This bishop has sat patiently on e7 for 25 moves whilst the other pieces have fought things out around it. But now it makes a star entrance

and puts White in a fatal pin on the d2 square. This wasn't luck: it was the logical outcome of Black's dynamic plan to smash the white centre.

33   ♖c2

There was nothing to be done. If 33 ♖xc6, hoping against hope for 33...♖xc6?? 34 ♕xd5, then 33... ♖xd2+ 34 ♔f1 ♕f2 is mate.

33   ...   ♗xd2

0-1

White is pole-axed after 34 ♖xd2 ♗b5+ 35 ♖d3 – the only move – 35...♖xd3 or 35...♗xd3+.

Game Five
J.Nunn - A.Sokolov
Dubai 1986
Sicilian Defence

From Game Four we can conclude that if Black manages to fend off White's initiative then he will have promising chances in the middlegame as his pieces will be on their strategically best squares, even if they took longer to get there.

On the other hand if Black judges things wrongly, he might get wiped out in 20 or so moves by an 'open position style' attack on his king, in which White's lead in development proves decisive. That is precisely what happens to Andrei Sokolov in Game Five, who at the time was rated number three in the world.

1   e4

Just as a house needs to be constructed on a firm foundation, so too does every plan for White need a solid beginning. The first stone to be laid in this case is 1 e4.

1   ...   c5

Around a third of all games after 1 e4 begin with a Sicilian Defence: and no wonder, as no other opening offers more chances to counter-attack right from the very first move.

2   ♘f3

White refrains from playing 2 d4 as after 2...cxd4 he must either reply 3 ♕xd4, when 3...♘c6 gains time by attacking the queen, or make a rather unappealing pawn sacrifice with 3 c3 dxc3 4 ♘xc3, with only a mild initiative for the pawn. Therefore White settles for an opening idea that proves good in 95% of cases: the development of his king's knight to f3.

2   ...   e6

In reply Black frees the e7 square for his knight or bishop and puts a rock-solid barrier on the diagonal that runs towards f7 – the square that White is most likely to target in the opening phase of the game.

3   d4

Only now: White regains control of the d4 square without needing to lose time with his queen or make any gambits.

3   ...   cxd4

If Black ignored White's last move then 4 d5 would nail down a space advantage in the centre.

4   ♘xd4

An excellent centre square for the knight, as the only way a pawn can dislodge it is with e6-e5, which would represent a serious loss of time as Black has already played 2...e6.

4   ...   ♘c6

Therefore Black finds another way to challenge the white knight.

5   ♘c3

The most active move that calls up reinforcements from the queen-side.

5   ...   a6

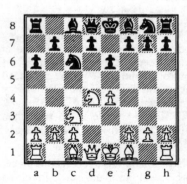

Whereas White brings out his pieces in direct, vigorous style, Black delays his development in order to achieve strategical objectives. Here for example he makes a useful little pawn move that facilitates the gaining of space on the queenside with b7-b5 in the future. If Black's plan works then it is praised as 'subtle' and 'sophisticated' and White's straightforward development is scolded as 'primitive' and 'old fashioned'. On the other hand, if Black's ideas fail he will be criticized for his 'over elaborate, time wasting play' while White's 'energetic, forceful play' will meet with approval from all commentators! Such is the inherent tension between the desire to put pieces on good squares and the need to get them working together quickly.

6   &e2

White continues to mobilize his pieces in accordance with classical precepts

6   ...   d6

...whilst Black sets up the Hedgehog centre so characteristic of the Sicilian Defence. It gives him less space than he usually achieves after 1 e4 e5, but it is not at all easy for an attacker to crack.

7   &e3

It has taken Nunn only seven moves to develop all four minor pieces and establish his centre: a very healthy state of affairs, as long as he can find a plan to exploit his activity.

7   ...   ₩c7

In contrast, Sokolov is in no hurry to develop his kingside. Here we see another point to 5...a6: the queen can go to this useful square where she has influence on the centre without being bothered by ♘b5.

8   f4

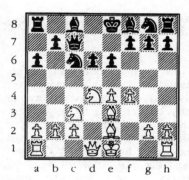

Having mobilized all his pieces White needs to find a way to use them. Nunn settles on the forthright idea of launching an assault on the e6 pawn, which in due course will amount to an assault on the black king.

8   ...   ♘a5?

Black takes his lackadaisical attitude towards development to an extreme. In fact he shows complete unconcern about events on the kingside. He wants to put his knight on c4, where it attacks both the bishop on e3 and the b2 pawn; it is reasonable to suppose White will respond with &xc4, when after ₩xc4 Black will have the bishop pair, which in the long term are a useful asset. But in the short term can Black really afford such a time consuming manoeuvre?

9   0-0

Two moves in one! The white king is evacuated from the centre and the rook is brought to f1, where it can support the f4-f5 advance.

9   ...   ♘c4

Black fearlessly continues his plan despite some ominous signs on the kingside.

10   &xc4

The knight is much too dangerous to be tolerated on c4.

10   ...   ♛xc4

Now the black queen sits on the weakest point in White's camp – the only centre square which cannot easily be defended by a pawn or covered by a piece. On the other hand, there is a Russian saying that 'one man in the field isn't an army' – and the queen doesn't have the support of any of the other black pieces.

11   f5

The white spearhead finally makes contact with the defensive wall. One player has already castled and has three minor pieces and a rook in play; the other player has only his queen in action. Despite its famous resilience Sokolov is asking way too much of the Sicilian set up.

11   ...   ♝e7

Black develops his bishop before the knight as he fears that after 11...♘f6 12 fxe6 fxe6 White will sacrifice the exchange with 13 ♖xf6! when 13...gxf6 14 ♕h5+ exposes the black king to the might of all the white pieces.

12   ♛g4

White's advantage is of a temporary nature: if Black succeeds in developing then he will even have the better game. Therefore Nunn cannot afford to waste time and strikes at both e6 and g7 with his queen.

12   ...   h5

This forces the white queen to retreat as if 13 ♕xg7? then 13...♝f6 and Black will win the knight on d4.

13   ♛f3

In fact the queen is by no means dismayed at being pushed back to the fine attacking square f3, especially as Black will never find a safe haven for his king on the kingside now that he has been cajoled into making the loosening move h7-h5.

13   ...   ♝f6

The bishop blocks the f file to meet the threat of 14 exf6 fxe6 15 ♕f7+, and at the same time attacks the knight on d4.

14   fxe6

Nonetheless, the f file will still prove to be a vital channel of attack for the white pieces.

14   ...   fxe6

After 14...♝xe6 Black's control of the key centre squares d5 and f5 would be severely weakened, which would allow the response 15 ♘f5 menacing a fork on d6.

15   e5!

A brilliant attacking move that clears the e4 square for the knight. No time is to be given to Black to develop his pieces.

15   ...   dxe5

Of course, if 15...♗xe5 16 ♕f7+ would soon be fatal for the black king.

16   ♘e4

The knight enters the fray with an immediate threat of 17 ♘d6+ winning the black queen.

16   ...   ♕c7

An astute defensive move: the queen returns to protect the second rank.

17   ♕g3!

Every player who aspires to being a great attacker needs venomous little moves as well as violent blows in his repertoire. Here Nunn pins the e5 pawn to prevent Black taking on d4 and introduces the idea of 18 ♕g6+ when if 18...♕f7 19 ♘d6+ wins the queen, while otherwise the black king will be subjected to a battering after a sacrifice on f6.

17   ...   ♘e7

Black has to cover the g6 square even though it means that the barrier on f6 will collapse.

18   ♖ad1

It isn't quite time for White to take on f6. Instead Nunn brings his last undeveloped piece into action. You can see that White now has both rooks in the game whilst Black's rooks are still passive. It is no wonder that Sokolov is unable to stem the tide of the attack as his army is simply outnumbered.

18   ...   h4

Black hopes to drive the white queen away from g3 and so win the knight on d4. He achieves his aim, but Nunn has calculated further.

19   ♘xf6+

First of all White wins the g7 square for his queen.

19   ...   gxf6

A necessary recapture after which both the white queen and knight are hanging.

20   ♕g7

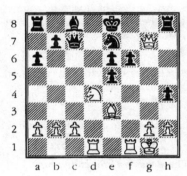

The point of Nunn's play: he attacks the rook and so gains time to dismantle the pawn barricades around the black king.

20   ...   ♖f8

Here is what might have happened after 20...♖g8: 21 ♕xf6 exd4 22 ♕f7+ ♚d8 (Black loses his queen after 22...♚d7 23 ♖xd4+ ♚c6 24 ♖c4+) 23 ♖xd4+ ♗d7 – the rook drops on 23...♘d5 24 ♕xg8+ – and now there is the elegant mating finish 24 ♕f8+! ♖xf8 25 ♖xf8 mate.

21   ♖xf6!

There is no need to move the knight: White has so many pieces involved in the attack that he can afford to give up one and still have an overwhelming advantage in firepower.

21   ...   ♖xf6

An abrupt end would be 21...♖g8 22 ♕f7+ ♔d8 23 ♘xe6+ with double, discovered checkmate!

22 ♕xf6

The last defender of f6 vanishes. Now Nunn gives the following variation after 22...exd4: 23 ♕h8+ ♔d7 24 ♖xd4+ ♘d5 25 ♕g7+ ♔e8 26 ♕g8+ ♔e7 27 ♖xd5! exd5 28 ♕g7+ when Black loses his queen after either 28...♔d6 29 ♗f4+ or 28...♔d8 29 ♗g5+.

22 ... ♕d6

Black tries his last trick: a pin on the knight on d4...

23 ♗g5!

...which White can simply ignore.

23 ... exd4

There was no longer any hope.

24 ♖xd4

Now it's a rook, queen and bishop attacking a king who is defended by a queen and knight. If the black king had adequate pawn cover this wouldn't be impossible odds; but when he is sitting between two open files and his back rank has collapsed a massacre is the only possible outcome.

24 ... ♘d5

Or 24...♕c5 25 b4! – breaking the pin on the rook as the queen must keep e7 defended – 25...♕c7 26 ♕h8+ ♔f7 27 ♖f4+ ♘f5 28 ♕h7+ wins the black queen.

25 ♖xd5! 1-0

A simple but elegant finale. if Black retakes with the pawn he loses his queen; if he retakes with the queen he loses his king to mate on e7. Sokolov wisely chose a third option: resigns.

Game Six
A.Shirov - J.Polgar
Buenos Aires 1994
Sicilian Defence

In the early 1900s there were many so called 'theme' tournaments in which it was compulsory to open with a prescribed Gambit line, most typically the King's Gambit. Such tournaments went out of fashion, perhaps because of the improvement in defensive technique which made gambits less effective and so less attractive in the eye of the chess public and patrons.

Nevertheless, the spirit of theme tournaments was revived in 1994 in Buenos Aires when a tournament was held in honour of the very strong Soviet Grandmaster Lev Polugaevsky. Not surprisingly, at this event open lines of the Sicilian were compulsory as Polugaevsky was the author of an original variation in the Najdorf Sicilian that justly bears his name. Although the Sicilian isn't a Gambit line it is the most exciting response to 1 e4: it leads to rich middlegame positions of which chess masters of the 19th century could never have dreamed.

It is no surprise that Shirov and Polgar, two of the most tactically minded players of the modern age, should produce fireworks when obliged to contest this aggressive opening.

1   e4

On move one it is way too early to decide on a kingside attack – unless of course you know your opponent is going to play the Sicilian!

1   ...   c5

It is difficult to name a great player of the second half of the 20th century who hasn't tried the Sicilian Defence at some point in their career: even World Champions with exceptionally solid styles such as Karpov and Petrosian have ventured it as Black in top class events.

2   ♘f3

White's best move can be found by a process of elimination. He doesn't want to develop his king's bishop until the situation in the centre clarifies; it would be impetuous to bring out the queen so early; if he plays 2 d4 then Black simply takes it. So that leads us to moves like 2 c3 (not bad, as it prepares 3 d4 to build a pawn centre, though it takes away the c3 square from the knight) 3 ♘c3 (a sound developing move) and 3 ♘f3. Of these three moves, White chooses the latter as it supports a quick challenge to the c5 pawn with 3 d4.

2   ...   e6

It is well known from the French Defence that the pawn on e6 forms a formidable barrier to any attack on f7. In contrast, Black has lost many games due to the pressure on f7 in the open game after 1 e4 e5 2 ♘f3 ♘c6 3 ♗c4.

3   d4

Not satisfied with having one pawn on the fourth rank White opens more lines for his pieces.

3   ...   cxd4

Black is obliged to exchange but can be pleased at having prevented White from establishing an ideal centre with pawns on both d4 and e4.

4   ♘xd4

Obviously the knight recaptures as 4 ♕xd4 would just lose time after 4...♘c6. Incidentally, this shows why the queen almost always does best to stay at home in the opening phase of the game. Paradoxically, her strength can be a weakness as she must always flee when attacked by a lesser piece rather than stand and fight her ground.

4   ...   ♘c6

Black has no intention of letting the knight remain undisturbed on d4, where it dominates the centre.

5   ♘c3

Even in complex modern opening systems you can find good moves by applying the rule of thumb that knights should be developed before bishops.

5   ...   d6

By delaying the development of her king's knight Black side-steps two possible attacking lines that occur after 5...♘f6: 6 ♘xc6 bxc6 7 e5 ♘d5 8 ♘e4 and the Sveshnikov Variation 5...♘f6 6 ♘db5 d6 7 ♗f4 e5 8 ♗g5. After the game move Black can answer 6 ♘db5 with the simple 6...a6 chasing away the knight.

6   g4

A very aggressive move. White's reasoning is as follows: 'Black has built a solid and compact pawn centre but hasn't challenged my space advantage there. Evidently my opponent is intending to play on the queenside and is happy to keep the status quo in the centre. Well, as that is the case I can immediately begin my plan of attack on the kingside; I don't have to worry about my centre being pressurized too much. It is reasonable to

suppose that Black will castle kingside – in the meantime I will castle queenside. Therefore I'll play 6 g4 beginning a pawn storm without any more ado'.

6   ...   a6

Black refuses to be panicked into rushing her pieces into the centre. Instead she makes a calm reply which facilitates a counter attack on the queenside.

7   ♗e3

Shirov continues his build up. He is now one step nearer to whisking his king away to safety on the queenside as a prelude to a kingside onslaught.

7   ...   ♘ge7!

A preferable deployment to 7...♘f6 for two reasons. Firstly, the knight cannot be attacked with g4-g5, when White would gain a move for his assault; and secondly on e7 the knight supports his colleague on c6 which means a queenside expansion is possible with b7-b5 without dropping a piece.

8   ♘b3

This looks like a flagrant decentralization, but White believes that the knight on e7 is badly placed and so, by avoiding an exchange of d4, denies it the centre post it would achieve after say 8 ♕f3 ♘xd4 9 ♗xd4 ♘c6 10 ♗e3 ♘e5.

8   ...   b5

A key advance for Black in the Sicilian Defence for a number of reasons. The mobile queenside pawns deny White's bishop the c4 square; they are ready to chase the white knight from c3, which will leave the e4 pawn less secure; and finally if White castles queenside they are all set to launch an attack.

9   f4

White presses ahead with his own attack and at the same time denies a black knight the use of the e5 square.

9   ...   ♗b7

A quiet developing move, but one containing poison as there is a latent threat against the e4 pawn, in conjunction with b5-b4 driving away the white knight.

10   ♕f3

Shirov defends e4 again and appears all set to continue his aggressive build up with g4-g5 and 0-0-0 followed by the advance of the h pawn. Still, the position of the white queen and rook on h1 on the same diagonal is distinctly uncomfortable – Black need only find a way to surprise the white queen with his bishop on b7...

10   ...   g5!

This brilliant offer of a pawn by the greatest ever female player completely upsets White's attacking plan.

11   fxg5

The sacrifice is best accepted, or else after 11...gxf4 White will suffer the same indignities as in the game without even having an extra pawn to console him.

11   ...   ♘e5

The first benefit of the pawn sacrifice: the black knight gains a fantastic centre post where it cannot be attacked by an enemy pawn.

12   ♕g2

The second benefit is the distress caused to the white queen, who must keep the e4 pawn defended as after 12 ♕e2 White has to reckon with the response b5-b4 followed by ♗xe4, destroying his centre.

12   ...   b4

Polgar makes forceful pawn strokes on both sides of the board, but her attention is very much focused on gaining control of the centre.

13   ♘e2

Having been forced to retreat, the knight can only choose its least bad square.

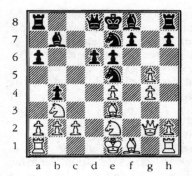

13   ...   h5!

The culmination of Black's artistic play with her pawns. It brings to mind Nimzowitsch's dictum that 'a move on the wing, but with the mind on the centre, betokens the hand of the master'.

14   gxh5

After 14 gxh6 ♗xh6 15 ♗xh6 ♖xh6 16 0-0-0 ♘7g6 Black has ample play for the pawn: her centre is solid and she can play for an attack on the queenside with a5-a4 etc. Meanwhile there is no white attack in sight and the black king is surrounded by staunch defenders. However, events in the game soon prove that this is the path Shirov should have taken.

14   ...   ♘f5

From being badly placed on e7 the knight suddenly becomes one of the stars of the show!

15   ♗f2

The bishop saves itself and guards the h4 square. If instead 15 ♗d2 ♘h4 followed by 16...♘hf3+ or 16...♗xe4 would be very painful for White.

15   ...   ♛xg5!

A spectacular entrance by the black queen which has a deeper point than merely regaining one of the pawns. If now 16 ♛xg5 ♘f3+ 17 ♔d1 ♘xg5 leaves White facing collapse on e4 as if 18 exf5 ♗xh1 wins the exchange.

16   ♘a5

White has relied on this move to save him and even win the game as after 16...♛xg2 17 ♗xg2 both the bishop on b7 and the knight on f5 are hanging and so 17...♖c8 18 exf5 wins at once for White.

16   ....   ♘e3!!

A terrible shock for Shirov. He is mated after 17 ♛xg5 ♘f3 – yes, it really is checkmate! This type of mate with two knights rarely occurs in practical play, so it is no surprise that even a tactical virtuoso like Shirov should miss it, especially as he was wrapped up in his own ideas of winning a piece.

If instead 17 ♗xe3 ♛xe3 leaves White unable to deal with the threat of 18...♘f3+ 19 ♔d1 ♛d2 mate, as well as 18...♗xe4, when his centre is ripped apart.

17   ♛g3

White tries to make the best of a bad job, but there is no satisfactory way to deal with the black knight's double attack on the queen and the c2 square.

17   ...   ♛xg3

After the magical tactical display in the early middlegame Polgar now diverts the course of the game towards an endgame in which she has a sizeable material advantage.

18   ♘xg3

With this method of recapture White gives his king the e2 square as a breathing hole.

18   ...   ♘xc2+

The fork of the king and rook by a knight on c2 is one of the disasters that often befalls a beginner, though rarely after such a sparkling build up!

19   ♔d1

The king goes to the d file so that he can at least try to prevent the knight re-emerging after its feast.

19   ...   ♘xa1

An inglorious fate for the rook which has been murdered in its bed.

20 ♘xb7

White snatches the bishop. If only he could somehow corner the black knight on a1 then he would have a good game.

20 ... b3

But this scotches White's plan as the pawn provides the knight with an escape route.

21 axb3

Also futile is 21 a3 ♘c2 and the knight hops out.

21 ... ♘xb3

Now White has no compensation at all for the exchange: in Grandmaster chess this makes his position already resignable.

22 ♔c2

Nevertheless Shirov, perhaps still in a state of shock at what has happened, plays on grimly.

22 ... ♘c5

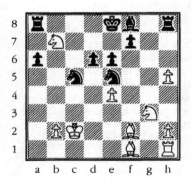

When you have a material advantage it makes sense to exchange pieces as the ratio of your army's strength in relation to your opponent's becomes more pronounced with every piece that vanishes from the board. On the other hand you shouldn't exchange pawns, as many pawnless endgames are theoretical draws, even when one player has an extra piece – for example, rook and knight versus rook without any pawns is a fairly easy draw for the defender.

23 ♘xc5

Nevertheless, in some sense White is pleased to exchange off his wayward knight that was deep in enemy terrotory.

23 ... dxc5

Black recaptures and now has a nice post for her knight on d4.

24 ♗e1

Perhaps he can generate some counterplay with 25 ♗c3, pinning the knight?

24 ... ♘f3

No: the knight heads for d4 to shut out the bishop.

25 ♗c3

The only faint hope for White is that his bishop pair can somehow support the passed pawn on h5.

25 ... ♘d4+

This effectively slams the door shut on White's scheme.

26 ♔d3

In such a hopeless situation he might as well advance his king fearlessly.

26 ... ♗d6

Polgar counter attacks against the defender of the h5 pawn.

27 ♗g2

Black wins very simply after 27 ♗xd4 cxd4 28 ♔xd4 ♔e7, followed by a6-a5 – saving the pawn from ♗xa6 in the future – and then ♖ag8 threatening ♗xg3, etc.

27   ...   ♗e5

The bishop defends the knight and meets the threat of 28 e5.

28   ♔c4

The king attacks the c5 pawn but it's all just bluff.

28   ...   ♔e7!

A fine reply as if 29 ♔xc5 ♖ab8! 30 ♗xd4 ♖hc8 is mate.

29   ♖a1

The last twitchings of a dead man.

29   ...   ♘c6

0-1

Here at last Shirov gave up as his king will suffer a fatal buffeting by the black rooks after 30 ♔xc5 ♗xc3 31 bxc3 ♖hc8.

Game Seven
M.Adams - V.Salov
Dortmund 1992
Sicilian Defence

The English Grandmaster Michael Adams has a distinctive style that Kasparov once described as 'Python-like'. You can judge whether this is an apt description by playing through the three games by Adams in this book. Certainly there is something snake-like in the way he aims to neutralise any attempt the opponent makes to play actively by gradually imposing a stranglehold upon the position. Only when the opponent's pieces have been reduced to passivity and he is helpless does Adams move in for the kill. In the present game his opponent, a top Grandmaster, plays the very dynamic Sveshnikov Variation but still can't prevent Adams from gaining complete control of the position with a series of apparently simple and unpretentious moves. I would recommend a deep study of Adams' games to anyone looking to improve their understanding of chess strategy.

1   e4

The first of many well established moves of theory. There are many players who regard the long opening variations so typical of modern chess as an unavoidable evil; on the other hand they often lead to middlegame positions which are full of life and character, whereas 'non-theoretical' or 'solid' opening systems all too frequently end up in dull or bland situations. Theoretical openings can enrich the creative side of chess.

1   ...   c5

It is a curious fact that the Sicilian often leads to a lively tactical battle, whereas the outcome in the mirror image pawn structure in the English Opening after 1 c4 e5 is a game much quieter and more positional in nature.

Of course it is a question of the extra tempo: in the Sicilian White can afford to play aggressively as he has an extra move, whereas in the English Black cannot afford to be so provocative.

2   ♘f3

The knight immediately joins in the battle for the centre by leaping to its favourite square.

2 ... ♘c6

In contrast to lines of the Sicilian in which Black sets up a small, reliable centre with e7-e6 and d7-d6, here Salov intends right from the outset to contest White's space advantage. Therefore he prefers to develop his knight rather than commit himself to any pawn moves.

3 d4

White removes the obstacle on c5 to gain ascendancy over the d4 square – but only for two moves!

3 ... cxd4

Black cannot allow the pawn on d4 to evade capture for if 3...e6 the black knight can be driven from its prized centre post on c6 with 4 d5.

4 ♘xd4

Traditionally in the Sicilian Defence White has supremacy over the four ranks in his half of the board, whilst Black is fortified on his own first three ranks with a 'no man's land' running between them on White's fifth rank. However, it soon becomes clear that this general rule doesn't apply here.

4 ... ♘f6

For now Black makes do with sound development and forces White to defend e4. If he had tried the immediate 4...e5 then 5 ♘b5 d6 6 c4 would give White firm control of the d5 centre point.

5 ♘c3

White supports his centre after which Black must choose between the safe and steady 5...e6 (or 5...d6)

and the more adventurous approach seen in the game.

5 ... e5

The defining move of the Sveshnikov Variation. At first glance it makes a lot of sense as Black:

♦ establishes his pawn centre and negates White's space advantage

♦ drives the enemy knight from its strong base on d4

♦ clears the way for the development of his king's bishop with gain of time, as 6 ♘xc6 bxc6 would only strengthen Black's centre.

6 ♘db5

This, however, is a very testing reply. The downside of Black's last move is that he has left himself with a backward pawn on the d file.

6 ... d6

Black deals with the positional threat of 7 ♘d6+ ♗xd6 8 ♕xd6 when White has the two bishops, but he remains afflicted with a backward pawn. Nevertheless, the practice of countless master games has shown that the pawn is very hard for White to win, despite the fact that it sits on an open file and cannot be defended by another pawn unless by some freak chance it got to d4.

7   &g5

It is often the case that the square in front of a backward pawn is a greater weakness, real or potential, than the pawn itself. Here the d5 square cannot be defended by a black pawn which means that White would love to get absolute control of it as a centre post for one of his knights. Therefore, it makes a lot of sense for him to use his bishop to pin and prepare to capture the knight that defends the d5 square.

7   ...   a6

Black chooses a good moment to drive back the knight as White threatened 8 &d5 followed by a knight fork on c7.

8   &a3

Black may have loosened his pawns in the centre with his bold play beginning with 5...e5, but at least he can be pleased to have driven the white knight to the edge of the board, which is a long, long way from the fabulous station where it began its career on d4.

8   ...   b5

Another dynamic pawn advance which:

♦ forces White to deal with the threat of 9...b4, forking his knights

♦ prevents the white bishop on f1 using c4 as an attacking square

♦ stops the manoeuvre &c4 and &e3, when the exiled knight returns to the centre

9   &xf6

White combines business with pleasure: he has to counter the threat of 9...b4 and does so by carrying out his plan to gain control of the d5 square. Naturally such an exchange has to be carefully assessed as White is parting with his excellent dark square bishop.

9   ...   gxf6

It looks ugly to recapture with the pawn but 9...♛xf6 wastes too much time: 10 &d5 ♛d8 – or else there is a fork on c7 – 11 c4! and White has a dangerous initiative.

10   &d5

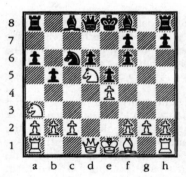

The fortunes of White's knights make quite a contrast – it is akin to one twin brother living in a palace and the other sleeping in a hole.

The ideal location for a knight is on a centre square from which it cannot be chased back by an enemy pawn; the worse situation is to be trapped on the edge of the board. Therefore the knight in the middle is delighted with the d5 square whereas his comrade is wretched on a3.

10   ...   &g7

Although his pawns on the kingside have been dislocated, it is by no means all bad news for Black: the bishop at least is grateful that a cavity has appeared for it on g7.

11   c3

The knight looks down and out on a3, but not for much longer as White clears the c2 square to allow the horse to return immediately to the centre.

11   ...   f5

Meanwhile Black finds a purpose for his doubled pawns: he can attack the white centre, dispose of the e4 pawn and still have another f pawn in reserve to spearhead a further assault along the f file.

12   exf5

White temporarily concedes control of the b1-h7 diagonal as he will gain time to recentralize his errant knight by attacking the bishop on f5 after ♘c2 and ♘e3. He also opens the diagonal a8-h1 which will prove of great use to his king's bishop.

12   ...   ♗xf5

Black gets his pawn back and completes the development of his minor pieces.

13   ♘c2

All as planned: the white knight returns to the centre and prepares to strengthen White's hold on the d5 square.

13   ...   0-0

Whilst the kingside isn't an ideal residence for the black king in view of the missing g pawn, the bishop on g7 is an excellent shield against any attack.

14   ♘ce3

White bolsters his knight on d5 and makes a side swipe at the black bishop.

14   ...   ♗e6

The bishop isn't too concerned at being compelled to retreat as in any case Black needed to clear the way for f7-f5 to achieve counterplay in the centre. The bishop selects e6 rather than g6 as here he is involved in the fight for the important d5 square.

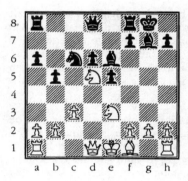

15   g3

All White's attention is focused on the d5 square. Therefore he prefers to spend an extra move in getting the king's bishop onto the h1-a8 diagonal rather than develop in routine style with 15 ♗e2.

In some cases it is essential to mobilize the pieces rapidly to avoid being overwhelmed by the opponent's superior firepower; but in other cases, as here, a more leisurely development is possible and indeed necessary. White has to put the pieces on the correct strategical squares rather than rush them out, or else he will lose all his opening advantage.

15   ...   ♘e7

Black for his part refuses to just sit and watch as White conquers the centre. He evacuates his knight from the long diagonal in anticipation of ♗g2 and puts more pressure on d5.

16   ♗g2

The bishop enjoys a splendid diagonal and already Black must attend to the threat of 17 ♘xe7+ ♕xe7 18 ♗xa8, winning the exchange.

16   ...   ♖b8

The rook prudently removes itself from the danger diagonal. On b8 it defends the b5 pawn in anticipation of an attempt by White to undermine the queenside with a2-a4.

17   0-0

At last White castles. He can be pleased with the coordinated action of his minor pieces which have an impressive hold on the d5 square. His long term plans include the preparation of the a2-a4 advance or ♕d2 followed by ♖ad1 to attack the backward d6 pawn.

On the other hand, Black's counterplay with f7-f5 shouldn't be underestimated.

17   ...   ♘xd5?

This exchange helps White as it enables him to slow down the f7-f5 break. It was better to play 17...f5 at once, when 18 ♘xe7+ ♕xe7 19 ♘d5 ♕d7 leaves the position delicately balanced.

18   ♗xd5!

The majority of players would automatically recapture with the knight, but Michael Adams didn't become one of the best five players in the world by making routine decisions.

A knight would look pretty on d5, but it wouldn't stop Black carrying out his plan with 18...f5. In contrast, after the game move Black can't move his f pawn without leaving the bishop on e6 en prise. Or if 18...♗xd5 19 ♕xd5 and Black still can't play 19...f5 as the pawn is pinned! Meanwhile White would be able to play ♖ad1 and ♘f5 with complete domination.

18   ...   ♔h8

Salov decides that it would be too slow to prepare f7-f5, if indeed it is still a feasible plan; so he changes track and looks to activate his king's bishop. If however 18...♗h6 then 19 ♗xe6 fxe6 20 ♕g4+ would force the awkward 20...♔f7 to defend e6. so first of all he moves his king to shelter on h8.

19   a4

Having defeated the plan of f7-f5 White turns his attention to the queenside. He aims either to create a black pawn weakness on a6 or to gain command of the a file for his rook.

19   ...   ♗h6

Now at least the bishop comes into the game, though a plan involving just the pieces cannot hope to be as effective as one which utilizes the centre pawn majority.

20 axb5

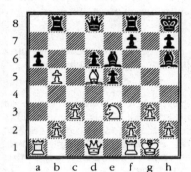

A critical moment as Black needs to find the correct response if he is escape from the deadly bind that Adams is weaving around him.

20 ... axb5?

Sometimes 'automatic recaptures' can be fatal blunders.

Now the white rook on a1 will gain a wonderful open file which it can use to penetrate the black queenside. It was imperative for Black to ease the pressure with multiple exchanges, namely 20...♗xe3! 21 fxe3 ♗xd5 22 ♕xd5 ♖xb5! 23 ♕d2 a5, when he should hold the endgame with queen and rooks. The classic recipe for escaping from a difficult middlegame is a swap of pieces.

21 ♘c2!

Salov won't be allowed a second chance to lop off the horse. Adams avoids the damage to his pawn structure that occurs after ♗xe3 and

f2xe3 and keeps the knight to restrain Black's pawns. In particular the break 21...b4 followed by the liquidation of the weak b5 pawn is prevented.

21 ... ♕d7

Black keeps the white rook out of the seventh rank, but there is also the sixth rank!

22 ♖a6!

Already Salov must meet the threat of 23 ♗xe6 fxe6 24 ♖xd6.

22 ... ♗h3

This looks like an attacking move, but in reality it is a desperate attempt to win time to hold his position together by hitting the white rook.

23 ♖e1

Carefully does it: 23 ♗g2 would uncover an attack on d6 and threaten 24 ♖xd6 but after 23...♗xg2 24 ♔xg2 ♕b7+ White has suddenly lost a rook!

23 ... ♗g5

As nothing is happening on the kingside the bishop begins a journey to the queenside in search of an aggressive role.

24 ♘b4

Things are much clearer for the white knight as it is beckoned towards the beautiful outpost square on d5.

24 ... ♗d8

'Chess is one long regret': No doubt Salov was wishing he had exchanged his wandering bishop for the powerful white knight when he had the chance back on move 20.

25 ♗e4

An all purpose move which

♦ vacates the d5 square for the white knight

♦ clears the way to threaten 26 ♖xd6

♦ introduces the idea of an attack on h7.

25 ... ♗b6

The bishop blocks the rook's attack on d6 and hopes to generate play against f2, but White's reply is crushing.

26 ♘d5

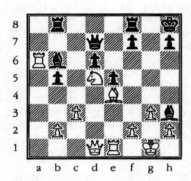

After a long wait the knight finally reaches the ideal square it was denied for strategical reasons back on move 18. Since that moment in the game the fortunes of the black bishop have deteriorated sharply. Now Black can't tolerate 26...♗d8 going back again as 27 ♕h5 – threatening mate on h7 – 27...f6 – here 27...f5 drops the bishop on h3 – 28 ♖ea1 planning 29 ♖a7 is overwhelming. Therefore Salov has to resort to tactical ideas to keep his position alive.

26 ... f5

This move is an integral part of Black's strategy in the Sveshnikov,

but here it comes as a desperate measure rather than a well thought out idea.

27 ♘xb6

The tactical point of Black's last move is that it seems as if White is just winning a piece, but after

27 ... ♕d8

...he has two pieces hanging which can't defend each other.

28 ♘d7!

However, it would have been contrary to logic for Black's wretched situation to provide him with a two-move escape clause. Therefore it is no surprise that White has a way to win an important pawn whilst maintaining all his other advantages.

28 ... ♕xd7

A necessary capture as the black rooks were in a fork.

29 ♖xd6

After seemingly endless pressure, Adams nets his first material gain.

29 ... ♕e7

The queen rushes to the kingside in an attempt to hold together the fractured defences around her monarch.

30 ♖d7

Just as the howls of a banshee are an omen of approaching death, so too the appearance of a rook on the seventh rank is a portent of doom for the defending side.

30 ... ♕g5

The queen must prevent ♕h5 by White, when either the bishop on h3 drops or catastrophe follows on h7.

31   ♗c2

Now the e5 pawn is hanging and if 31...♖fe8 a possible finish would be 32 f4! exf4 33 ♕d4+ ♔g8 34 ♗b3+ – here we see why the bishop was placed on c2 – 34...♔f8 35 ♕h8+ and mates.

31   ...   e4

This at least forms a solid barrier to the white bishop, but the white rooks and queen can rampage along the seventh rank.

32   ♕d4+

The queen heads for a7 with gain of time.

32   ...   ♕f6

It demonstrates the hopelessness of Black's predicament that he can only dream about being allowed to defend the rotten endgame after 33 ♕xf6+ ♖xf6.

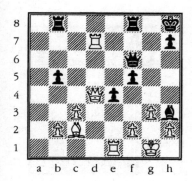

33   ♕a7

Adams isn't interested in the endgame as he knows that his onslaught along Black's second rank will soon be irresistible.

33   ...   ♕h6

He cannot let the h7 pawn drop.

34   ♖a1

The other white rook hurries to join in the fun on the seventh rank.

34   ...   b4

A last gasp of activity by Black that White quite rightly ignores.

35   ♕d4+

Another queen check on d4, and this time it clears the way for the rook to reach a7.

35   ...   ♕f6

Back again, but this time White has no need to avoid the exchange of queens.

36   ♖aa7

It is a testimony to Adams' brilliant positional understanding that he can outplay top notch opposition in this fashion.

36   ...   ♕xd4

There was no longer any way to defend h7.

37   cxd4   1-0

Black gave up as besides being completely busted in a general sense he has no answer to the threat of mate in two beginning with 38 ♖xh7+ which doesn't at least drop the bishop on h3.

Game Eight
V.Anand - G.Kasparov
World Championship,
New York 1995
Sicilian Defence

1   e4

This is the ideal way to begin a game of chess whether you are looking to start a big attack or maintain a small advantage going into the middlegame.

1 ... c5

A fighting reply which ignores the pawn on e4 and looks for counterplay on the queenside. This is a radically different philosophy from the approach of most masters in the first half of the 20th century, who regarded it as almost behoven of Black to copy White's first move with 1...e5 to offset his space advantage in the centre.

2 ♘f3

This represents a great increase in the knight's efficiency: on g1 it controlled a maximum of three squares, whereas on f3 this has risen to eight squares – and two of them are centre squares.

2 ... d6

An all purpose move which stabilizes Black's centre, opens a diagonal for his queen's bishop and makes the d7 available for his knight. Most importantly of all he prepares ♘f6 without having the knight pushed back by e4-e5.

3 d4

White conquers the d4 square in order to increase the mobility of his minor pieces.

3 ... cxd4

Naturally White's strong centre pawn should be eliminated.

4 ♘xd4

Now the knight is extremely well placed to support any plan of attack that White might conceive. On the other hand, Black has the consolation that White has been prevented from building a broad pawn centre.

4 ... ♘f6

When deciding what to play, top priority should always be given to a sound developing move that contains an immediate threat. Now White must attend to the defence of e4.

5 ♘c3

It's worth remembering that knights tend to know where they belong at an earlier stage in the game than bishops. The knight is highly unlikely to find a better square than c3, where it defends e4 and is in no danger from an immediate attack. Instead the e4 pawn could have been defended by 5 ♗d3, but this is far less efficient as the bishop might soon find it would be better placed on c4 or e2.

5 ... g6

Rather than develop the bishop to e7 with 5...e6 and 6...♗e7, Kasparov decides on a kingside fianchetto. This is the famous Dragon Variation. It has many good points, but first we should appreciate the risk that the World

Champion is taking in his quest for counterplay:

He is creating a target on g6.

The pawn on g6 encourages White to castle queenside and launch an attack with h4-h5.

He is delaying his development

It takes two moves to put the bishop on g7, compared to only one to play ♗e7, if we accept that e7-e6 freeing up the e7 square is a useful move in its own right.

His centre pawns are less flexible.

The move e7-e6. which is an integral part of the typical small Sicilian centre, becomes problematical as Black has committed himself to a fianchetto and so cannot keep the d6 pawn defended with ♗e7. Even more inappropriate would be e7-e5, which in many other systems is useful to control d4 and f4, but here would shut in the bishop besides leaving d6 weak.

6   ♗e3

Despite the drawbacks outlined in the previous note the black bishop will be excellently placed on g7 both for defence and attack. Therefore White decides on a plan to exchange it off with ♕d2 and ♗h6 in the future. This represents White's most ambitious response to the Dragon Variation – in effect he is trying to refute outright 5...g6.

In the meantime the bishop supports the knight on d4.

6   ...   ♗g7

This bishop has the potential to exert enormous pressure as White has traded his d pawn and so cannot

use it to plug the a1-h8 diagonal on d4.

7   ♕d2

White continues with his plan to challenge the black bishop with ♗h6. At the same time he gives himself the option of castling queenside as the prelude to a pawn rush against the black king.

7   ...   ♘c6

The knight joins in the battle for the centre and at the same time rules out 8 ♗h6? in view of 8...♗xh6 9 ♕xh6 ♘xd4, winning a piece.

8   f3

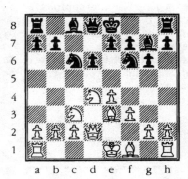

This useful pawn push supports the attacking move g2-g4 and is also a precaution against 8...♘g4, when Black not only prevents ♗h6 but also threatens to eliminate White's valuable dark square bishop.

8   ...   0-0

In some sense, Kasparov is castling his king into danger as White is gearing up for a kingside advance. On the other hand Black has a lot of active pieces and the situation in the centre is far from stable; therefore it will be hard for

White to concentrate his forces sufficiently for an attack on the black king without things falling apart for him elsewhere.

9   &c4

If he wants to pursue his dream of a kingside assault White has first of all to think about restraining his opponent's activity as after 9 0-0-0 Black can play 9...d5 when the focus of the battle shifts to the centre. On c4 the bishop deters d6-d5 and may prove useful in attacking f7 in the future.

9   ...   &d7

Nevertheless, the white bishop is also a target sitting unprotected on an open file and Kasparov intends to harass it with ♖c8 followed by moving the knight from c6 with a discovered attack. In this way he will speed up his counterplay in the centre.

10   h4

At last White feels ready to begin his pawn offensive on the kingside.

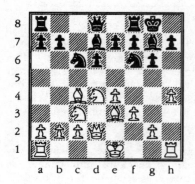

10   ...   h5

A well respected chess precept says that you shouldn't move pawns on your weaker side. This is especially the case when facing a pawn storm in front of your king – any alteration in the defensive wall of pawns is likely to create a protruding weak spot on which the advancing pawns can base their break through. Here for example it looks as if Black is helping White's cause by exposing the h5 pawn to attack by g2-g4.

However, in this specific situation it should be borne in mind that there is already a target for White's pawns to attack – the g6 pawn. Practice has shown that if White is allowed to advance h4-h5 and then break open the h file he gains a vigorous attack. By playing 10...h5, Black is almost encouraging g2-g4, but at least after the reply h5xg4 the white centre is crumbling which means that Black should have more chances of striking an effective counterblow elswhere.

Nevertheless, 10...h5 remains a double-edged concept and it is open to debate whether or not he should play it. Of course, the fact that Kasparov was prepared to play it in a World Championship match is a great endorsement.

11   &b3

White removes his bishop from the vulnerable c4 square in anticipation of Black's next move.

11   ...   ♖c8

Having defended his kingside to his satisfaction, Kasparov now puts his rook on an excellent open file.

If White responds by castling queenside then Black's ideas include ♘e5 and ♘c4, putting the knight on the weakest square in White's pawn structure, when after the exchange &xc4; ♖xc4 he has not only gained the bishop pair but also removed any tactical threats to f7. A more radical idea for Black should White castle queenside is the preparation of the exchange sacrifice ♖xc3!? This would be particularly effective after White has committed his queen to an attack on the kingside so that he has to recapture b2xc3, when the pawns defending his king are shattered. Alternatively, Black could simply increase the pressure on the queenside with a7-a5-a4.

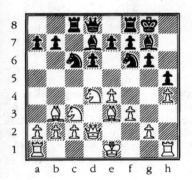

12   ♘xc6?!

Anand avoids all the tactical themes for Black described in the previous note that require the use of the c file. But it is at a high cost as this exchange considerably increases Black's control of the centre and is seldom a good idea for White in the Sicilian Defence. Having come so far he should have boldly castled queenside, faced Black's counterplay head on and trusted that his attack on the kingside would prevail. It is no surprise that Anand was keen to do something unusual in order to surprise his magnificently prepared opponent. Nevertheless, this wasn't

a good time to leave familiar territory.

12   ...   bxc6

Now the c file is blocked but in return Black has got another pawn in the centre, which gives extra dynamism to his position. Furthermore he can attack down the b file and also try to exploit the position of the bishop on b3.

13   ♗h6

This proves to be the final flourish of White's projected attack on the kingside. From now on he will act purely on the defensive in trying to hold together the shaky foundations of his centre position.

13   ...   c5

The black pawns begin to show their teeth with the threat of 14...c4, which would seriously embarrass the white bishop.

14   ♗c4

The bishop has little choice but to return to c4 to block the pawn.

14   ...   ♛b6

In Kasparov's capable hands the drawbacks to the faulty exchange 12 ♘xc6 begin to snowball. Here the black queen is deployed to an excellent attacking post with gain of time by attacking b2.

15   ♗xg7

At least White has managed to exchange off Black's dark-squared bishop which would otherwise have wreaked havoc down the long diagonal after White's next move.

15   ...   ♚xg7

Now once again White has to attend to the threat on b2. Kasparov himself suggests that White can bail out with 16 0-0-0 ♛b4 17 b3 ♝e6 18 ♘d5 ♘xd5 19 exd5 ♛xd2+ 20 ♖xd2 when the exchange of queens has safeguarded White's position.

16   b3

Anand prefers to keep the tension by avoiding the queen swap, but Black is able to brush aside his supposed light-squared blockade.

16   ...   ♝e6!

The bishop threatens to tear up White's queenside pawns with 17...♝xc4 18 bxc4, when the c4 pawn would be a constant liability.

17   ♘d5

One can sympathize with White's reluctance to strengthen Black's control of d5 with 17 ♝xe6 fxe6, an exchange which also grants the black rook on f8 an open file. Nevertheless this was the best chance to keep the balance as the attempt to play actively just leads to disaster.

17   ...   ♝xd5

An unwelcome exchange for White as the natural response 18 ♝xd5 allows 18...e6 19 ♝c4 ♖fe8 followed by 20...d5, when Black's pawns conquer the centre.

18   exd5

Anand hopes that things will remain quiet long enough for him to develop his rooks, but Kasparov of course is in no mood for delays.

18   ...   e5!

Now White must either let Black gain supremacy over the dark squares in the centre or else open lines with the move he plays in the game.

19   dxe6

Now all the pent up dynamism in Black's fortress bursts forth.

19   ...   d5!

The obvious move was the recapture 19...fxe6. especially as White cannot reply 20 ♝xe6? because of 20...♖ce8. But if Black is going to exploit his lead in development then he needs to keep the e file open as an avenue of attack for his rooks – and he needs the white king to remain stuck on e1.

Therefore rather than taking pawns Kasparov concern is to make the idea of castling impossible or unacceptable for White, so that his prey cannot escape from the e file. With this in mind he advances his centre pawns to disrupt White's queenside pawns and make it unfit to be a future residence for his king. At the same time White will be prevented from castling kingside after Black's next move.

Remember that the pawn count is irrelevant if Black succeeds in mating White down the e file!

20   ♝e2

The d5 pawn is taboo: 20 ♗xd5 ♖fd8 21 c4 fxe6 and Black wins a piece.

20 ... c4!

All as planned: the black queen now covers the g1 square and so rules out castling kingside by White, whereas the disintegrating pawn structure on the queenside makes this a suicidal escape route for the beleaguered white monarch.

21 c3?

A fatal loss of time. If 21 0-0-0 cxb3 22 axb3 ♕xb3 is horrible, but 21 ♖d1 bringing up reinforcements might well have saved the day. White could then facilitate castling kingside with ♕d4 followed by 0-0.

21 ... ♖ce8!

The battle will be won down the e file: a magnificent channel of attack for the black rooks.

22 bxc4

Instead 22 exf7 ♖xf7 would just speed up Black's plan of doubling rooks on the e file.

22 ... ♖xe6

The signs are ominous for the white king: how can he resist the attack along the e file when almost half his army are absent from the battle on a1 and h1?

23 ♔f1

Here 23 cxd5 is a futile exercise in pawn grabbing that merely helps the black knight join in the attack after 23...♖e5 24 ♔f1 – or else 24...♖fe8 wins the bishop – 24...♘xd5 threatening 25...♘e3+ with a massacre.

Therefore Anand elects to move the white king away immediately to prevent 23...♖fe8 from pinning and winning the bishop. The alternative was 23 0-0-0 – this looks ghastly and so it is: 23...♖b8 – threat 24...♕b1 mate – 24 ♗d3 dxc4 and the bishop has no where safe to move to keep b1 defended as if 25 ♗c2 ♕b2 mate.

23 ... ♖fe8

In preparing one of my earlier books on miniature chess games I noticed that Garry Kasparov has made a career out of sacrificing pawns to get his rooks into play whilst those of his opponents are still slumbering. Here the doubled rooks will prove irresistible down the open file.

24 ♗d3

The bishop must flee as 24 ♖e1 dxc4 leaves White completely paralyzed by the pin on the e file. In that case the simplest way for Black to exploit his advantage would be to play ♖d6 and then ♘d5 with a fatal check to follow on the e3 square. In this variation and the game continuation you will see that the white bishop is continually outclassed by the black knight due to its inability to fight for the dark squares such as e3 and g3.

24	...	dxc4

Now White can hardly refuse the pawn offer, for if 25 ♗c2 ♖d6 wins in the style of the previous note above: Black intends 26...♘d5 followed by 27...♘e3+ with a lethal infiltration on the dark squares, and the exchange of queens doesn't even help White: 26 ♕f2 ♕xf2+ 27 ♔xf2 ♖d2+ wins the bishop.

25	♗xc4	

White hopes that the attack on the rook will at least slow down Black's onslaught, but Kasparov has prepared a killer move.

Black has a tremendous lead in development: he has both rooks in the fray whilst White's rooks are still inactive on a1 and h1. Nevertheless this advantage won't last forever: if Black fails to seize the moment then White can remedy the situation by bringing both rooks to the defence of his king. So Black must find a way to immediately press home his temporary advantage. The target of course is the white king: Black must either mate or win a decisive amount of material before White can develop his rooks. Is there a way for Black to open up lines, say with a piece sacrifice?

Even if Black gave up a piece to get at the white king, in real terms he would still have an enormous advantage in fire power: two rooks against a bishop.

Therefore it is entirely logical to offer the knight with

25	...	♘e4!

The black knight attacks White's queen and at the same time threatens 26...♘g3 – which, believe it or not is checkmate! If 26 fxe4 then the open lines prove decisive: 26...♖f6+ 27 ♔e1 ♖xe4+ 28 ♗e2 – or if 28 ♔d1 then simply 28...♖xc4 when there is no good answer to 29...♖d6 winning the queen – 28...♕f2+ 29 ♔d1 ♖xe2! 30 ♕xe2 ♖d6+ and Black wins the white queen.

Nor can Black decline the sacrifice with 26 ♕e1 as the devilish little move 26...♖d6! wins on the spot: the threat is 27...♘d2+ winning the queen – to say nothing of the bishop on c4 – and if 27 fxe4 then 27...♖f6+ 28 ♔e2 ♖xe4+ wins the queen. It is no wonder that Anand preferred to resign straight-away.

The analysis that justifies this sacrifice might appear complicated, but essentially it is a case of a black queen and two rooks attacking a white king who is only protected by the queen. These are hopeless odds when all the lines are opened up.

0-1

Game Nine
M.Adams - J.Benjamin
New York 1996
Sicilian Defence

1 e4

One day a computer may decide that the best way to open a game of chess is 1 a3, in order to prevent Black pinning the knight on c3 after 43...♗b4 (and not 1 e4? because of 38...♖f5! winning the g5 pawn). But until that moment arrives the best the human mind can come up with is 1 e4 freeing the queen and bishop.

1 ... c5

In the early days of chess history, when 1...e5 seemed almost as compulsory for Black as 1 e4 for White, the Sicilian was dismissed as an 'Irregular Opening'. Nowadays it is recognised as being not only fully sound but also the most exciting response to 1 e4.

2 ♘f3

The only possible objection to this excellent developing move is that it obstructs the pawn on f2, which could otherwise go to f4 and control the e5 square. As pawns have been described as the 'soul of chess' this might seems a serious drawback, especially if we recall that after 1 d4 White is always very respectful to his c pawn: he makes a point of advancing 2 c4 (or 2 ♘f3 and then 3 c4) rather than obstructing the pawn with 2 ♘c3.

It is indeed possible for White to play 1 e4 c5 2 f4 or 2 ♘c3 and then 3 f4. However, it doesn't mean that he is neglecting his pawns when he

plays 2 ♘f3, as he has another great pawn advance in mind: d2-d4.

If contrast after 1 d4 d5 2 ♘c3 ♘f6 White cannot play 3 e4 unless he wants to make a rather dubious gambit after 3...dxe4 4 f3 so in that case White does better to avoid putting the knight on c3 in favour of 2 c4 (or 2 ♘f3 ♘f6 3 c4) so that he can apply pressure on d5.

Therefore we can conclude that White isn't neglecting his pawns after 2 ♗f3: he is simply more in love with the advance d2-d4 than f2-f4.

2 ... e6

In good Sicilian style Black fights for the d5 square, opens up e7 for his pieces and clears a diagonal for his king's bishop.

3 c3

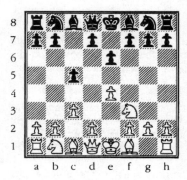

Rather than activate his knight after 3 d4 cxd4 4 ♘xd4, White decides to build a pawn centre: a good idea as having pawns abreast on d4 and e4 will put Black under long term positional pressure. (Indeed Grandmaster Bent Larsen has gone as far as claiming that 3 d4 is a blunder for White in the Sicilian, as after 3...cxd4 he has lost all chance of building a broad centre!) The only drawback to this plan is that the pawn on c3 deprives the queen's knight of its favourite square in the opening.

3 ... ♘f6

It makes sense for Black to attack the e4 pawn as it lacks its natural defender in the shape of a knight on c3.

4 e5

White removes the threat with gain of time by counter attacking the knight. On the other hand, his centre won't be as flexible as it would have been if he maintained pawns on both d4 and e4.

4 ... ♘d5

Black immediately exploits the fact that White has committed himself to 4 e5 by putting the knight in the gap on d5.

5 d4

All according to plan: White supports the pawn on e5 and at the same time open lines for his pieces.

5 ... cxd4

A necessary exchange as otherwise the white pawns might roll forwards with 6 c4 and 7 d5.

6 cxd4

The only sensible recapture as the whole point of White's opening strategy has been to maintain a pawn presence on d4.

6 ... b6

As the way out via e6 is blocked Black seeks another method of development for his light-squared bishop.

7 ♗c4

There are no such problems for White's light-squared bishop: it can be developed in straightforward and aggressive fashion by attacking the knight.

7 ... ♗a6

Black decides to challenge White's bishop rather than play 7...♗b7 when 8 0-0 ♗e7 9 ♗xd5 ♗xd5 10 ♘c3 ♗b7 – or else White doubles Black's pawns with 11 ♘xd5 exd5 – 11 d5! gives White the initiative in the centre.

8 ♗xa6

It was also possible to inflict doubled pawns with 8 ♗xd5 exd5 but they are difficult to attack – for example if 9 ♘c3 ♗b4 and then ♗xc3. Furthermore, White would be unable to castle due to the bishop on a6 controlling the f1 square. Therefore Adams prefers to simply exchange bishops.

8 ... ♘xa6

Black recaptures the piece and can be pleased at having exchanged off White's 'good' bishop – i.e. the bishop which isn't obstructed by his own centre pawns, which are both on dark squares.

Nevertheless the knight has been forced by the transaction onto the inferior a6 square. It will be difficult for Black to find a suitable role for this piece in any future plan.

9   0-0

Having settled matters in the centre to his satisfaction Adams safeguards his king and centralizes the rook.

9   ...   ♗e7

Here the bishop is securely positioned and wards off any attacking ideas with ♘g5.

10   ♘bd2

The beginning of a little strategical plan to exploit the only weaknesses in Black's otherwise solid set up: the e4 square and a knight's move beyond it the d6 square.

10   ...   0-0

It is always a relief for Black when he can whisk his king away from the centre without having suffered any major accidents.

11   ♘e4

A centre square where it can sit with impunity is always a delight for a knight. Here the white knight can only be challenged with f7-f5, but this would weaken the black kingside. The black knight on d5 also resides contentedly on a 'pawn-proof' square.

11   ...   ♘ac7

In contrast this knight finds itself 'surplus to requirements' – there is only one great square for a black knight and the other knight is already sitting on it.

12   ♗g5

Black has a firm grip on the light squares in his half of the board, but the d6 square is only defended by the black bishop. So Adams makes a wise decision to offer the exchange of bishops.

12   ...   f6

Benjamin decides to keep his bishop, but now a slight weakness appears in his kingside structure.

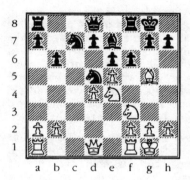

13   exf6

The nature of the position now changes. White's strong pawn on e5 vanishes, which increases the freedom of action of the black pieces; at the same time the hole on d6 ceases to be a serious issue. But how can Black recapture on f6 without compromising his position in some way?

13   ...   ♘xf6

Of Black's four possible recaptures, this makes the most sense as it not only challenges the white knight on e4 but also clears the way for the neglected knight on a6 to reach the d5 square.

14   ♗xf6

The only way for White to keep control is by giving up his bishop for the knight. It is important to remember that a well placed knight in the centre is often more valuable than a bishop. Besides, White wants to keep the tension in the position and the exchanging sequence 14 ♘xf6+ ♗xf6 15 ♗xf6 ♕xf6 leads to a position that looks fine for Black as he can attack down the f file.

14 ... gxf6

After 14...♗xf6 the black bishop is just staring at the d4 pawn and is unable to inflict any damage on the white position – in fact it is even getting in the way of the black queen, who would like to use the f6 square to begin a counterattack. Therefore 15 ♖c1, etc. would keep a slight, but enduring edge for White.

For this reason Benjamin prefers to recapture with the pawn. It strengthens his hold over the e5 square but leaves his kingside slightly open to attack.

15 ♖c1

Adams calmly takes control of the open file and obliges his opponent to make an important strategical decision.

15 ... d5

Black correctly drives the white knight from the centre, even though the knight on c7 will remain bereft of an active centre square for the rest of the game. Instead 15...♘d5 looks right at a superficial level, but 16 ♘c3! is another example on the theme of wise exchanging: after 16...♘xc3 17 ♖xc3 White is ready to pulverize the black centre with d4-d5! when his opponent cannot avoid being left defending at least one very weak pawn.

16 ♘g3

The knight retreats sadly from its formerly inviolable centre post, but it is destined to play a starring role in a kingside attack after Black's inferior reply.

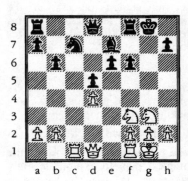

16 ... ♕d7?

It may seem harsh to describe this as a fatal mistake, but Adams' brilliant play in what follows makes it hard to suggest any decent defence. Basically, Black makes a little queen move to 'tidy up' his position and it proves to be a serious loss of time. After 16...♗d6 White's next move in the game, 17 ♘h4, could be answered by 17...♗xg3! exchanging the bishop for the knight. This would seriously reduce White's initiative, as not only does the knight on g3 prove to be a fearsome assailant in the game, but also the blocking of the g3 square after 18 hxg3 would prevent a white rook using it as the base to launch an attack down the g file.

17 ♘h4

A useless decentralisation?

Whereas beginners often make idle attacking gestures or aimless manoeuvres with the pieces on the wings, here Adams puts his knight on h4, but his thoughts are very much on the centre. He is clearing the way for his next move 18 f4 which will increase his control over the e5 square. And just to show that Adams really is thinking about the centre, if 17...f5 then 18 ♘f3 follows and suddenly White has the e5 square for his knight. Here it is worth reminding ourselves that moves by the pieces can be retracted, but moves by the pawns can't: White can retract ♘h4, but Black can't change his mind about the pawn advance f6-f5.

| 17 | ... | ♗d6 |

A solid defensive move: Black activates his bishop, adds another defender to the knight and clears the second rank so that his queen can come to the aid of his king.

| 18 | f4 | |

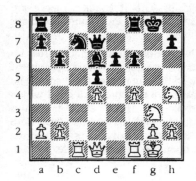

What more could be asked from a pawn move? In one stroke White:

♦ threatens to ram Black's centre at some point with f4-f5

♦ prepares to bring the rook into the attack along the third rank with ♖f3

♦ prevents Black easing his game by exchanging pieces with 18...♗xg3.

| 18 | ... | f5 |

White wouldn't have rushed into f4-f5, even if Black had played a quiet move such as 18...♔h8; but it would have been a permanent threat hanging over the black position after a series of preparatory moves such as ♘h5 and ♖f3.

Therefore Benjamin decides to rule it out immediately and prepares a positional threat of his own: namely ♘e8, ♘f6 and ♘e4, when the feeble knight on e4 has become a monster on e4. White would find it exceedingly difficult to draw the game if the Black knight got to e4. Therefore immediate counter-measures are called for!

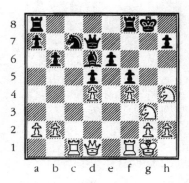

| 19 | ♘h5! | |

Again Adams sends a knight to the edge, but with the centre foremost in his thoughts.

It is a sign of the efficiency of White's strategy that in carrying out his own plan he 'by accident' confounds his opponent's idea. Now the black knight can be eliminated if it ever gets as far as f6. Another bonus of having the knight on h5 is that it defends the f4 pawn, which frees the rook on f1 to join in an attack and also makes possible the manoeuvre ♘f3 and ♘e5, as Black won't be able to reply ♗xf4.

19   ...   ♛f7

This looks awkward for White, as if 20 ♘f3, aiming to put the knight on e5, or 20 ♖f3, bringing the rook into the attack, the white queen no longer defends the knight on h5 and it can be taken by the black queen. So it appears that White has to give up his attacking aspirations and retreat with 20 ♘g3, when Black would have a fine game after 20...♘f6 and 21...♘e4.

20   ♖f3!

You can't carry out any strategical plan without being aware of tactical features. This essential strengthening of the white attack is only possible because White has calculated that if 20...♛xh5 21 ♖g3+ wins the black queen by a discovered attack. This might not seem like an important tactic, but it is in fact the decisive moment in the game: Black's last move is revealed

to be an important loss of time and his position slides downhill. With hindsight, 19...♔h8 should have been preferred, when the black queen keeps the bishop defended and the c6 square safe from the white rook on c1.

20   ...   ♔h8

The king moves off the open g file and so makes 21...♛xh5 a real threat. Still, it soon becomes clear that the king is by no means safe on h8.

21   ♖h3

Adams sends a third piece to the edge of the board – and once again the aim is to strengthen his control of the centre. He wants to recentralise the knight on h4, and so ensures that after ♘f3 his rook will take over defensive duty of the other knight on h5 from the queen.

The rook also threatens to attack h7 in combination with a future ♘g5 or ♘f6 if Black's pieces are distracted from their control of these squares.

Note that these manoeuvres by Adams are only possible because of the static situation in the centre. The pawns are rigidly interlocked which means that Black can't launch a violent break out whilst the white pieces are involved in ponderous manoeuvres on the kingside.

21   ...   ♖g8

The lack of harmony in Black's camp is evident from the fact that the rook is needed to fight for the g file but at the same time its presence on g8 actually removes some of Black's defensive resources by preventing his king using the square as a possible escape hatch.

22   ♘f3

The knight is delighted to return to f3 as new attacking vistas have opened up on e5 and g5.

22   ...   ♛e7

Black has to waste more time with his queen to avoid being hit by 23 ♘g5. Here is what would have happened if he had tried to bring his knight to the defence of his king: 22...♘e8 23 ♘g5 ♛d7 24 ♘xh7! and the black king is stripped of all its pawn cover as Black loses his queen after either 24...♔xh7 25 ♘f6+ or 24...♛xh7 25 ♘g3.

23   ♛e2

If at once 23 ♘e5 ♘xe5 24 fxe5 ♘e8 gives Black chances to save the game, as the e5 square is blocked and the e6 pawn cannot be attacked from the front any more. Instead Adams plays a quiet but lethal preparatory move: White plans to put his knight on the commanding e5 square, when if Black responds ♝xe5 he can now recapture with the queen, at the same time giving a fatal check to the black king who has no way to escape.

23   ...   ♘e8

This knight has had a wretched game. It supports Tarrasch's dictum that 'if one piece stands badly, then the whole game stands badly'.

24   ♖c6

Adams increases the pressure inexorably on both wings and in the centre. Now the black bishop is a helpless target as if it moves then ♖xe6 follows.

24   ...   ♛d7

Ideally Black would like to challenge the white knight on h5, but this is what would happen:

24...♘f6 25 ♘xf6 ♛xf6 26 ♖xd6 and Black is a piece down; or

24...♘g7 25 ♖xd6! ♛xd6 26 ♘f6 and Black is suddenly defenceless against the threat of 27 ♖xh7 mate, unless he gives up his knight with 26...♘h5 27 ♖xh5. The white rook proves its worth on the h file.

25   ♘e5!

This powerful entrance is far superior to retreating the rook. If now 25...♝xe5 26 ♛xe5+ ♘g7 27 ♘f6 ♛xc6 28 ♖xh7 mate!

25   ...   ♛e7

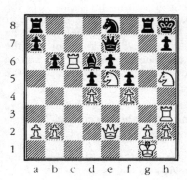

Now White has every piece on an excellent square. The queen is sitting quietly on e2 from where she is ready to orchestrate an attack on either the queenside, kingside or the centre. The knights are both aggressively placed on the fifth rank; one of them is on the ideal outpost square on e5 whilst the other is eyeing the weakened dark squares in Black's camp on f6 and g7. The rooks are also finely placed, especially for lateral or sideways action: on c6 one rook is exerting pressure on the black bishop – a key defender of the loose dark squares – whilst the other rook on h3 is ready to swing to the g file or e file at a moment's notice.

So everything is perfect in White's camp. But how is he to make further progress, when every piece is already on its optimum square?

In almost every game, no matter how positional the build up, a moment comes when it is necessary to press home the advantage with a tactical operation. White needs to gain ascendancy over the dark squares e5, f6 and g7 when the black king will find himself in the firing line at the end of the weakened dark square diagonal. If he could get his queen to e5 he would achieve his aim, but alas the black bishop is guarding this square and the white knight is also in the way.

Is there a sacrifice which allows White to get his queen to e5?

26   ♖xd6!

This is it! White eliminates the black piece that is offering the most dark square resistance and also wins

time to get the knight out of the way of his queen with his next move.

26   ...   ♘xd6

This is forced for if 26...♛xd6 27 ♘f7+ wins the queen.

27   ♘c6   1-0

The old rule holds firm: when you have lost control of squares of one colour disaster strikes on a square of the other colour. By attacking the black queen White gains a decisive move to utilize the e5 square. Now Benjamin didn't wait to see the triumphant check on e5 as after 27...♛f8 28 ♛e5+ ♖g7 – forced – 29 ♘xg7 ♛xg7 30 ♛xd6 he is a whole knight down for nothing.

3 Judging the Time Factor: Diverse Ideas after 1 e4

I have never in my life played the French Defence, which is the dullest of all openings.

Steinitz

In planning a chess strategy there is always a tension between what the player wants to do and what he needs to do. For example, a course of action which offers great future prospects can prove hazardous in the short term.

In the previous chapter Sokolov thought it would be nice to have the bishop pair: he achieved his aim, but he didn't have long to enjoy his bishops as he was quickly mated. Nunn was able to use the time that Sokolov spent on acquiring the bishops to build up a brisk attack on his king. This is a classic example of a player misjudging the time factor.

It is all a matter of fine judgment, but the nature of the pawn structure tells us a lot about whether we should be thinking about long term goals or have our minds concentrated on the pressing needs of the position.

It can be said that there are three types of pawn structure or position: open, closed and semi open.

In open positions, of which one obvious example is that reached after 1 e4 e5, there are lots of active possibilities for the pieces. A violent fight soon erupts for control of the centre, which means that the emphasis is on rapid development as any delay in getting the pieces out can be fatal. The pieces have to a certain extent to be rushed out, even if they don't occupy the most ideal positions for the middlegame, so as not to be outnumbered.

In contrast, in closed positions development can be more leisurely as a blocked centre reduces the danger of a sudden, overwhelming attack. In fact, it could be said that development must be slower: it is important to put the pieces on the right squares. Closed positions often feature a lot of concealed manoeuvring of the pieces – and if they are on the wrong squares to start with this can ruin the whole of the middlegame. One example of a closed position is that reached in the French after 1 e4 e6 2 d4 d5 3 e5 c5 4 c3. Black can now take the liberty of developing his queen with 4...♛b6 where she is strategically well placed in attacking d4, as the blocked centre means that the White pieces can't launch an attack without a great deal of preparation.

Semi-open positions – or if you prefer, semi-closed positions – fall between these two extremes. In fact there is hardly any position, no matter how closed, that doesn't have some features of an open game and vice versa. Therefore it is vital to stay alert to danger at all times.

In this chapter we'll look at diverse openings after 1 e4 in which the players assessed the time factor with various degrees of success. In some cases there is an immediate tactical battle in the style of the open game; in others slow manoeuvring is to the fore.

Game Ten
A.Shirov - E.Bareev
Wijk aan Zee 2003
French Defence

1   e4

A bold, attacking genius like Alexei Shirov has no fear in pushing his king's pawn two squares forwards. Perhaps you aren't always as lucky in your games as the Latvian-born World Championship finalist, but if you want to exercise your powers of calculation in a lively fight then this is the first move for you.

1   ...   e6

The Russian Evgeny Bareev has been consistently among the top ten highest rated players in the world since the late 1990s and at the time of writing has reached an all time high of Number Four in an Elo list of 2003. His style of play is very different from that of Shirov's: he looks to play a steady game and slowly outplay his opponent. It is no wonder that the French Defence, which blocks the centre and puts the emphasis on concealed manoeuvring, has always been his opening of choice.

2   d4

White accepts the space that is offered to him as more space means greater mobility for the pieces and therefore the greater chance to demonstrate tactical fantasy.

2   ...   d5

Black completes his central pawn barrier. In contrast to lines after 1 e4 e5, the white king's bishop will find it almost impossible to attack the f7 square, which is notorious for being the weakest point in Black's position in the opening phase. (Incidentally, the weakest point in White's position is the f2 square).

The main drawback of the French Defence for Black is that his own bishop on c8 isn't very amused at finding its way into the world blocked by the pawn on e6. For this reason the bishop often proves a nuisance for Black and is often dubbed his 'problem piece'. However, you can't have everything: security always comes at the price of less activity for one or more pieces.

3   ♘c3

Here again style is reflected in the choice of move. A less overtly aggressive player might have preferred 3 ♘d2, the Tarrasch Variation, in order to avoid the possibility of the knight being pinned by 3...♝b4 – after 3 ♘d2 it would be silly to play 3...♝b4 as White could simply reply 4 c3.

3   ...   ♘f6

As mentioned above, Black could have played in more adventurous style with 3...♝b4. But such an approach would weaken the black kingside and isn't to Bareev's taste. He prefers to develop his king's knight and attack e4 in approved classical style: indeed this variation is called the 'Classical Variation'.

4   e5

Shirov maintains his space advantage. Instead 4 exd5 exd5 would be no more than equal as Black's queen's bishop suddenly has an open diagonal.

4   ...   ♘fd7

The best square for the knight as in conjunction with Black's next two moves it puts pressure on the white centre.

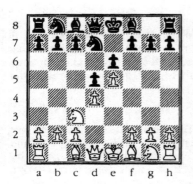

5   f4!

White supports the e5 spearhead with a second pawn bastion. If he had continued developing in routine style with 5 ♘f3 then after 5...c5 followed by ♘c6 he would find it hard to prevent his centre evaporating.

5   ...   c5

It is vital that Black generates counterplay by undermining the d4 pawn. This is an especially attractive target as the presence of the white knight on c3 prevents it being supported by c2-c3.

6   ♘f3

White must support his centre or else it will be overthrown by 6...cxd4, etc.

6   ...   ♘c6

Bareev steps up the pressure by forcing White to attend once again to the threat to d4.

7   ♝e3

An essential strengthening as White would lose both time and position after 7 ♝e2 cxd4 8 ♘xd4 ♘xd4 9 ♕xd4 ♝c5.

7   ...   cxd4

Not forced, but Black wants to clarify the situation in the centre so that he can utilize the c5 square for his bishop.

8   ♘xd4

The scope of the bishop on e3 is somewhat curtailed by White's own pawns on e5 and f4, but it is still needed in the fight for the dark squares against Black's bishop. Therefore quite wrong is 8 ♝xd4? when after 8...♘xd4 9 ♘xd4 ♝c5 Black is already preparing to overrun the dark squares.

8   ...   ♗c5

This puts the white knight in a pin and threatens 9...♕b6 which would be most awkward in view of the double attack on d4 and b2.

9   ♕d2

The best reply which defends the bishop on e3 and clears the way for castling queenside.

9   ...   ♗xd4

The exchanging sequence initiated by Black is logical as he has less space and so every piece that disappears will ease the congestion in his position.

10   ♗xd4

If Black now plays 10...0-0 then it is worth White spending a tempo on 11 ♗e3! to keep his excellent dark-squared bishop.

10   ...   ♘xd4

Of course an arch strategist such as Bareev isn't going to allow the bishop to escape!

11   ♕xd4

Now White has a marginal advantage: as so often in the French

Defence the black bishop on c8 is the worst minor piece on the board.

11   ...   ♕b6

Nevertheless, in an endgame it would be very hard to prove that the inferiority of the black bishop would give White any real winning chances. Therefore Bareev is quick to offer the exchange of queens.

12   ♕d2

An aggressive riposte: White is willing to gambit one or more pawns on the queenside in order to gain a lead in development and keep the queens on the board.

12   ...   ♕xb2

A bold but necessary capture as against a slower move White would simply have castled queenside with the initiative and no material deficit.

13   ♖b1

The black queen has to be forced to a3 in order for White to gain time for an attack with his knight.

13   ...   ♕a3

The only way for the queen to save herself.

14   ♘b5

White must play fearlessly, as if he is content to develop his pieces Black will curb his attacking options with 14...a6! gaining control of the b5 square.

14   ...   ♕xa2

The black queen completes her feast on the queenside. Now White is committed to win the game by attack as in the long term Black's passed pawns will prove decisive.

15   ♘d6+

This check is the correct way to disrupt the black king. Instead 15 ♘c7+? would be a serious mistake as after 15...♚d8 both the white rook and knight are hanging.

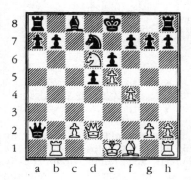

15 ... ♚f8

The obvious reply, but 15...♚e7, keeping the option of bringing the king's rook into the game was a serious alternative. At first glance it looks like a blunder as White has 16 ♕b4 in reply, threatening a discovered check on the king, but after 16...a5! 17 ♘f5+ ♚d8 18 ♕e7+ ♚c7 19 ♕d6+ ♚d8 would be a sharp draw. Alternatively after 16...a5 White has 17 ♘xc8+ ♚d8 when he is temporarily a piece up but his attacking is running out of steam as both the queen and knight are hanging and 19 ♕xb7 allows 19...♖b8 when moving the white queen to safety drops the rook on b1 with check.

16 ♖d1!

It looks strange to remove the rook from the b file, but Shirov intends to castle and then attack along the f file with f4-f5. If Black withdraws his queen in an attempt to prevent White castling, as occurs

in the game, then the rook on d1 will be well placed to support an attack along the d file based on c2-c4.

16 ... ♕b2

The queen heads back to b6 in order to obstruct the harmonious build up of White's attack. She goes via b2 to restrain for a moment the advance c2-c4, as White obviously has no wish to exchange queens.

17 ♗e2

Shirov patiently develops his bishop as he sees that Black's next move won't solve his defensive problems.

17 ... ♕b6

The queen is now stopping White castling, but it all begins to fall apart after White's reply.

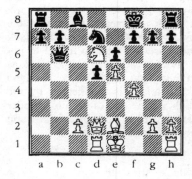

18 c4!

With a lead in development White strives to open lines. This is a painful move for Black to meet as if 18...dxc4 19 ♘xc8 ♖xc8 20 ♕xd7 nets a piece.

18 ... d4

This has the merit of keeping the d file at least temporarily closed, as

White has no wish to exchange queens by taking on d4, but the black pawn now blocks the a7-g1 diagonal so that castling is on the cards again for White.

19   &f3

White mustn't hurry as if 19 0-0? d3+ wins a piece. So first of all he has to move the bishop out of the way. He does so in a very efficient manner by attacking b7 again.

19   ...   a5

Having failed in his bid to stop White's build up, Bareev can only put his trust in his passed pawn to save him. Unfortunately for him it will be a long time before this pawn becomes threatening.

20   0-0

Finally White has achieved his aim. His king leaves behind the dangers of the centre and the rook on f1 is now ready to join in the onslaught down the f file. The black pieces are too uncoordinated to put up much resistance: neither rook is playing any useful role and the bishop on c8 is blocked in by the knight. It is therefore no wonder that sacrificial combinations soon become feasible.

20   ...   d3+

Black tries to get his queen involved in the thick of the action. It is difficult to recommend any other move, as for example if 20...&c5, aiming to free the bishop, then simply 21 &xd4 gives White a huge advantage.

21   &h1

In contrast to the black king's peril, the white monarch can watch the drama unfold in perfect safety.

21   ...   &d4

The queen takes up a fine centre post where she helps keep the d file blocked and rather optimistically guards the a1 square in anticipation of the advance of the passed pawn. In due course she can be supported by moves such as &c5 and &d7. But with his next move Shirov completely upsets Black plans.

22   &b5!

An unexpected and very strong riposte. It was difficult to foresee as the knight already appeared to be on its optimum square on d6 and it is notoriously difficult to see backward moves by knights. If now 22...&xc4 Black is doing White's work for him by opening the c file. The game could continue 23 &d6 &d4 (or 23...&c2 24 &e3 intending 25 &c1 to pick up the bishop on c8) 24 &c1 &b6 25 &c7 and White has a very strong attack.

22   ...   &c5

The black queen has no choice but to retreat from her ideal square.

23   &xd3

Now the blockade in the centre has collapsed and with it all Black's hopes of a successful defence.

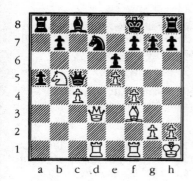

Let's compare the deployment of the white and black pieces.

Rooks. One white rook is in control of the only open file and the other rook is centralised and ready to back up an attack with f4-f5. The black rooks are still sleeping in the corners of the board.

Knights. White's knight is highly dynamic and about to re-enter the commanding d6 square. The black knight is a target and can't move on pain of ♕d8 mate.

Bishops. White's bishop enjoys a long diagonal; the black bishop hasn't a single move.

Queens. Both queens are well placed for the fight ahead.

Kings. The white king is enjoying a quiet life and gets in no one's way. The black king blocks in his own rook and is a ready target.

White has achieved all this at the cost of one pawn – an absolute bargain.

23 ... g6

Black makes an escape route from the dangerous f file for his king on g7, which will in turn free the rook on h8. He also tries to dissuade White from staging a breakthrough by guarding f5 again, but it will be to no avail.

24 ♘d6

Back again, and this time with the threat of 25 ♘xc8, winning a piece.

24 ... ♘b6

The knight runs for its life but it will also prove to be a target on b6.

25 ♖b1!

Another change of front. Black's queen is all that is holding his position together. So White plans to force it backwards so that his own queen gets control of d4: as will be seen this is a vital centre square.

25 ... ♔g7

Now Black threatens to develop with 26...♗d7 when if 27 ♘xb7 ♕xc4-with the king on f8 this could have been answered by ♕d6+ picking up the knight. Therefore White must act fast to keep the black pieces bottled up.

26 ♖b5!

The black queen is evicted from her strong square and at the same time the rook takes up a post where it will prove very powerful in the final combinative phase of the game.

26 ... ♕c7

This is the only square that is safe from the marauding white pieces.

27 ♕d4!

White's queen assumes control of the centre dark squares with gain of time by hitting the knight.

27 ... ♘d7

A miserable retreat after which the black bishop is boxed in again.

28 f5!

With all his pieces on their optimum squares it is time for White to strike hard to finish the game. It can only be done with sacrifices to pierce the defensive barriers around the black king.

28 ... gxf5

If Black had ignored White's thrust with 28...a4 then all the same he clears a way forwards with 29 fxe6 fxe6 30 ♗g4, without even needing to sacrifice.

29 ♘xf5+!

Now we can see clearly why Shirov wanted his queen on d4.

29 ... exf5

If Black declined the offer with 29...♔f8 he would soon be pulverized by 30 ♘d6 and 31 ♗h5, when the f7 pawn drops.

30 e6+

A deadly discovered check which rips open the king's defences.

30 ... ♘e5

A desperate move, but after 30...♘f6 31 ♖xf5 ♕e7 – what else? – 32 ♗d5! the knight on f6 is suddenly attacked three times, with a quick mate looming after the unstoppable 33 ♖xf6.

31 ♖xe5

Now the threats include 32 ♖c5+ winning the queen.

31 ... f6

The only way to struggle on but it's a forlorn hope against a maestro of tactical chess such as Shirov.

32 ♖xf5

The rook is wreaking havoc along the fifth rank. Now Black has to contend with 33 ♕xf6+ and mate next move.

32 ... ♖f8

At last a black rook makes a contribution to the game, but it is way too late to make any difference to the outcome.

33 ♗d5

White defends his passed pawn, which keeps the wretched black bishop entombed on c8, and uncovers an attack by the rook on f1 against f6.

33 ... ♕e7

The queen fights valiantly but with so little help from the other piece is unable to rescue the situation.

34 ♖h5!

The f6 square is defended three times and not vulnerable to attack by the white bishop as it is on a dark square. Therefore White uses his greater mobility to focus on a softer target – the h7 pawn, against which the bishop can also apply its powers.

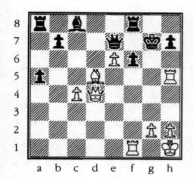

34 ...   ♔h8

If 34...♖h8 35 ♖g5+ ♔h6 36 ♖xf6+ ♔xg5 37 ♕f4+ and mate next move.

35 ♗e4

Now the h7 pawn is doomed and with it all hope that the black king will find shelter from the onslaught.

35 ...   ♗xe6

I guess that Black was determined to at least develop this bishop before resigning, but it is hardly a star entrance.

36 ♖xh7+

The rook has had a wonderful career on the fifth rank, but of course every rook aspires to go to the magical seventh rank, especially if it wins the opponent's queen!

36 ...   ♕xh7

The black queen has done a heroic job defending the king whilst too many other pieces have been mere bystanders.

37 ♗xh7

Not only winning the queen but also clearing the e4 square for a double attack.

37 ...   ♔xh7

Bareev could resign but decides to let his opponent show him the win.

38 ♕e4+   1-0

White picks up the bishop with a crushing material advantage. A fine handling of the initiative by Shirov – he used the whole board for his manoeuvres and was patient or forthright according to the demands of the position.

Game Eleven
N.Short - J.Timman
Reykjavik 1987
French Defence

1   e4

It is impossible to achieve anything in a chess game if you have a contemptuous attitude towards the pawns. They may be the weakest unit on the board but they play a vital part in any strategy. Already the pawn on e4 is marking out White's territory.

1   ...   e6

The French Defence is one of the most reliable responses to 1 e4. Black sets up a solid pawn chain in the centre which shields the weakest point in his position: the f7 square. He also opens the diagonal of the king's bishop: only the queen's bishop is left feeling aggrieved by being shut in.

2   d4

It is often the aim of chess strategy to put another pawn in the centre alongside the furthest advanced pawn. Thus in the Ruy Lopez after 1 e4 e5 2 ♘f3 ♘c6 3 ♗b5 White is striving in the long term for d2-d4; in the Queen's Gambit he compliments 1 d4 with 2 c4. Such a strategy is by no means confined to the opening. Thus if White has a pawn structure with a pawn on e5 he will often strive if at all possible for f4-f5 or d4-d5.

When two pawns are placed adjacent to each other they command the two squares directly in front of them and the two squares diagonally to either side. That is a lot of expensive real estate in the centre!

They are also in the most flexible state to respond to an attack: if one of the pawns is attacked a pawn chain can be formed with its fellow by advancing one square forwards.

Therefore it is no wonder that White takes the opportunity to put a second pawn on the fourth rank with 2 d4 – something he isn't allowed to do unchallenged by a black pawn in either the Sicilian or after 1...e5.

2   ...   d5

In view of what has been said above it is no wonder that Black immediately breaks up the happy union of White's centre pawns.

3   ♘c3

Very economical: Short develops a knight and defends the e4 pawn.

3   ...   ♗b4

The most aggressive response as it renews the threat to e4 by pinning the knight.

4   e5

White saves his pawn from capture and consolidates his space advantage.

4   ...   c5

An example from Black of the 'put another pawn next to your most advanced pawn' rule. Now that White has committed himself to the pawn chain d4/e5 it should be attacked at its base, which for the moment is d4. It is less effective to attack it from the front – here the e5 pawn – as the furthest advanced pawn has more freedom and therefore more power to fend off the attack: he can advance or exchange himself or even be sacrificed without worrying about the disruption he might be causing further up the pawn chain.

5   a3

A good moment to force the bishop to clarify its intentions on b4.

5   ...   ♗xc3+

Black gives up his wonderful king's bishop, the ideal guardian of his dark squares. On the other hand he inflicts doubled pawns on his opponent: in particular the pawn on c3 will be hard to defend.

6   bxc3

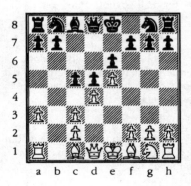

The pawn on c3 would have made classical players of the 1920s shudder – though admittedly they would also have looked askance at Black giving up his beautiful dark-squared bishop. In reality, both players have gained something of equal value from the exchange on c3 – of course, if this wasn't the case either White would avoid this line or Black wouldn't play the Winawer. White has the ascendancy on the dark squares and doesn't have to worry about losing control of the d4 square: the c3 pawn is – statically speaking – weak, but it is performing a useful role in bolstering the d4 square. So Black's assault on the centre with c7-c5 has been seriously blunted. This gives White more freedom to carry out operations of his own, most likely on the kingside.

Black for his part has a clear target on which to base his own strategy: the weakling on c3.

6 ... ♘e7

Already we can see how White's space advantage has an adverse effect on Black's piece deployment: the black knight is denied its normal f6 square and has to make do with e7.

7 ♘f3

Although it looks impressive the white pawn centre might crumble if it isn't properly supported by the pieces. Therefore the rapid development of the knight is preferred to 7 f4.

7 ... ♛a5

Black strikes straightaway at the Achilles' Heel in White's pawn structure – the c3 pawn.

8 ♛d2

It may look odd to use the powerful queen to defend the pawn when 8 ♗d2 was available, but White wants to keep as an option an alternative development of the bishop with a3-a4 and then ♗a3. If now 8...cxd4 9 cxd4 ♛xd2+ 10 ♗xd2 and despite the slight weakness on c2 White has the more promising position due to his bishop pair.

8 ... ♗d7

An interesting alternative to natural development with 8...♘bc6. It introduces the positional threat of 9...♗b5 when Black exchanges his so-called 'bad' bishop – whose mobility is impeded by his own pawn pawn centre on d5 and e6 – for his opponent's 'good' bishop. In that case the light squares in White's camp would begin to look rather sickly as almost all his pawns are on dark squares – in particular the c4 square would become an excellent outpost for a black knight.

9 ♖b1

Short is alert: he acts immediately to prevent 9...♗b5 and at the same time attacks the b7 pawn.

9   ...   &c6

An unusual square for a bishop as it is deployed to a blocked diagonal. However, Black has decided on the following set up: &c6, &d7 and then 0-0-0, when his king is relatively safe. If instead he had played 9...b6 then a well timed d4xc5 would have opened lines of attack against his king.

10   &d3

A sound developing move amid all the elaborate schemes. White wants his bishop on d3 rather than e2 so that the c2 pawn is defended should Black exchange on d4 then play &c8. Furthermore, the bishop can answer &f5 with &xf5 breaking up Black's pawns; or if Black castles kingside it is ready to engage in combinations against h7 – a square that lacks the usual protection of a knight on f6. Black can repel the bishop with c5-c4, but in fact White would welcome this clarification of the situation in the centre.

10   ...   &d7

The knight clears the way for queenside castling and is ready to support an attack on White's centre with f7-f6.

11   0-0

White has more or less completed his development and has a safe king and a space advantage. On the minus side his bishops are as yet no great attacking force and the weakness on c3 remains.

11   ..   c4

Black decides to close the position on the queenside to prevent White ever opening lines for his bishops with a future c3-c4.

12   &e2

Now that White no longer has to worry about the pressure on the d4 square he can turn his attention to increasing the space advantage on the kingside. This can be done by carefully preparing the pawn advance f2-f4.

12   ...   h6!

A little pawn move but one of tremendous value. Black takes measures against White's plan of f2-f4 by denying the white knight the g5 square, as after 12...0-0-0 there follows 13 &g5! &df8 14 f4 h6 15 &f3, when White can prepare g2-g4 with the idea of edging further up the f file with g2-g4 and f4-f5. Such a series of pawn moves isn't without its hazards for White – after all, he is dismantling the defences in front of his king. But assuming he is careful and keeps the initiative the positional benefits will outweigh the dangers. The idea behind f4-f5 is to attack the pawn on e6. If e6xf5 in reply then g4xf5, and the white pawns are mobile and powerful. If instead Black allows f5xe6 then White can put further pressure on e6 with moves such as &f4, etc.

13   h4

If the position in the centre was open this pawn advance would be highly doubtful, but here an attempt by Black to exploit the loosening of his kingside means opening lines with f7-f6 which could well favour the white bishops – just look at Black's inert bishop on c6!

It is all a matter of fine judgment as according to circumstances any pawn advance by either player can be good or bad. Thus the main point of 13 h4 is to restrain Black from playing g7-g5 at a suitable moment.

As we shall see in the game Jan Timman, a world class Grandmaster, gets it wrong – he opens lines in an inappropriate situation.

13   ...   0-0-0

Black completes his first mini-strategic plan by putting his king behind the wall of pawns on the queenside.

14   &dl

'If you don't know what to do, wait for your opponent to come up with a plan – it's sure to be wrong!' said Tarrasch. Short eggs Black on to attack his centre with this refined waiting move, which clears the e file and so makes it possible for the e6 pawn to be attacked from the front.

14   ...   f5?

Too ambitious. Instead after a solid move such as 14...&b8 it is difficult to see what progress White could make.

15   exf6

White is grateful to his opponent for allowing him to open up the e file as this means he can pressurize the backward pawn on e6.

15   ...   &xf6

Black is still intent on playing actively – indeed the threat of 16...&e4 looks strong. But in fact the defensively minded 15...gxf6 was to be preferred to keep hold of the e5 square. Then if 16 &e1 &f8 holds everything together.

16   &e1!

The queen steps back from the looming attack by the knight and at the same time hits the e6 pawn.

16   ...   &e4

Timman presses on with his plan. At least on e4 the knight temporarily shields the e6 pawn.

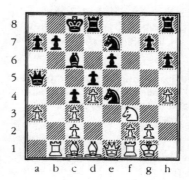

17   &b4!

The rook defends c3 by blocking out the black queen. Now White has much the better of it as his knight will enjoy the wonderful e5 square.

17   ...   &hf8

Timman refuses to panic. He centralizes his last undeveloped piece and prevents White from building up the pressure with &f4.

18   &e5

A dream square for a knight: a centre post from which it cannot be evicted by a hostile pawn. The black knight on e4 doesn't have this luxury as sooner or later it can be chased away by f2-f3.

18 ...   ♛c7

The black queen returns to the second rank to bolster the defences. In particular once the knight is driven back from e4 she is needed to answer ♘xc6 with ♛xc6 to keep the e6 pawn from capture by ♖xe6.

19 ♗g4

One by one the white pieces find excellent attacking squares, which makes Black rue opening the position with 14...f5.

19 ...   ♖f6

Timman switches to solid defensive play by using the rook to aid the beleaguered e6 pawn.

20 f3

At last White removes the knight and so opens the way for a headlong assault against the e6 pawn.

20 ...   ♘d6

The only square for the knight. Now how is White going to increase the pressure? He comes up with a wonderful idea that is in some ways harder to see than a queen sacrifice.

21 ♗h3!

An insidious little move with the evil intention of 22 ♘g4, when the rook must retreat and the e6 pawn is lost, as if 22...♖g6 23 h5 etc.

21 ...   ♗d7

In order to counter the threat Black is obliged to defend the e6 pawn again as 21...h5 22 ♗g5 is too horrible to contemplate.

22 ♖f2!

Easy chess: Short methodically increases the pressure. Now the rook is ready to swing over to e2 when the e6 pawn faces a deadly discovered attack.

22 ...   ♘c6

Black must challenge the white knight and does so in the most time saving manner by also attacking the rook.

23 ♖b1

The rook is by no means unhappy at being forced to retreat as its role on b4 has become irrelevant. The nearer it is to the e1 square the better!

23 ...   ♘f7

This attacks the white knight a third time and so forces it to make a decision: what piece should it exchange itself for?

24 ♘xd7!

Short shows excellent judgement. It is better to keep Black boxed up than to seize material immediately, as after 24 ♘xf7 ♖xf7 25 ♗xe6 ♖e7 26 ♖e2 ♖de8 White has won a pawn but all the black pieces have suddenly become very active.

The black bishop doesn't look too impressive, but it is the chief guardian of the e6 square – the focal point of the whole struggle.

24   ...   ♛xd7

The queen is far less comfortable than the bishop in defending e6 as the bishop on h3 is bearing down heavily along the diagonal.

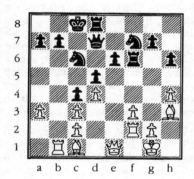

25   ♗f4!

A beautiful example of strategy being supported by tactics.

White wants his bishop on the diagonal h2-b8 for three reasons. Firstly, the bishop adds to his control of the centre square e5. Secondly, it can be used to terrorize the black king, whose escape to the safety of a8 is now prevented. And thirdly, just by moving out of the way the bishop gives the rook on b1 the chance to enter into the attack on the vulnerable e6 pawn via e1 at some later point.

Of course, none of this would be possible if Black could simply reply 25...♖xf4 and take the bishop. But here 26 ♗xe6 would then win the black queen.

This is brilliant, high level positional play, but there is no mystery here, is there? It is just a case of having the following silent conversation with yourself:

"I'd like my bishop on f4 – can I put it there?"

"No, I can't because it loses a piece to 25...♖xf4."

"But wait! Wouldn't Black lose his queen to 26 ♗xe6 if he took the bishop?"

"Yes, that's right! So let's go ahead with 25 ♗f4!"

25   ...   g5

Alas this has come one move too late to prevent the powerful redeployment of the white bishop.

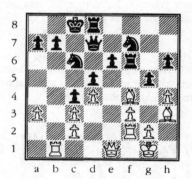

26   ♖e2!!

Short extracts maximum benefit from the potential pin on the black queen. Again, this might seem like magic but it is entirely logical. Continuing our imaginary conversation, White says to himself "I guess I have to retreat my attacked bishop. I'd prefer to play 26 ♖e2 to attack the weak pawn on e6 but that's life! Hey, wait a second, if I played 26 ♖e2 and he took my bishop, what exactly would he do after 27 ♖xe6?''

Once you have looked at 26...gxf4 27 ♖xe6 for a little while you will realize that Black has no good move at all – either he takes the rook and loses his queen to the pin after 27...♖xe6 28 ♗xe6 or else he saves his queen and lets White take a whole rook for nothing with 27 ♖xf6 when White will be the exchange and a pawn up.

The next time you see a strong but 'impossible' move don't reject it straightaway – give it a little thought, say 30 seconds, to see if it could possibly be made to work. If there is any chance of it working, delve a little deeper. You might have to reject it, but if you don't then you will have found a 'magic' move like 26 ♖e2!!

26   ...   ♖e8

Black can only bolster his defences and hope that Short doesn't come up with any more inspired attacking moves!

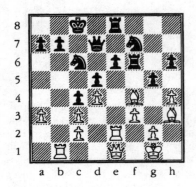

27   ♗h2!

Don't forget the bishop is now hanging – 27 hxg5? ♖xf4 would be highly embarrassing! White tucks

the bishop away on a secure square and gives himself the option of ♕g3 when the queen and bishop would strike terror in the black king down the long diagonal.

27   ...   gxh4?

Timman seeks counterplay by clearing the g5 square for his knight and thereby introducing combinative play down the g file. However, Short is able to neutralize Black's threats with some precise play. It then emerges that the g5 pawn was playing an important defensive role by controlling the f4 square. Once it has vanished, the way is clear for White to use his pawn on f3 as a battering ram to besiege the e6 pawn.

If Black had sat tight he would still have had a solid defensive position. White could have tried to increase the pressure on the e6 pawn with ideas such as ♕g3 and ♖be1, but there would have been nothing clear.

Therefore Black should have secured his king's position with 27...b6 and 28...♔b7, when the threat from the bishop on h2 is reduced – the black king can run to a8 or even a6 if things got dangerous.

28   ♕xh4

White recaptures and clears the e1 square for his queen's rook with gain of time by hitting the rook on f6.

28   ...   ♘g5

Black responds with two threats of his own:

a positional threat of 29...♘xh3+ exchanging off White's strong bishop that is heaping misery on e6;

a tactical threat of 29...♖xf3! tearing open White's kingside for if 30 gxf3 ♘xf3+ wins the white queen.

29 ♗g4!

No problems: White deals with both threats with this patient, unruffled move.

29 ... ♕g7

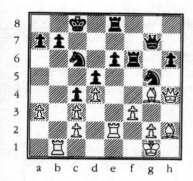

This is the move on which Timman placed his hopes and it certainly looks like a powerful one. Black defends his knight and plans 30...h5 when

(a) if 31 ♕xh5 ♖h8 traps the white queen!

(b) if 31 ♗xh5 Black puts a nasty pin on the bishop with 31...♖h8 when he threatens to exploit the killer pin on the g file and the pin on the h file to win White's queen in one move: 31...♘xf3+!

Now it would be easy for Short to be bullied by these threats into settling for the safe 30 ♕h5, when he keeps some advantage. Nevertheless, everything cries out for White to complete the last part of the positional jigsaw by putting his queen's rook on e1 – but can it be made to work tactically?

30 ♖be1!

Remember what we said above about the importance of having a look at moves that you want to play but are 'impossible' for tactical reasons.

White thinks: 'I have the safe move 30 ♕h5, but ideally I'd love to play 30 ♖ae1 as it puts enormous pressure on e6. However, I would lose my queen after 30...h5 31 ♕xh5 ♖h8. Well that's not strictly true as I can make an escape square by giving up a bishop with 32 ♗xe6+ ♘xe6 though it would still be hopeless a piece down after 33 ♕g4 ♕xg4 34 fxg4. In fact I've just noticed I could also fight on with 32 ♖xe6 as after 32...♖xh5, 33 ♖e8+ is double, discovered check mate!

Hold on, I might be doing more than fighting on – perhaps I'm even winning after 32 ♖xe6! I should think about this carefully. How does Black capture my queen after 32 ♖xe6 – if 32...♘xe6 I take again with 33 ♖xe6 and Black still can't take my queen with 33...♖xh5 because of 34 ♖e8 mate. If instead 33...♖xe6 34 ♗xe6+ ♔d8 then my queen escapes with 35 ♕xd5+: I have three pawns for the exchange and a huge attack on the black king. That must be winning: 30...h5 isn't any good for Black.

That means I can play the move I want to play: it is tactically sound!'

30 ... b6

Timman admits that 30...h5 was no more than a very clever bluff. He has therefore failed to disrupt White's strategical build up on the e file and can only brace himself for the coming attack. To this end he makes a bolt hole for his king on b7.

31 ♕h5

Now White rules out h6-h5 altogether and attacks the black rook on e8.

31 ... ♕d7

An inglorious return to defensive duty by the black queen.

32 f4!

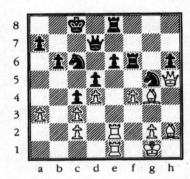

White's position is a marvel of co-ordination. Every piece is exerting pressure along the e file, either:

(a) through directly attacking the e6 pawn

(b) causing discomfort to its defenders

or

(c) being ready to launch a follow up attack on the black king once the barrier on e6 has been breached.

Now the time has come for White to clinch the win by using his pawns to prise open the e file. It was necessary to foresee the strength of the exchange sacrifice that follows.

32 ... ♘e4

The knight must plug the e file as 32...♘f7 33 f5 is horrible.

33 ♖xe4!

It would have been crazy for White to have allowed the black knight to reach the e4 square if he hadn't had this sacrifice ready.

33 ... dxe4

Black must capture the rook even though his centre is fatally dislocated.

34 d5!

The point: Black's defences crumble as 34...♕xd5 just drops the queen to 35 ♕xd5.

34 ... ♘d8

The black pieces huddle together trying to prevent disaster on e6...

35 ♕e5!

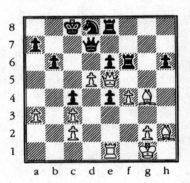

...but it is the dark-squared bishop waiting quietly on h2 which will provide the decisive impetus for White's attack. The black rook on f6 is hanging and if 35...♖g6 36 f5! ♖xg4 37 ♕b8 is mate.

35 ... ♖f5

A desperate offer to return the exchange in order to prevent the killer 36 f5! advance.

36 dxe6!

Short rightly ignores the rook as if 36...♖xe5 37 exd7+ would be a massacre.

36 ... ♕d2

Black counterattacks and even threatens mate in one move!

37 ♕xe4!

But this simple riposte wins at once as the rook on e1 is defended and Black has no way to save his own rook on f5 without allowing a lethal discovered check.

37 ... ♖d5

If 37...♖xe6 38 ♗xf5 wins one rook and fatally pins the other.

38 e7+

The white bishops and passed pawns are a ferocious combination.

38 ... ♔c7

The black king flees from one discovered check by a bishop...

39 f5+ 1-0

...but the second is too much. After 39...♔c6 or 39...♔b7 White's simplest way to win is 40 ♖d1! when retreating the black queen allows 40 ♕xd5+ while 40...♕xd1+ 41 ♗xd1 is hopeless – the rook can't even recapture on d1 as it is pinned.

Game Twelve
V.Topalov - E.Bareev
Dortmund 2002
French Defence

1 e4

First and foremost in the opening White tries to seize control of the centre as a prelude to a quick mating attack. Failing that he will try to prevent his opponent developing his pieces or inflict a structural weakness somewhere; if all else fails he will make do with a space advantage and try to outwit his opponent in the middlegame. Whatever White's intentions, you can't find a better starting move than 1 e4.

1 ... e6

Black is prepared to concede space in return for the security that a blocked centre confers. In particular the f7 square – the most vulnerable in the black camp – is shielded from attack down the a2-g8 diagonal.

2 d4

White achieves maximum freedom for his pieces by putting both centre pawns on the fourth rank.

2 ... d5

A necessary challenge or else White will have a free hand in the centre.

3 ♘c3

The boldest way to defend e4. More solid was 3 ♘d2 but it would shut in the bishop on c1 and so make an immediate attack less viable for White.

3 ... ♘f6

Again Black puts pressure on the e4 point. He would like to cajole White into playing 4 exd5, when after 4...exd5 the bishop on c8 has an open diagonal. However Topalov finds a more aggressive response.

4 ♗g5

White pins the black knight and gets the bishop outside of his pawn structure. This means that after 4...♗e7 5 e5 ♘fd7 6 ♗xe7 ♕xe7 7 f4 White has built a pawn centre on the dark squares without having to worry about shutting in his bishop – it has already been exchanged off. However, Bareev chooses another path that avoids this line.

4   ...   dxe4

This prevents White from setting up the cramping pawn centre as occurs after 4...♗e7 5 e5, as described in the previous note. On the other hand such a move is described as 'conceding the centre': Black voluntarily relinquishes the strong point on d5 and leaves White with a space advantage due to the pawn on d4.

5   ♘xe4

White regains the pawn and puts the knight on an excellent square in the centre.

5   ...   ♘bd7

Meanwhile Black ensures that he can recapture on f6 with a knight in order to keep up the fight for the e4 square.

6   ♘f3

At last White begins the development of his kingside. The knight is sure to find itself well placed on f3 in all scenarios that may arise from the position.

6   ...   ♗e7

Bareev breaks the pin on the knight. His aim is to exchange off several minor pieces and so increase the freedom of action of those that remain on the board.

7   ♘xf6+

There is no opportunity to conserve pieces for a later attack as after 7 ♘g3 c5! Black would easily equalize by eliminating the d4 pawn.

7   ...   ♗xf6

Now Black hopes for 8 ♗xf6 ♘xf6 when he is well on the path to equality.

8   h4!

Topalov meets his opponent's intention to simplify half way. If now 8...♗xg5 9 hxg5 another piece has disappeared but on the other hand White has pressure along the h file and the g5 pawn excludes the black knight from its best square by controlling f6. Black quite rightly regards this as an unacceptable concession.

8   ...   c5

Having been frustrated in his bid to simplify on the kingside, Black reverts to his stock plan in this type of position: the elimination of the pawn on d4 which constitutes White's space advantage in the centre.

9   ♕d2

White cannot maintain a pawn centre, but he hopes that the superior mobility of his pieces will allow him to drum up an initiative. Therefore he continues his build up with a view to castling queenside. Instead 9 dxc5 ♛c5+ 10 c3 ♛xc5 would be fine for Black who has brought his queen to a strong square.

9 ... cxd4

White's only pawn in the centre vanishes. Undoubtedly this is a great positional achievement for Black. The big question is whether he can complete his development before White manages to strike a telling blow with his more dynamic pieces. In particular, he has to solve the problem of the passive bishop on c8.

10 ♘xd4

Here we see another point of 9 ♛d2: the bishop on g5 is defended so that Black can't win a pawn by taking twice on g5.

10 ... h6

Bareev decides that he has endured the tension on f6 for quite long enough and so forces the exchange of bishops.

11 ♗xf6

A critical moment has arrived: will the active white pieces come out on top, or has Black's simplification drained too much energy from his opponent's initiative?

11 ... ♘xf6

It appears that the exchange of two minor pieces has eased the black position, as his centre remains solid and there is no apparent danger on the kingside. But trouble strikes from an unexpected direction.

12 ♛b4!

Now is the moment for decisive action. The routine 12 0-0-0 would be far inferior as after 12...0-0 Black would be ready to counterattack in the centre with e6-e5. Black must therefore be stopped from castling at all costs.

12 ... ♘d5

Bareev forces the white queen away from the b file so that he can develop his bishop as in the game without allowing ♛xb7.

13 ♛a3

The white queen persists in obstructing Black from castling kingside: it is White's only advantage so he must extract maximum benefit from it.

13 ... ♛e7!

There was no time to waste in challenging the white queen as Topalov already planned to smash through the centre after 14 0-0-0 and 15 c4.

The best way to defuse an attack is by offering the exchange of queens.

14 ♗b5+!

White continues to harass his opponent as Black only needs to be left in peace for one move to enable him to castle with a perfectly safe game.

14   ...   ♗d7

Naturally Black is happy that he can exchange off this passive piece for White's active bishop.

15   ♗xd7+

This gives Black a difficult choice: either he can renounce castling immediately by recapturing with the king, or else he can spend valuable tempi (that is, moves) on playing 15...♕xd7 and then putting the queen back on e7.

15   ...   ♔xd7?

After this the black king will be a perpetual target for the white pieces. It appears that 15...♕xd7 was the correct choice, as after 16 0-0-0 ♕e7 17 ♕a4+ ♕d7 there is no obvious way for White to profit from the dance of the two queens.

16   ♕a4+

Here 16 ♕xe7+ ♔xe7 would be the completely wrong plan for White. The black king would be well placed in the centre for the endgame rather than a target.

16   ...   ♔c7

The king chooses a square where he doesn't interfere with the development of his rooks, as would be the case after 16...♔c8 or 16...♔d8.

17   ♖h3!

An excellent wing deployment of the rook. Black was hoping for 17 0-0-0 when 17...♕b4! smothers the white queen and so forces a very welcome exchange.

17   ...   a6

Black guards the b5 square and prepares to activate the rook on a8 without allowing ♕xa7. The move he would really like to play is 17...♕b4, but after 18 ♖c3+! his king is in trouble despite the exchange of queens: 18...♔d8 – of course taking the rook can't be captured without dropping the queen – 19 ♕xb4 ♘xb4 20 ♖b3 ♘c6 21 ♘xc6+ bxc6 22 ♖b7 and the white rook is dominant on the seventh rank.

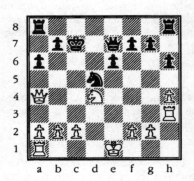

18   ♖b3!

White brings his rook into the attack and prevents the simplifying 18...♕b4+. Now Black has to stop the threat of 19 c4 which would drive his knight from the centre post where it holds off White's attack.

18   ...   ♕c5

A bold entrance by the black queen as now 19 c4? drops a piece to 19...♕xd4.

19   0-0-0!

Here castling is both a strong defensive and aggressive move. It safeguards the king and protects the knight on d4 a second time, thereby freeing the queen from the task. The idea of c2-c4 becomes attractive, though it would take some preparation as the pawn is pinned at the moment; still, it is a potential threat and with his next move Bareev immediately opposes it. Meanwhile the rook on d1 is ready to join in the attack and as will be seen the e1 square which the king has just vacated becomes a strong attacking post for the queen.

19   ...   b5

Black makes space for both his king and queen on the b file and obstructs the projected c2-c4 advance. But as will be seen the black queenside is much too fragile to withstand the pressure. He might have played 19...♖hd8 bringing up reinforcements: indeed, it might be said that if that move loses than everything loses.

Note that Black has to avoid 19...♘b6. which apparently forces the exchange of queens, in view of 20 ♘xe6+! fxe6 21 ♕f4+ ♚c8 22 ♖c3 winning the black queen as 22...♘c4 23 ♖xc4 doesn't help.

20   ♕a5+

The only square for the queen, but quite sufficient to build up the attack.

20   ...   ♕b6

The black queen is relieved to get off the c file where she is perpetually in danger of being pinned against the king, but Black has reckoned without White's superb reply.

21   ♕e1!

A brilliant retreat, which sends the queen backwards in order to go forwards! One threat is 22 ♕e5+

♚b7 23 ♕xg7, simply picking up a pawn on the kingside.

21   ...   ♚b7

Black avoids the check on e5, but now his king and queen are bunched together again on the same file which almost invites a pin.

22   ♕e2!

Already White threatens 23 ♘xb5 axb5 24 ♖xb5 picking up the queen. This is far better than 22 c4? ♖hc8! when the pin on the white king frustrates the attack.

22   ...   ♚a7

Perhaps Bareev imagined that he had avoided disaster by tucking his king away on a7. Indeed, he only needs time to develop his rooks, say with 23...♖hd8 and 24...♖ac8 and all danger will be passed. But Topalov won't allow him even a one move respite from the attack.

23   ♘xb5+!

It is worth repeating that not only is this sacrificial combination very powerful, it is also necessary as otherwise all White's advantage will evaporate.

23   ...   axb5

Of course this was an offer that couldn't be refused.

24   🖲xb5

Now the black king has lost all its pawn cover. Both black rooks are on their starting squares, so the material situation where it matters is

White: Two rooks and a queen

Black: A queen and knight

These are hopeless odds for the defender when the king is totally exposed to attack.

24   ...   ♛c6

The variations are grim for Black: 24...♛a6 25 🖲dxd5 exd5 26 ♛e7+ and mate next move or 24...♛d6 25 🖲d4 when 26 🖲a4 is unstoppable.

25   🖲dxd5!

The next stage in the winning combination: White removes the defensive knight and opens the e file for his queen.

25   ...   exd5

Now the attack versus defence balance sheet reads:

White: queen and rook

Black: queen

26   ♛e7+

White has to play precisely as he has only two units left with which to finish the game.

26   ...   ♚a6

The king limps forwards but cannot escape its fate.

27   🖲b3!

A quiet but lethal move. Black has no good answer to 28 ♛a3+ followed by mate.

27   ...   ♛b6

The queen has to give herself up for if 27...♛a4 28 ♛b7+ and mate in one move.

28   🖲a3+

Accurate to the end. Instead 28 🖲xb6+ ♚xb6 might allow Black some activity based on 🖲xa2.

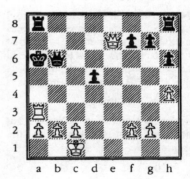

28   ...   ♛a5

Here's a pretty finish in which the black king gets mated back on his starting square: 28...♚b5 29 ♛d7+ ♚c5 30 🖲c3+ ♚d4 31 🖲d3+ ♚e5 32 ♛xd5+ ♚f6 33 🖲f3+ ♚e7 – 33...♚g6 34 ♛f5 mate – 34 🖲xf7+ ♚e8 35 ♛d7 mate.

29   🖲xa5+

At last White takes the booty...

29   ...   ♚xa5

...as now the black king is blocking the attack on a2 by his rook and so there is no counterplay.

30   ♛xf7   1-0

So the game didn't end in mate, but here Bareev decided to call it a day as White has a queen and six pawns for two rooks and three pawns, with more black pawns about to tumble. These are hopeless odds in all but a blitz game.

Game Thirteen
R.Ponomariov - S.Conquest
Torshavn 2000
Caro-Kann Defence

1   e4

'Best by test' claimed Bobby Fischer about this move, and few would dare to disagree with him – though it is only fair to point out that whether he was 'testing' 1 e4, 1 d4, 1 c4 or even 1 b3 the result was usually a brilliant win for the American genius. Any mainstream opening gives scope for demonstrating style and strength, not just 1 e4.

1   ...   c6

The Caro-Kann defence. Black plans to challenge White's proud e4 pawn with d7-d5 without losing time with his queen – as occurs after 1...d5 2 exd5 ♛xd5 3 ♘c3 – or shutting in his queen's bishop as in the French with 1...e6 2 d4 d5. The Caro-Kann is a very solid defence, but every opening move has its drawback and in this case you could ask Black's queen's knight what it

thinks about having its natural square on c6 taken away by a pawn.

2   d4

By putting a second pawn on the fourth rank White achieves maximum freedom of movement for his minor pieces.

2   ...   d5

Black releases his queen's bishop and prepares to break up White's pawn centre.

3   ♘c3

White prefers to keep the position open rather than block the centre with 3 e5 when a more manoeuvring game would result. Such decisions are primarily a matter of style as in both cases White would have a slight advantage, but of a different type: more space (after 3 e5) or livelier piece play (as in the game).

3   ...   dxe4

Black has to exchange pawns before deploying his pieces as after 3...♘f6 the riposte 4 e5 would be awkward.

4   ♘xe4

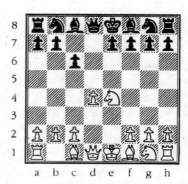

A knight loves to be on a centre square where it cannot be attacked by pawns. Here the only way to dislodge the knight with a pawn would be by 4...f5, but this would create ugly weaknesses on the e5 and e6 squares.

4 ... ♗f5

As the white knight is so beautifully placed on e4 it is no wonder that Black's strategy here focuses on using the pieces to drive away the knight. Besides the game move, which has the virtue of developing the bishop whilst hitting the knight, other methods are 4...♞bd7 and then 5...♞gf6 or even 4...♞f6 straightaway, not worrying about the doubled pawns after 5 ♞xf6+ gxf6 or 5...exf6.

5 ♞g3

The knight has to retreat and does so in the most time efficient way by harassing the black bishop.

5 ... ♗g6

The black bishop stays on the more active diagonal and keeps out of the way of the other pieces. Consider the alternative moves for the bishop:

(a) on c8 it obstructs the queen's rook

(b) on d7 it prevents ♞d7

(c) on e6 it gets in the way of e7-e6. which stops the king's bishop getting into the game.

Yes, the g6 square was made for the bishop!

6 h4

The question arises: Why does White select a loosening pawn move on the wing when he has the sound developing move 6 ♞f3 at his disposal? It seems as if he is neglecting the centre and making the kingside unsuitable as a future residence for his king.

The point is that Black isn't putting any immediate pressure on the centre, so White can afford to take some liberties with his development. Therefore, he takes the opportunity to gain space on the kingside and threaten 7 h5, which causes some trouble for the black bishop. In the long term the white king can go to the queenside and be safe there.

How does Ponomariov know all this? Is it obvious through looking at the position that White can afford to take a 'timeout' from his development?

No, it isn't at all obvious. A move like 6 h4 had to be tried and tested for decades in master games before it became accepted as a standard part of opening theory. A player of the 1920s would have looked askance at this apparently frivolous pawn move. That is why every player needs some knowledge of opening theory – that is, he or she has to be aware of what has worked and what hasn't worked in previous games.

6 ... h6

Black makes a bolt hole for his bishop as otherwise 7 h5 would be painful. If instead 6...h5 then 7 ♘1e2! planning 8 ♘f4 to hit the bishop and the h pawn (for a third time!) would be highly awkward.

7 ♘f3

White could have played 7 h5 straightaway, but he rightly prefers to keep the option of harassing the bishop with 8 ♘e5 as well as 8 h5 on the next move.

7 ... ♘f6

The alternative was 7...♘d7 to prevent Ponomariov's next move, when 8 h5 ♗h7 9 ♗d3 ♗xd3 10 ♕xd3 is slightly advantageous to White who can complete his development with ♗d2 and 0-0-0.

8 ♘e5

The knight takes the chance to seize a strong centre square.

8 ... ♗h7

A necessary retreat as Black can't tolerate his kingside pawns being smashed up after 8...♘d7 9 ♘xg6 fxg6.

9 ♗d3

Most players would automatically play 9 ♗c4, a sound developing move with a strong threat: mate on f7. But things are by no means clear after 9...e6 as at some point Black can utilize the d5 square with ♘d5, when the knight is blocking the centre and can't easily be expelled by c2-c4 – White's own bishop is in the way of the pawn. Ponomariov prefers a different approach which continues to hound the black bishop on h7.

9 ... ♗xd3

If 9...♕xd4 10 ♘xf7! is the clever point as 10...♔xf7? 11 ♗g6+ would cost Black his queen to the discovered check. A possible continuation after 10 ♘xf7! would be 10...♗xd3 11 ♘xh8 ♕e5+ 12 ♗e3 ♗h7 – apparently the knight is trapped on h8, but...13 ♕d8+! ♔xd8 14 ♘f7+ ♔e8 15 ♘xe5 and White emerges the safe exchange up.

10 ♕xd3

White regains his piece and moves one step closer to castling queenside.

10 ... e6

Despite the loss of time with his light-squared bishop, Black is pleased to have exchanged it off as his pawn structure would otherwise have impeded its action.

11 ♗f4

A strong deployment for the bishop in support of the knight on its centre outpost. Now White is ready to complete the mobilization of his pieces with 12 0-0-0, but Conquest tries to throw a spanner in the works...

11 ... ♕a5+

You should never make a check just for the sake of it, unless it happens to be checkmate! Black's idea is that the presence of the black queen on a5 will make it harder for White to secure his king as 0-0-0 will drop the a2 pawn to ♛xa2.

12 c3

White also has the quandary of how to block the check. After 12 ♗d2 ♛c7 White has gained nothing time-wise as the black queen is better on c7 than d8: he has merely put his bishop on a square where it has less scope than on f4. The game move is also not without drawbacks as the white king will now have a slightly less secure pawn front after castling queenside.

12 ... ♛a6

As he has less space and is slightly behind in development Black decides that swapping queens will ease his position.

13 ♞e4

White acquiesces in the exchange of queens but on his own terms: he will get rid of his poorly placed knight on g3 and inflict doubled pawns on his opponent.

13 ... ♞xe4

Black changes his mind about the queen exchange as he evidently believes the price is too high after 13...♛xd3 14 ♞xf6+ gxf6 15 ♞xd3, when his kingside has suffered some slight damage. Still, this was his best course of action – the middlegame proves to be by no means easy for the black king with queens still on the board.

14 ♛xe4

The queen is now excellently centralized and can play a leading part in any plan that White should choose. Meanwhile the black queen is stopping the white king from castling on either wing – if 0-0-0 then ♛xa2 – but she is out of contact with the centre.

14 ... ♞d7

This forfeits the right to castle but otherwise it is difficult to see how Black could have developed his pieces. In any case the knight couldn't be left unchallenged for too long on e5.

15 ♞xd7

Now White's initiative will have a ready made target in the black king.

15 ... ♚xd7

After 15 moves Black has only his queen developed, unless of course you consider his king to be well centralized on d7! Such a state of affairs is only possible in a blocked position – if the position was open then Black would face an immediate cataclysm.

16 ♖h3!

In view of his space advantage, White is able to swing his rook to an attacking square in the centre via h3. Black cannot copy the trick as his own pawns are too far back to permit such a manoeuvre.

16 ... ♖c8

Black is desperate to develop his kingside but if 16...♗e7 immediately then 17 ♕e5 with ideas of both 18 ♕xg7 and 18 ♕c7+ is troublesome.

17 ♗e5!

If now 17...♗e7 18 ♗xg7 wins a pawn. Ponomariov will only permit his opponent to develop the bishop if he concedes a weakness in his centre with f7-f6. An essential part of any strategy is preventing your opponent playing good moves unless the price is right.

17 ... ♕c4

Conquest decides he needs his queen to be in touch with the centre. Here she will lend a hand in defending the e6 square after the enforced weakening that follows.

18 ♖f3!

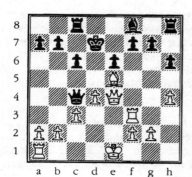

White's strategy can be summed up as follows:

Stage one: make Black impair the defence of e6 with f7-f6.

Stage two: triple all the major pieces pieces against e6.

Stage three: break through the barrier with ♖xe6.

Stage Four: checkmate the defenceless black king.

18 ... f6

Alas, Black cannot maintain his pawns in a compact formation as here is what would have happened upon 18...♔e8: 19 ♕f4! f6 20 ♗xf6! gxf6 21 ♕xf6 and White wins the rook in the corner after either 21...♖h7 22 ♕g6+ or 21...♖g8 22 ♕f7+.

19 ♗g3

Now that the desired chink in Black's armour has appeared the bishop is happy to retreat.

19 ... f5

Now the threat of 20 ♕g6 infiltrating to f7 via the hole on g6 forces Black to relinquish his control of the e5 square.

20 ♕c2

The queen retires a safe distance as very embarrassing would be 20 ♕f4 g5! 21 hxg5?? hxg5 when suddenly Black wins a rook because if 22 ♕xg5 ♖h1+.

20 ... g5

Black hopes to distract White from a concerted attack on e6 with a demonstration by the pawns on the kingside. The immediate threat is 21...f4, shutting the white bishop out of the game.

21 ♗e5!

This nips in the bud Black's plan with gain of time by attacking the rook.

21 ... 🜚g8

Unfortunately for Black his rook has to give up the h file for if 21...🜚h7 22 🜚xf5! exf5 23 ♕xf5+ picks up the rook with two pawns as a bonus.

22 b3!

The mechanics of White's winning plan begin to take shape. First of all he will drive the black queen away from the defence of e6.

22 ... ♕d5

The ideal square for the queen, but alas she can only stay here for one move.

23 c4

This pawn advance not only chases the queen from the centre but also supports a possible d4-d5 thrust to smash open the black king's defences.

23 ... ♕a5+

The queen has little choice but to return to the wilderness of the rook's file as the queen exchange brings no respite after 23...♕e4+ 24 ♕xe4 fxe4 25 🜚f7+, when Black's pawns are wretched and the white rook is supreme on the seventh rank.

24 ♔f1

The white king is not only secure on f1 but is defending g2 should Black venture 24...gxh4.

24 ... ♗e7

If 24...gxh4 25 🜚xf5! is crushing as 25...exf5 26 ♕xf5+ ♔d8 – or else the rook on c8 drops – 27 ♗f6+ wins the black queen by discovered attack. But now Black threatens 25...g4 followed by 26...♗xh4 when his counterattack is in full swing.

25 hxg5!

This stroke destroys the momentum of Black's kingside advance as 25...hxg5 26 🜚h3 leaves White with uncontested control of the h file. As a general rule, the player with the better minor piece can count on winning the struggle for an open file. In this scenario the fact that the white bishop controls the h8 square prevents any challenge by the black rooks.

25 ... 🜚xg5

Rather than concede the h file Black aims for frontal pressure with his rooks against g2. However, White finds his opponent's counterplay far easier to contain now that there is no mass of advancing black pawns.

26 🜚d1

Finally Ponomariov develops his queen's rook and in doing so avoids the trick 26 🜚e1? 🜚xg2! 27 ♔xg2 ♕xe1 when he would have to start thinking about how to save the game.

26 ... h5

Black prepares to ram the white kingside with h5-h4 once White has been provoked into g2-g3. He is reluctant to play 26...罝cg8 immediately as after 27 g3 he has to contend with the threat of d4-d5 breaking up his centre; whereas with the rook still on c8 he can answer 27 d5 with 27...cxd5 when White can't recapture as the c4 pawn is pinned.

27 ♕e2

At last Ponomariov is set to apply the power of his heavy pieces – the queen and rooks – against the ragged pawn on e6. White has only one advantage in the position, but it is an enormous one: the terrible situation of the black king. If his king were tucked away on a8 then Black would have nothing to fear; in fact he would have rather the better chances as he can drum up an attack down the g file. But as things stand his monarch is going to be subjected to an overpowering onslaught.

27 ... ♕a6

If Black could only get his queen over to the kingside he would greatly increase the potency of his counterplay and perhaps even succeed in saving the game. Unfortunately it all remains a dream as for example after 27...♕d8 28 d5! is killing. The awkward looking game move is designed to counter 28 d5 as 28...cxd5 29 cxd5 ♕xe2+ would be paradise for Black.

28 ♗f4

Most efficient: the approach to e6 is cleared with gain of time.

28 ... 罝g6

Naturally the rook retreats to a square where it guards the vulnerable pawn.

29 罝e3

White's plan nears completion as once he plays 罝de1 the defence of e6 will be at melting point.

29 ... 罝cg8

The only hope is counterattack along the g file

30 g3

...but White sets up a pawn barrier that is supported by three units – the pawn on f2, rook and bishop. Thus it can hold the black rooks at bay long enough for decisive action to take place on the e file.

30 ... h4

The last throw of the dice by Black.

31 罝e1

At first glance Black's attack looks just as menacing as White's – in fact perhaps even more so, as his rooks have the aid of the h4 pawn which can be used to undermine g3. But there is a vital difference which gives White a decisive advantage: he is playing with the help of his queen. Any strategical plan in the middlegame requires the assistance of the queen: and here Black's is sitting idly on a6 whilst White's is in the thick of things on the e file. It is no wonder that Black suffers a quick catastrophe.

31   ...   ♗b4

Black would be torn apart after 31...c5 – belatedly involving the queen in the defence of e6 – 32 d5! when the pin on the e file is lethal. The game move is a forlorn attempt to distract a white rook from the e file.

32 ♖xe6!

The brilliant culmination of White's well conceived strategy which began with 17 ♗e5!

32   ...   ♗xe1

In such positions all you can do is grab material and hope your opponent makes a mess of the attack.

33 ♖e7+

It is almost always a bad sign when the opponent's rook reaches the seventh rank, even when the king is safely hidden away; here it can only lead to a quick massacre.

33   ...   ♔d8

Instead 33...♔c8 34 ♖e8+ mates after either 34...♖xe8 35 ♕xe8 or 34...♔d7 35 ♕e7.

34 ♗c7+

Step by step the black king is hunted down. This may seem like a long process, but remember that Black's options are very limited, which greatly reduces the complexity of any calculation White had to make before choosing 32 ♖xe6.

34   ...   ♔c8

But now White has run out of useful checks. Has he messed up the attack?

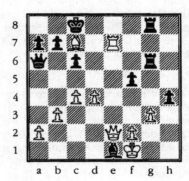

35 ♕e5!

No, as it is by no means necessary to check. This is a tremendous centralization with the direct threat of 36 ♕xf5+ and mate next move. More insidiously the white queen eyes a mate on c7 once the square is vacated by the white bishop.

35   ...   b5

The black king needs air as 35...♖f8 36 ♗d8 – threat 37 ♕c7 mate – 36...♗a5 37 ♗xa5 leads to mate on c7. A similar disaster occurs in the game.

36 ♗d8!

The pseudo sacrifice of the bishop ensures that the black king can never use the bolt hole on b7.

36   ...   ♗a5

The only reasonable attempt to defend the dark squares.

37 ♖c7+

Nevertheless, the king can't resist the close range attention of the white bishop, rook and queen with only a solitary bishop offering any sort of cover on the second rank.

37   ...   ♔b8

Walking into a discovered check is every king's nightmare, but 37...♗xc7 38 ♕xc7 and 37...♔d8 38 ♕e7 are both mate.

38   ♖xc6+   1-0

Black resigned as the queen is lost. It is somehow fitting that Ponomariov's demolition of the Caro-Kann culminates with the removal of the pawn on c6!

Game Fourteen
V.Kovacevic - Y.Seirawan
Hoogovens, Wijk aan Zee 1980
Pirc Defence

1   e4

Ever since its creation this has been the favourite way for White to begin a game of chess...

1   ...   d6

...whereas this move would never be found in a 15th century chess manuscript. Black's wants to fianchetto his king's bishop on g7, where it will put pressure on the white centre. His system of development for his kingside therefore involves ♘f6, g7-g6 and then ♗g7. So first of all he defends the e5 square in order to avoid having his knight attacked as occurs after 1...♘f6 2 e5, when we are in the realms of the Alekhine Defence.

2   d4

Naturally White isn't going to refuse all the free space on offer in the centre.

2   ...   ♘f6

Thanks to his precaution on the first move Black's knight can sit on its best square without being harassed.

3   ♘c3

White defends e4 without wasting time. Nevertheless, in contrast to the King's Indian Mainline as occurs after 1 d4 ♘f6 2 c4 g6 3 ♘c3 ♗g7 4 e4, White has had to renounce building a broad pawn centre with c2-c4. Therefore it is reasonable to assume that he will try to exploit the advantage of the first move in a direct manner with piece play, as he has less to hope for from long term pressure on the centre.

3   ...   g6

All according to plan: Black makes way for his bishop on g7.

4   ♗e2

This quiet looking move belies White's aggressive intentions. A different, and more promising method of direct attack, was 4 ♗e3 intending after 4...♗g7 to offer the exchange of dark-squared bishops with 5 ♕d2 and 6 ♗h6.

4   ...   ♗g7

The kingside fianchetto breathed new life into Black's defences to 1 d4 back in the 1930s and 1940s. The rise of the Grunfeld, King's Indian and Benko Gambit removed forever any danger that chess would be 'played out' – the dreaded 'draw death' predicted by Capablanca.

It is no wonder that here Black tries the same type of set up against 1 e4.

5   g4

Black is putting no immediate pressure on the white centre, so Kovacevic decides that he can afford to start an instant attack with his pawns on the kingside. This is a highly ambitious and double edged approach to say the least: if Black manages to begin a counterattack, where is the white king going to hide?

A safe alternative was 5 ♘f3.

5   ...   c6!

Seirawan is unruffled by his opponent's attacking gesture and calmly prepares counterplay on the queenside with b7-b5. He avoids castling kingside, at least for the time being, as this would play into White's hands. The black king would be a nice target on g8 once the h file is blasted open. For example 5...0-0 6 g5 ♘fd7 7 h4 followed by 8 h5 would more than justify White's attacking set up.

Sometimes classical ideas of development – such as castling – have to be delayed or even abandoned altogether. The great American Master Pillsbury once remarked that you should castle because you want to or because you have to, but never just because you can.

6   g5

White continues with his attacking plan, which at least has the merit of dislodging the black knight from its best square.

6   ...   ♘fd7

The knight elects to stay in the centre as to retreat back to g8 would be dismal indeed.

7   h4

White presses on with his kingside assault...

7   ...   b5

...and the black counterattack is launched on the queenside.

8   h5

White has been deprived of his natural prey on the kingside, as the black king has remained stubbornly on e8. However, he can yet justify all his pawn advances from a strategical perspective if he is allowed to play 9 h6! driving the black bishop back to f8, where it is buried.

Seirawan's reply is directed against this threat.

8   ...   ♖g8!!

A brilliant positional move. Now Black is ready to answer 9 h6 with 9...♗h8, when the black bishop remains on its excellent diagonal. In that case White would have achieved nothing by blocking the kingside whilst Black would have plenty of dynamic chances on the queenside.

9   hxg6

White thinks that gaining possession of the h file will be great for his rook but he in for a big surprise. With hindsight it was better to keep the tension on the kingside and avoid the exchange.

9   ...   hxg6

Now Black is no longer troubled by events on the h file and can think about his own expansion on the queenside.

10   ♘f3

Better late than never: White finally develops his knight.

10   ...   b4

Pawn power in action: in a mirror image of White's attack on the kingside, the black pawn drives the knight away from its centre square.

11   ♘b1

An abject retreat, but still preferable to putting the knight out in the wilderness on a4.

11   ...   a5

Seirawan's whole strategy is based upon loosening White's defences to the bishop on g7. If he could strike out with other pawn advances such as c6-c5! or a4-a3! he would be delighted.

12   a4

Of the next few moves it becomes clear that White has run out of dynamic ideas and is trying to achieve a draw by blocking everything up. His pawn structure loses all flexibility, he weakens the e5 square and he removes all obstacles (he would call them 'targets'!) from the sights of the black bishop on g7. On the other hand he hopes that the lack of open lines will prevent Black from making any winning breakthrough – after all, it is White who controls the only open file on the board with his rook on h1...

12   ...   c5

A key attack on the centre after which White concedes the open diagonal to the bishop on g7 without a fight.

13   d5

The shutters come down on the centre light squares.

13   ...   ♘b6

'Where is this knight going?' you may ask. The answer is: nowhere! The idea is to vacate the d7 square to make possible Black's next move.

14   c4

The mission to seal the light squares is accomplished. He could have played actively with 14 c3, but he has missed Black's reply.

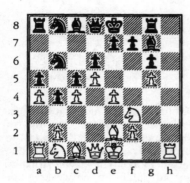

14 ...   ♔d7!!

Without this brilliant clearance move White's strategy would have succeeded. There is only one way through the light square defensive wall, and that is via the h file.

15 ♘bd2

The irony is that White has built such a strong fortress on the queenside that he cannot possibly remove the barricades to get at the black king.

15 ...   ♖h8

The black rook returns gleefully to the h file as the first step in the planned invasion of White's position.

16 ♖g1

An echo of Black's 8...♖g8, but whereas the white rook proved a lonely figure on the h file, its black counterpart will enjoy the close support of the queen.

16 ...   ♔c7

Black has no need to hurry. He clears the way for the development of his queen's knight to d7 as the next stage in softening up White's centre.

17 ♖b1

White plans b2-b3 followed by ♗b2 in order to challenge the black bishop.

17 ...   ♖h3

The first black piece crosses into enemy territory and vacates the h8 square for the queen.

18 b3

A slight glimmer of hope as 19 ♗b2 would claim back some of the dark squares he so casually gave away in the opening...

18 ...   ♛h8!

...but Black puts paid to the idea. He we see the magnificent flexibility of the queen: she works in combination with the bishop diagonally and the rook laterally.

19 ♘f1

Having been frustrated in his plan of ♗b2, Kovacevic has to find an alternative way to develop the bishop. He therefore clears the way to f4.

19 ...   ♘8d7

At last Black develops his queen's knight – after 19 moves! Of course it's all very different from 1 e4 e5 when the knight's services are required immediately upon 2 ♘f3 ♘c6. In closed positions there is more time to choose the strategically best squares for the pieces as a delay in development is less likely to lead to trouble.

20 ♗f4

Meanwhile the white bishop wakes from a 20 move slumber only to find itself in a nightmare position.

20   ...   ♘e5!

This clears the way for ♗d7 followed by the active deployment of the rook on a8. The next couple of moves are a lesson in the art of wise exchanging.

21   ♘xe5

The first piece to disappear is the white knight which was doing a good defensive job on the kingside.

21   ...   ♗xe5

...and now Seirawan wants to be rid of White's bishop which is fighting for control of the e5 square. Whilst it is true that Black also loses his own powerful bishop in the process he will be more than compensated in seeing his queen become master of all the dark squares.

22   ♗xe5

White has no wish to leave the black bishop dominating the long diagonal.

22   ...   ♛xe5

Now the pawn on e4 is hanging. How can it be defended without making any concessions to Black?

23   f3

This amounts to positional surrender as White's dark squares become horribly weak but there was no good alternative.

23   ...   ♗d7

Black frees his rook on a8 with the last quiet move before he decides it is time to launch an outright attack against White's flimsy defences.

24   ♛c2

White's king can't make a dash for the queenside as if 24 ♔d2 ♛c3 is mate. With the game move he prepares 25 ♛b2 to challenge the black queen.

24   ...   ♛d4

Black's grip on the dark squares is gradually tightened.

25   ♖g2

The rook flees to the second rank for if 25 ♖g3 ♖xg3 26 ♘xg3 ♛g1+ 27 ♘f1 ♛xg5 leaves White a pawn down.

25   ...   ♖h1

The rook infiltrates even further into the white camp.

26   ♖f2

White hopes that his rook will be well placed here. It not only defends the second rank and the knight who is barricading his king but also supports counterplay with f3-f4.

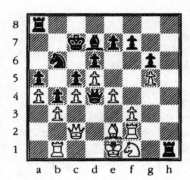

26   ...   ♕h8!!

The queen appeared excellently placed on d4, where she surveyed all the dark square holes in the white centre and on the wings. But a game of chess is won not through having one piece on a great square but rather through coordinating the action of all the pieces. Therefore Black retreats the queen so that she adds her power to that of the rook in exploiting the h file.

27   f4

White can't stand his slow death any longer and so launches an attempt at activity in the centre. Naturally such an approach hastens the end as the white defences become even more stretched.

27   ...   ♕h4

The pin on the rook will prove highly unpleasant for the white king.

28   ♖d1

White fights on grimly. If you have a losing position it is often best to centralize all your pieces and hope for the best – not all your opponents will be as inspired as Seirawan in finishing off the game!

28   ...   f6!

At last it is time for Black to use his pawns to break open lines. The winning theme will be: mate to the white king. Meanwhile Black's own king is perfectly safe on c7.

29   gxf6

This leads to the opening of the e file with dire consequences for the white king but if he allowed f6xg5 then the f file would become open with equally fatal results.

29   ...   exf6

Black recaptures and is poised to attack the e4 pawn with ♖e8 and f6-f5.

30   e5

White takes the bull by the horns and opens the position himself as he can see no answer to the black threats outlined above. Not surprisingly it leads to a quick defeat.

30   ...   fxe5

The one thing Black mustn't do is allow counterplay after 30...dxe5? 31 d6+.

31   fxe5

White hopes that 31 exd6+ or 31 e6 will generate some initiative, but Seirawan is not to be distracted by this sideshow.

31   ...   ♖f8

A very belated but devastating entrance by the rook into the game. The threat of course is 32...♕xf2+.

32   exd6+

Perhaps Black will take the pawn, when 33 ♕xg6+ will follow in a flash?

32   ...   ♔b7!

The black king retreats into complete safety. The extra white pawn on d6 is of no relevance whatsoever as White has no answer to the pin on f2.

33   ♗d3

The only way to defend f2. After Black's reply we see that the passive looking bishop was actually performing a vital defensive role in blocking the e file.

33   ...   ♖e8+

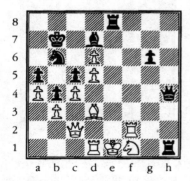

0-1

Here the game ended abruptly. If 34 ♔d2 ♕xf2+ while 34 ♗e2 allows Black to exploit the double

pin on e2 and f2 to win with 34...♖xf1+! 35 ♔xf1 ♕h1 mate. A pretty finish, but not as breathtaking as some of Seirawan's positional moves in the game!

Game Fifteen
V.Anand-J.Lautier
Biel 1997
Scandinavian Defence

1   e4

No objection is possible to this move which seeks to exploit in direct style White's one and only advantage: the initiative, or the right to move first. All ambitious players should have this move in their repertoire, as the resulting open positions will teach them all about tactics. Furthermore, as Reti remarked, the foundation of positional play is a knowledge of combinations.

1   ...   d5

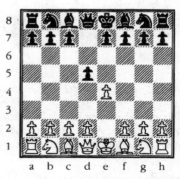

Lautier issues a direct challenge to the e4 pawn, which ensures White will be unable to build and maintain a wide centre with 2 d4. In a general sense this should make Black's development easier; the only drawback is the inevitable loss of time in regaining the proferred pawn.

2   exd5

The pawn must be taken as after 2 e5 Black could cut off the support of the pawn with 2...c5, preventing 3 d4. Besides, Black could develop his bishop in good style to f5.

2   ...   ♕xd5

A sound alternative was 2...♘f6 aiming to recapture on d5 with the knight, but Black prefers to regain the pawn forthwith even though the queen now becomes an object of attack.

3   ♘c3

Here we see the immediate drawback to Black's opening scheme: White gets to make a solid developing move at no expense in time, as the black queen must move again.

3   ...   ♕a5

A wise choice of square by the queen: it is to be expected that White will play d2-d4 sooner or later and then there will be a pin on

c3 that Black can hope to exploit with a future ♗b4 or ♘e4.

4   d4

The only way for White to take advantage of Black's loss of time is to prepare a bold and energetic deployment of his pieces.

4   ...   ♘f6

Black may have taken liberties with his development, but one good feature of his opening scheme is that he can put his knight on its best square without worrying about being driven back by e4-e5.

5   ♘f3

Anand continues his build up and adheres to the classical recipe that knights should be developed before bishops: this is especially appropriate as Black has yet to commit himself to a fixed pawn structure.

5   ...   c6

A farsighted move which restrains a possible breakthrough in the centre with d4-d5 and also clears an escape route for the queen to c7 or d8 should she ever be menaced by the manoeuvre ♘e5 and ♘c4, or similarly ♗d2 followed by moving the knight from c3 with a discovered attack on the queen.

6   ♗c4

In contrast to his opponent's elaborate opening scheme, White brings his pieces to aggressive posts in straightforward style.

6   ...   ♗f5

It makes sense to put the bishop on an active square before playing e7-e6 which would shut it inside the black pawn structure.

If Black is now left to his own devices then he will achieve a very solid and harmonious development with e7-e6, ♘bd7, ♗b4 and 0-0-0. In that case things could even turn unpleasant for White as the d4 pawn is a target for the rook on d8, all the more so as the knight on c3 prevents the supporting move c2-c3. The constant need to defend c2 against ♗xc2 would also prove irritating for White.

7   ♘e5!

In view of the considerations above, White must take the chance to play dynamically which his lead in development grants him: this is no place for slow moves such as 0-0 or ♗f4.

7   ...   e6

Black meets the threat to f7 and opens the diagonal for his king's bishop.

8   g4

Only thus as he cannot afford to play slowly. There are no structural weaknesses in the black camp, so White has to keep the momentum of his initiative by seizing space and causing embarrassment to the black

pieces. The perfect way to do this is with a general advance of the kingside pawns. The namby-pamby 8 0-0 would be wholly inappropriate here!

8   ...   ♗g6

The bishop retreats and once again the onus is on White to keep up the pressure, or else Black will mobilise all his pieces with a good game.

9   h4!

Now the unpleasant idea of h4-h5 hangs over the bishop, when its flight to e4 will prove to be fraught with danger.

9   ...   ♘bd7

Seeing no remedy to White's push on the kingside, Black makes the best of things by challenging the strong white knight.

10   ♘xd7

It should be noticed that White's pawn advances, although threatening the disruptive h4-h5, have not only slowed down his development but also loosened his kingside structure and left his king sitting in the centre. If White loses control of the position then these factors will give Black good chances. Therefore the correct maintenance of the initiative is vital. Here for example White's dynamism would soon fizzle out after 10 ♘xg6 hxg6.

10 ... ♘xd7

The obvious recapture, but 10...♔xd7 would have been a tough nut to crack: the knight remains on f6 ready for action in the centre and it is by no means clear how White could get at the black king as the breakthrough d4-d5 is firmly restrained.

11 h5

White presses on with his plan before Black has the chance to soften up his pawns by playing h7-h5 himself.

11 ... ♗e4

The only safe square for the bishop. If now 12 f3 ♗d5 achieves nothing for White.

12 ♖h3!

If you want to be World Champion you should never miss the chance to bring your rooks into

play whilst those of the opponent are still slumbering. Only in this way can Anand preserve the dynamism in his position as the rook is well placed on h3 not only to swing into action in the centre but also because it defends c3 against attack by ♗b4.

12 ... ♗g2

Black seeks to gain time by attacking the rook as after 13 ♖g3 ♗d5 he is ready to play 14...♗d6.

13 ♖e3

The rook reaches a good centre square, but is it well placed or merely a target for the black pieces? The answer to this question will decide the game, as Lautier and Anand are diametrically opposed in their assessment of the situation and strive to the utmost to prove they are right.

13 ... ♘b6

Black hits the bishop on c4 as a prelude to his attacking scheme involving ♘d5 and ♗b4.

14 ♗d3

Instead after 14 ♗b3 the bishop loses control of the a6 square, which might allow Black at some point to play ♕a6! threatening ♕f1+, when the black queen and bishop unexpectedly co-ordinate their action. With the bishop on d3 White has available the strong idea of ♗d2 followed by a discovered attack on the black queen with ♘b5. Immediate action is therefore required from Black.

14 ... ♘d5

It looks as if Black's opening has been a complete success, as both the white rook and the knight are under attack. However, he has evidently forgotten that one of his pieces has wandered off deep into enemy territory on g2...

15   f3!

A metal gate closes on the reckless bishop. If now 15...♘xe3 16 ♗xe3 and there is nothing to be done against the threat of 17 ♔f2 ♗h3 18 ♕h1 winning the hapless cleric when White will have two minor pieces or a rook.

15   ...   ♗b4?

The bishop is also cornered in the variation 15...♘xc3 16 bxc3 ♕xc3+ 17 ♗d2 ♕xd4 18 ♔f2, though here Black would emerge with three pawns for it after 18....♗xf3 19 ♔xf3. This was the best fighting chance for Black, despite the fact that in the middlegame a bishop normally proves more valuable than three pawns.

16   ♔f2!

The king sidesteps the pin and begins to hunt down the stranded bishop.

16   ...   ♗xc3

Black must try to inflict as much damage as possible on the white

position, as if 16...♗h3 17 ♘xd5 ♕xd5 18 ♔g3 will win a piece for nothing.

17   bxc3

White captures one bishop and prepares to feast on the other.

17   ...   ♕xc3

A powerful entrance that hits both the rook on a1 and the d4 pawn. If only the other black pieces could give a little more help to their hard working queen and knight! But alas, the rook on h8 is still asleep and the bishop on g2 is barely alive.

18   ♖b1!

Calmly does it: Anand now has every piece performing a defensive or attacking role, including the king. This superb co-ordination allows him to resist the marauding black queen.

18   ...   ♕xd4

Black picks up a second pawn and prevents 19 ♔xg2 in view of 19...♘xe3+ when it is White who suffers a disastrous loss of material.

19   ♖xb7!

Besides trapping the bishop on g2 there is a second theme to White's winning strategy: a direct, tactical exploitation of the superior activity of his pieces, which work together like a well drilled army.

19   ...   ♖d8

Black's king cannot flee the centre as if 19...0-0? 20 ♗xh7+ wins the queen by discovered attack. Therefore Black can only play a sound centralizing move and hope for the best.

20   h6!

Every white piece is doing its duty so now is the moment to use a pawn to demolish Black's defensive wall on the kingside.

20   ...   gxh6

No better is 20...♘xe3 21 ♗xe3 ♕e5 22 hxg7 ♖g8 23 ♕c1! – defending the bishop on e3 and so threatening 24 ♔xg2 – 23...♕h2 24 ♗f4 ♕h3 25 ♗g3 and having shut out the black queen White is ready to launch a mating attack with 27 ♕a3 or 27 ♕g5.

21   ♗g6!!

A stunning blow but entirely in keeping with the logic of the position. White is justified in

looking for a sharp method of beating off the black attack as he has such a huge advantage in firepower – the black bishop on g2 and rook on h8 are effectively out of the game.

Black is mated if he accepts the queen offer: 21...♕xd1 22 ♖xe6+ ♘e7 (22...♔f8 allows mate one move sooner with 23 ♗xh6+ ♔g8 24 ♗xf7) 23 ♖exe7+ ♔f8 24 ♗xh6+ ♔g8 25 ♗xf7 mate.

21   ...   ♘e7

Evidently preferring to lose in less spectacular style, as the release of the pressure on e3 means that the bishop on g2 is abandoned to its fate.

22   ♕xd4

Now Black's onslaught peters out and it becomes a question of counting the number of pieces and pawns.

22   ...   ♖xd4

Lautier hopes to fight on after 23 ♗b2? ♖d2+ or 23 ♖xe6 hxg6...

23   ♖d3!

...but Anand exchanges off Black's active rook. In a winning position you should always choose the simplest rather than the most spectacular way to finish the game.

24   ...   ♖d8

If 23...♖xd3 24 ♗xd3 with the double threat of 25 ♔xg2 and 25 ♖b8+ winning the rook.

24   ♖xd8+

Again the no-nonsense approach to winning. Instead 24 ♗a3? looks crushing but after 24....♘xg6 25 ♖xd8+ ♔xd8 White sees to his dismay that after 26 ♖b8+ ♔d7 the rook on h8 is defended by the knight!

| 24 | ... | ♔xd8 |

Now the knight can block on the first rank after 25 ♖b8+ ♘c8, but disaster awaits on another part of the board.

25 ♗d3

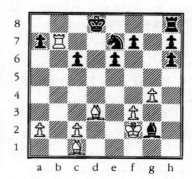

1-0

Black resigned as the bishop is finally lost after 25...♗h1 26 ♗e2 followed by 27 ♔g1.

You may have noticed that two pieces didn't move at all during the game: White's bishop on c1 and the black rook on h8.

However, the bishop was by no means sleeping on c1: it played an important role by supporting the rook on e3 against the attentions of the black queen; and later on it took an active interest in a mating attack that Black could only prevent at the cost of losing his trapped bishop. In contrast the rook on h8 contributed nothing to Black's game. Lautier's attack looked intimidating, but with one of his most powerful pieces sitting out the struggle on its starting square it is no wonder it failed. This is why the co-ordination of the pieces is the theme that underlies all strategy in chess.

4 Strategy under the Microscope: 1 d4 d5

An eye for the Microscope betokens the master.

Marco

The classical recipe in chess is to fill the centre with pawns as quickly as possible, and bring out the pieces promptly to support the pawns. That means 1 e4 e5 or 1 d4 d5. White is pleased with this 'first come, first served' arrangement: it means that the advantage of moving first is likely to stretch right into the middlegame, or even the endgame.

For Black, however, it is a rather different story. After for example 1 d4 d5 2 c4 e6 he or she might have to spend the next 50 or so moves trying to prove that White's pressure on the queenside doesn't add up to much or that the bishop shut in on c8 isn't so bad after all. Of course, some players are delighted to engage in such a positional struggle as Black – first of all they look to negate White's advantage, then they soften him up with careful manoeuvring and finally they emerge triumphant, often without having taken any big risks or given their opponent the slightest hope of victory. The result can be a very satisfying strategical performance – see for example Karpov's win over Korchnoi in this chapter.

But we'll start with a fine win as White by Karpov's successor as World Champion.

Game Sixteen
G.Kasparov - T.Petrosian
Bugojno 1982
Bogo-Indian Defence

1   d4

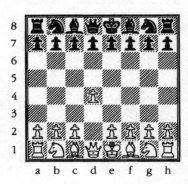

When this game was played Garry Kasparov was still a young man. Nevertheless, he already had an opening repertoire that included 1 e4, 1 d4 and 1 c4. As he has achieved equally great success with all three first moves, it is impossible to claim that one is superior to the others. Lesser mortals, who have neither the time, inclination or strength of memory to learn all the openings should settle on just one first move and study it in depth. Whatever first move you choose it can be handled according to your preferred method of play and temperament. The move 1 e4 has no monopoly on aggressive chess, whilst 1 d4 doesn't have to lead to positional battles. Style will out, no matter how you begin a game of chess.

Nevertheless, despite your own style of play you have to adapt it to circumstances if you are going to be a complete chess player. At the start of his career Kasparov was renowned for his brilliant sacrifices, yet in this game there are no fireworks. After seizing the advantage in the opening he slowly and carefully increases the pressure on the queenside. He doesn't look for a kingside attack or a spectacular tactical blow, as that is not what the position requires.

Tigran Petrosian, a former World Champion, is reduced to a state of complete paralysis. Kasparov was very proud of this game as it showed he had reached the highest level in the art of positional chess.

1   ...   ♘f6

You can't do better than this: Black develops without leaving any immediate structural target for his opponent.

2   c4

As Black has avoided 1...d5, White takes the chance to increase his pawn wedge in the centre.

2   ...   e6

This clears the way for the development of the king's bishop

and at the same time prepares to challenge White's space advantage.

3   ♘f3

To a certain extent the value of a developing move at the start of a game has to be taken on trust. As yet there are no clear plans: according to the set up Black chooses White might decide to attack either on the queenside, or on the kingside or in the centre. A hundred years or more of master chess has taught us that wherever White eventually decides to attack it will almost always be a good idea to have a knight on f3.

3   ...   ♗b4+

A useful check: Black develops his second minor piece and after only three moves is ready to castle.

4   ♗d2

Also possible was 4 ♘c3, but Kasparov prefers to offer the exchange of bishops. His reasoning is that Black is going to play d7-d5 at some point, in order to neutralize White's space advantage. When that happens, a certain dark square weakness is going to appear in the black camp. Furthermore, after the exchange of bishops Black will be left with his 'bad' bishop – the light-squared bishop, which will be obstructed by a pawn centre on e6 and d5.

4   ...   ♛e7

Petrosian doesn't want to waste time by withdrawing his bishop, but neither is he in a hurry to exchange on d2 as after 4...♗xd2+ 5 ♛xd2 d5 White has a free hand in the centre to continue 6 ♘c3 and then 7 e3 etc. keeping a pleasant edge.

In contrast, if White now tried for immediate action in the centre with 5 ♘c3 then Black would be able to force off another pair of pieces with 5...♗xc3 6 ♗xc3 ♘e4. Generally speaking every exchange suits Black as he has less territory within which to accommodate pieces than White.

5   g3

White would drop a pawn for nebulous compensation after 5 ♗xb4 ♛xb4+ 6 ♘bd2 ♛xb2. The game move is modest looking, but White's strategy will be built around the pressure exerted by the king's bishop situated on g2.

5   ...   ♗xd2+

Now that he has deterred White from a rapid expansion in the centre Petrosian decides to exchange bishops.

6   ♛xd2

At first glance the alternative recapture 6 ♘bxd2 conforms more with the law of rapid development. But it would be a pity to put the knight on d2 when it has a much better post on c3. Besides, the white queen is getting out of the way of

her rooks and is marginally better placed on d2 than d1.

6   ...   0-0

Castling is a sound option. Instead Black could try to disrupt White's build up with 6...♘e4, but White keeps a slight edge after 7 ♛c2 ♛b4+ 8 ♘bd2 ♘xd2 9 ♘xd2 followed by ♗g2.

7   ♗g2

If you want to understand why things go so well for White and so badly for Black in what follows, you only need to keep a special eye on the fortunes of this bishop and its opposite number on c8.

7   ...   d5

At last Black challenges the white centre. Unfortunately next move he fails to stand his ground.

8   0-0

The king feels very safe sheltering behind the bishop as a fianchetto position is one of formidable strength.

8   ...   dxc4

Black is in too much of a hurry to simplify. He believes that he can equalize next move with c7-c5, when all the centre pawns vanish. Whilst it is true that positions without centre pawns and a symmetrical pawn structure on the wings tend to be drawish, Petrosian has underestimated the danger from the white bishop on g2.

It was far better to keep up a barrier to the white bishop with 8...♖d8! Then play could go 9 ♕c2 – defending c4 and getting the queen off the same line as the black rook – 9...♘c6!? 10 cxd5 exd5 11 ♘c3 ♗g4. Black would then have active pieces to compensate for his slightly disjointed pawn structure on the queenside. The white bishop, which becomes a monster in the game, would be kept under control.

9   ♘a3!

Excellent! White intends to recapture on c4 with his queen's knight and so doesn't lose any time with his development. If instead 9 ♘e5 then 9...c5 gives Black good chances to escape as White would have two pieces still asleep on the queenside.

9   ...   c5

As planned, though the elimination of White's strong centre pawn fails to solve Black's problems as it opens a highway for the white pieces to attack down the d file.

10   dxc5

The correct capture as it entices the black queen to a square where she is exposed to *tempo* (or time) gaining attacks by the white pieces.

10   ...   ♕xc5

After this recapture it seems like Black has almost equalized. As there are no centre pawns White's winning chances depend entirely on using the greater mobility of his own pieces to put the black pieces under pressure.

11   ♖ac1

Now White is sure to regain the pawn with a slight but definite initiative due to his more active pieces.

11   ...   ♘c6

Black cannot defend the c4 pawn as if 11...b5 12 ♘d4 ♘d5 – the only move – 13 ♘dxb5 and in any case the c4 pawn will be lost, leaving Black a pawn down.

12   ♘xc4

If there is a secret to Kasparov's success it is that he always manages to get his rooks into play before his opponent's. The fact that White will now have his rook bearing down the c file, whilst Black's is sitting idly on a8, will mean that White will enter the middlegame with good chances.

12   ...   ♕e7

Understandably Black is keen to get his queen out of the firing line of the rook on c1, but this allows White to impose a fatal bind. He had to play actively with 12...♖d8 when after 13 ♕c2 he can develop his queenside with 13...♗d7. White could continue to probe with 14 ♕b3, but this would be nothing compared with the pressure he is able to apply in the game.

13 ♘fe5

The bishop on g2 is unleashed. Now Black will be unable to solve the fundamental problem of Queenside openings: how to develop the queen's bishop without allowing White strong pressure on the b7 pawn.

13 ... ♘xe5

This exchange leaves White in mastery of the c file but there was little choice, for example if 13...♗d7 14 ♘xd7! – even better than inflicting a weak pawn on c6 with 14 ♘xc6 – 14...♕xd7 15 ♕xd7 ♘xd7 16 ♘d6! leaves Black unable to avoid disaster down the long diagonal on either b7 or c6.

14 ♘xe5

The move Black wants to play is ♗d7, which develops the queen's bishop and clears the way for the rooks to enter into the game. But there is a twin reason why this is impossible here: after 14...♗d7 White can either win a pawn with 15 ♗xb7, or even better play 15 ♖c7, when the pin on d7 is likely to cost Black a piece. For the rest of the game Kasparov uses these two threads – pressure against b7 along the diagonal and against c7 along the c file – to keep the bishop boxed in on c8. This isn't a problem for just the black bishop – it is a catastrophe that affects all the other black pieces as they are unable to be properly coordinated, either for defence or counterplay.

14 ... ♘d5

In view of the above it is no wonder that Petrosian would be more than happy to give up a pawn to free his position. If now 15 ♗xd5 exd5 16 ♕xd5 ♗h3 and all the black pieces come to life after 17...♖fd8 etc. Black's previously entombed bishop on c8 suddenly becomes the best minor piece on the board and his rooks enjoy open lines.

15 ♖fd1!

Kasparov refuses to accept the bait. He now has all his pieces well placed and working together.

15 ... ♘b6

Black is unable to unwind, as after 15...♖d8 16 e4 or equally 15...♗d7 16 ♘xd7 ♕xd7 17 e4 he loses a piece due to the pin on the d file. This is all thanks to the rook on d1, which like every other white piece is helping to prevent Black from developing.

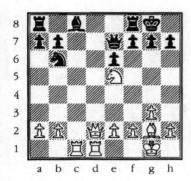

16   ♕a5!

The queen leads from the front: here she is immune from attack and ties the black rook down to the a7 pawn. Furthermore, she also deters Black from driving away the white knight from e5 with 16...f6 as after 17 ♘c4 ♘xc4 18 ♖xc4 there is no good way for Black to prevent an invasion of the seventh rank with 19 ♖c7, since the queen is controlling the c7 square.

16   ...   g6

Having lost the battle to play ♗d7, Black makes a hole for his king which avoids any back rank mating tricks. As White doesn't have a dark square bishop the loosening of the squares f6, g7 and h6 isn't a great issue – Black is far more concerned with the weakness of another dark square on c7, as this can be exploited by the white rooks and queen.

There is also a specific idea behind Petrosian's move: namely, to exchange off a pair of rooks with 17...♖d8. As a rule, if a player has a cramped position every exchange will help him as it leaves his remaining pieces with more room in which to function.

17   ♖d3!

Keeping a former World Champion under lock and key requires great accuracy. It would only take one careless move by White for Petrosian to break the grip. Now Black is prevented from playing 17...♖d8, as after 18 ♕c5! ♕xc5 19 ♖xd8+ ♕f8 20 ♖xf8+ ♔xf8 21 ♖c7 his pawn structure on the second rank will be massacred by the white rook. Now imagine if Kasparov hadn't moved his rook to the third rank but played the plausible move 17 e4, to restrain the black knight. Then 17...♖d8 eases Black's game, as 18 ♕c5?? fails to 18...♖xd1 CHECK!! – 19 ♖xd1 ♕xc5.

17   ...   ♘d5

Back again: perhaps this time White will be tempted by 18 ♗xd5, when 18...exd5 19 ♕xd5 ♗f5 brings Black's game to life.

18   e4!

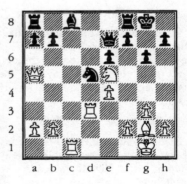

After all this talk of White's pressure against b7 it might seem odd to shut in the bishop. But chess strategy is all about exchanging one advantage for another, and trying to come out best in the 'deal'. Whilst it is true that the bishop is obstructed, in return White drives away the enemy knight from its centre square, where it not only shields the d file but also prevents an intrusion by a white rook on c7. Thus the white rooks are very happy with 18 e4: the white bishop much less so, but overall the white pieces benefit from the move.

18   ...   ♘b6

The knight has to retreat here as 18...♘f6 allows an immediate invasion with 19 ♖c7.

19   ♗f1!

The golden rule in such positions is not to hurry. Black is unable to do anything constructive and so White patiently improves his game by bringing the bishop to an open diagonal.

19   ...   ♖e8

Black can only mark time with his pieces and hope that his defences hold firm.

20   ♖dd1

Kasparov has won many brilliant attacking games with sacrifices, but he also knows when to play quietly. The rook clears the way for the bishop and is more secure on d1 than d3.

20   ...   ♖f8

Black continues with his waiting policy. He has no real choice as any attempt to develop leads to immediate defeat: for example if 20...♗d7 21 ♘xd7 ♘xd7 22 ♖c7 puts the knight in a fatal pin, for if 22...♖ed8 23 ♗b5 attacks the piece a third time. Here we see one point of 20 ♖dd1 – the way has been cleared for the bishop to go to b5.

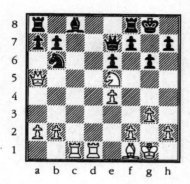

21   a3!

When you have every piece on an ideal square, but can't see any way forwards, have a look around for a little pawn move. Pawns can be fearsome battering rams, going before the pieces in an all out attack, or they can be as subtle as the proverbial little straw that breaks the camel's back. Here Petrosian, a brilliant defender, has managed to resist the temptation to create any pawn weaknesses in his camp – therefore there are no obvious targets for the white pieces. But even he cannot cope with the slow, but inexorable, advance of White's queenside pawns. Once White gets a pawn to a5, forcing back the knight, Black's defences will crumble.

21   ...   ♔g7

Black is entirely helpless. Rather than move his rook to e8 and f8 again he decides to move his king forwards and backwards.

22   b3

As if to emphasize the hopelessness of Black's predicament the pawns move forwards as slowly as possible.

22 ...   ♚g8

Has Black really got nothing better to do than move his king backwards and forwards? Let's look at the evidence, beginning with Black's pieces on the queenside:

Black's rook on a8. Has one square, but if 22...♖b8, 23 ♕xa7 wins the knight.

Black's bishop. Has one square, but if 22...♗d7 23 ♘xd7 ♘xd7 24 ♖c7 soon wins a piece.

Black's knight. Has one square where it isn't captured by a pawn, but after 22...♘d7 23 ♘xd7 ♗xd7 24 ♖c7 will cost a piece.

So Black has no moves at all on the queenside which don't lose at least a piece.

On the kingside:

The *black king* can move from g8 to g7 and back again.

The *rook on f8* can shuffle backwards and forwards to e8 and f8.

The *black queen* can go to e8, f6 or g5, but any of these moves allow a rook invasion with 23 ♖c7.

So Black really is reduced to moving his king or the rook on f8. Such is the power of Kasparov's quiet, but precise positional play. We can only marvel that he managed to pull this off against one of the greatest strategical players of all time.

23   a4

Despite Black's paralysis the game has to be finished off, just as a spider has to inject venom into its prey and not just tie it up. If Black passes again, then White can simply move his queen from a5 and then play 25 a5, when the black knight is forced onto d7, where it is fatally pinned as we have seen in the comments above.

23   ...   ♖d8

Black is induced by the looming threat to try an active move, but it is immediately punished.

24   ♕c5!

1-0

Even if you have a strategically excellent position, you should still be on the look out for strong tactical opportunities, as they will save you a lot of effort.

There is no need to prepare a4-a5 as the offer to exchange queens destroys Black's defensive set up. If 24...♕xc5 25 ♖xd8+ ♕f8 26 ♖xf8+ ♔xf8 27 ♖c7 is horrendous for Black – not only is he menaced with 28 a5, winning the knight, but his kingside pawn structure is going to collapse after 28 ♖xf7+. That is too much for flesh and blood to bear, so Petrosian resigned.

Game Seventeen
V.Kramnik - P.Svidler
Linares 1998
Catalan Opening

1   ♘f3

As this almost always proves to be the best square for the knight, it makes a lot of sense to put it here immediately.

1   ...   ♘f6

Black responds with the identical developing move. Whether he intends to play classically by putting pawns in the centre or counterattack with 2...g6 and 3...♗g7, the knight will be well placed to support his plan.

2   c4

White begins the fight for the d5 square...

2   ...   e6

...and Black at once opposes him.

3   g3

As an active development with ♗c4 or ♗b5 has been ruled out by

putting a pawn on c4, Kramnik decides to aim his bishop at the centre via g2.

3   ...   d5

A key decision that will determine the type of middlegame reached. Black occupies the centre with his pawns rather than trying to control things from a distance with his pieces after 3...b6 4 ♗g2 ♗b7.

4   d4

White won't allow his opponent a free hand in the centre. Note that he isn't offering a pawn sacrifice as after 4...dxc4 he can easily regain his pawn, most simply by 5 ♕a4+ and 6 ♕xc4.

After the game move the space situation is equal, as both players have a pawn on their fourth rank; but Black faces the eternal dilemma in the Queen's Pawn Openings: how does he develop his light-squared bishop without creating a serious weakness in his queenside pawn structure?

4   ...   ♗e7

At least Black has no problems with this bishop. It is safely and comfortably slotted into e7, a useful gap in his pawn structure.

5   ♗g2

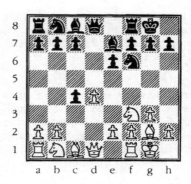

Whereas a knight needs to be securely placed right in the centre to be at maximum efficiency, a bishop is often happy overseeing things from a distance. Try a little experiment: swap around White's kingside minor pieces so that the knight is on g2 and the bishop on f3. You will see that the bishop has become more vulnerable to attack on f3 without becoming any stronger; whereas the knight has lost most of its power to control the centre by stepping back to g2.

5   ...   0-0

Black has developed sensibly and quickly: already his king can be removed from the airy centre and placed behind a wall of pawns.

6   0-0

White follows suit. It would make no sense trying to castle queenside and then throwing pawns at the black king, as the bishop on g2 is pointing the wrong way for a kingside attack.

6   ...   dxc4

All is well in the black camp apart from the problem alluded to above: how does he find a fitting role for the bishop on c8, without compromising his position in some way? If the bishops on c1 and c8 just vanished in a cloud of smoke then Black would be equal, but unfortunately chess games are decided by logic and common sense rather than magical spells. Therefore Svidler begins a plan to activate his bishop, but it is at a cost: the d5 barrier is dismantled which gives White's pieces, especially the bishop on g2, extra scope.

7   ♕c2

Now White is sure to regain his pawn as after 7...b5? 8 a4! Black's pawns will be split up, as 8...c6 9 axb5 cxb5 10 ♘g5! leads to disaster – he cannot prevent ♗xa8 with 10...♘d5 in view of 11 ♕xh7 mate.

7   ...   a6

Black however has no intention of holding onto his pawn. His idea is to use the time White spends in recapturing the pawn to get his bishop onto b7, where it is well placed on an open diagonal.

8   ♕xc4

White regains his pawn and at the same time clears the way for action along the c file – the Achilles Heel of Black's position.

8 ... b5

Not a pretty looking move as it leaves holes on c6 and c5, which can no longer be protected by a pawn; but on the other hand it wins time for Black's plan.

9 ♕c2

In retreating, the queen chooses a square where she both maintains pressure along the c file and has influence on the e4 square.

9 ... ♗b7

So Black has solved the problem of how to activate his queen's bishop: this is a great positional achievement, as many games have been lost due to the bishop sitting idly on c8.

10 ♗f4

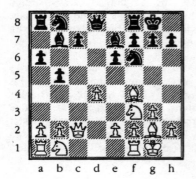

Nevertheless, it takes a mistake for White to lose the advantage of moving first, and Kramnik has done nothing wrong. Therefore, just as energy can be transformed but never

destroyed, White's advantage has changed from having the better queen's bishop to having the better pawn structure. This means that he can attack the pawn on c7, a vulnerable pawn which can never be supported by another pawn unless it reaches c4 – which is the stuff of fantasies unless White totally loses control of the position. Much more likely is that Black will escape by playing c7-c5, and then exchanging his weak pawn for White's strong pawn on d4. If that happened without White gaining any significant advantage elsewhere then Black would equalize at once. Therefore the battle now focuses on Black's attempt to rid himself of the weak pawn and White's efforts to prevent him. Already Black must deal with the threat of 11 ♗xc7.

10 ... ♘d5

It was also possible to activate the queenside pieces with 10...♘c6 11 ♘c3 ♘b4, but Svidler wants to eliminate White's bishop.

11 ♘c3

A good developing move with a direct threat: 12 ♘xd5 ♗xd5 13 ♗xc7 winning a pawn.

11 ... ♘xf4

The only consistent move as after 11...♘xc3 12 ♕xc3 Black has clearly lost time – he has made three moves with his knight to capture an enemy knight that has only moved once.

12 gxf4

Who has gained the most from the exchange on f4? Let's weigh up the evidence.

For Black:

♦ he has dealt with the immediate attack on c7

♦ he has exchanged a knight for a bishop – generally speaking a good swap

♦ he has somewhat weakened the white kingside

For White:

♦ he has gained time for development whilst Black was arranging the exchange

♦ his grip on the centre, particularly e5 is strengthened by the transfer of the pawn from g3 to f4

♦ with his dark square bishop exchanged, he can put his pawns on dark squares without worrying about blocking it in.

As will be seen, in the game Kramnik is able to make better use of the plusses from the exchange than Svidler.

| **12** | ... | ♘d7 |

At last Black develops his queen's knight. If he can break out with c7-c5 he can expect complete equality – or even more due to his bishop pair.

| **13** | ♖fd1! |

The rook arrives on the d file to prevent 13...c5 which would lose to 14 dxc5 ♗xc5 and now either 15 ♘e5! or 15 ♘g5! – threatening mate on h7 – would cost Black a piece.

| **13** | ... | ♗xf3 |

Instead 13...♕c8!? sidesteps potential trouble on the d file and defends b7: this would rule out any tricky discovered attacks on either the queen or bishop. Play could then go 14 ♘e4 c5 15 dxc5 ♘xc5 16 ♘xc5 ♕xc5 17 ♕xc5 ♗xc5 18 ♖ac1. So far we have been following a game of Karpov's as Black against Ribli. Black has liquidated his weak pawn and almost equalized, though he still has to tread carefully as White's rooks are very active.

| **14** | ♗xf3 |

Black has given back the bishop pair, as he hopes that this will facilitate the advance c7-c5. But as Kramnik demonstrates, now that his king's bishop has no rival he can impose a strong bind on the light squares.

| **14** | ... | ♖b8 |

The rook has to save itself, but as it does nothing on b8 this is a rather miserable move that indicates all is not well with the coordination of Black's pieces.

15   e3!

In contrast, White's pawn structure accords well with his light-squared bishop – all his centre pawns are now on dark squares, whilst the bishop controls all the open lines.

15   ...   ♘f6

By putting the knight on f6 Svidler concedes that he won't be able to force through c7-c5 in the near future.

16   ♖ac1

White's position is now a model of harmonious co-operation. In particular his rooks have both found better roles than their black counterparts: the rook on f8 is passive whilst the other rook stares uselessly at its b5 pawn.

16   ...   ♕d6

Of course if 16...c5? 17 dxc5 uncovers an attack on the black queen and stays a pawn up.

17   ♘e2!

It is absolutely essential to stop Black getting rid of the backward pawn with 17...c5.

17   ...   ♖fc8

The battle over the c5 square continues – on it the outcome of the game will be decided. Black is ready to advance c7-c5 again, with complete equality: how can Kramnik keep up the pressure?

18   e4!

White decides the moment is right to utilize his centre pawns: and no wonder as he has all his pieces on their most effective squares. Meanwhile the black rooks are bunched together on the queenside and cannot resist a push in the centre.

18   ...   ♕d7

The queen has to retreat in the face of the fork 19 e5, winning a piece.

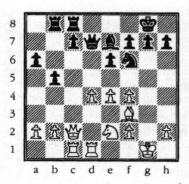

19   d5!

A key advance that ensures the black knight is driven away from the centre and opens up the d file for the white pieces. If immediately

19 e5 the knight would jump to a fine centre square with 19...♘d5! when lines are blocked.

19 ... exd5

The white pawn juggernaut cannot be left unopposed in the centre.

20 e5!

Excellent: the black knight has been prevented from going to d5 and so it is chased back to a wilderness on e8 where it remains for the rest of the game. Instead 20 exd5?? would be totally wrong: the white *pawns* would be split and lose their mobility and the white *pieces* would be deprived of the d file and in particular the d5 square. Nor would the black knight be obliged to retreat anywhere.

20 ... ♘e8

A dismal retreat, after which Black's resistance in the centre comes to an end.

21 ♖xd5

White regains his pawn with ascendancy over the light squares.

21 ... ♛h3

Black's only active piece is his queen. Therefore Svidler uses her to launch a counterattack against the white kingside, which has been slightly weakened by the advances in the centre; and being a gifted tactician he manages to generate some interesting counter chances. Nevertheless, he must have been aware of the Russian proverb 'One man in the field isn't an army'.

22 ♗g2

White meets the threat to his bishop in the most economical way by attacking the black queen.

22 ... ♛h4

Black hopes to get the chance to play 23...c5! when the backward pawn vanishes – and with it the weak square on c6 – and the white knight is deprived of d4. Apparently the white knight cannot move from e2 as the f4 pawn is attacked, but...

23 ♘d4!

...the maintenance of a stranglehold on the light squares is more important then the f4 pawn.

23 ... ♛xf4

Black might as well take the pawn, as after 23...c5? he would lose a piece to 24 ♘f5 as the queen can't remain defending the bishop.

24 ♘c6

The triumph of White's light square strategy. The knight is on a wonderful square where it

♦ attacks a rook and bishop

♦ controls d8 and so prevents Black fighting for the d file with his rooks

♦ blocks Black's freeing move c7-c5

It is no wonder that Black is desperate to dislodge the knight, even at the cost of the exchange.

24 ... ♗h4

Svidler battles hard. He threatens 25...♗xf2+! winning a pawn, for if 26 ♕xf2 ♕xc1+.

25 ♖cd1!

There is absolutely no need to hurry to win material with 25 ♘xb8. Kramnik avoids the trap above and prepares to bring his rook to d4 to harass the black queen, who is being pushed around – that's what happens to a queen when she has inadequate support from her other pieces.

25 ... ♖b6

Black battles hard to stay alive, but the superior coordination of the white pieces is overwhelming – you only have to look at the passive rook on c8 and the knight on e8 which has no safe moves to realize this is the case.

26 ♖5d4

After this simple move the black queen has no good retreat square.

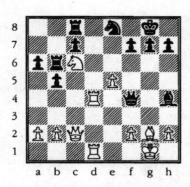

26 ... ♖xc6

The only survival chance and quite a good one, as White has several chances to go wrong. If instead 26...♕g5 then 27 ♕e4! unexpectedly traps the bishop on h4, while after 26...♕h6 27 ♕f5 ♖a8 – the rook has nowhere safe to flee – 28 ♘e7+ ♗xe7 29 ♗xa8 Black is not only the exchange down but threatened with 30 ♕d7, winning a piece.

27 ♗xc6!

The correct way to recapture as after 27 ♕xc6 ♗xf2+ 28 ♔h1 ♗xd4 or 27 ♖xf4 ♖xc2 28 ♖xh4 ♖xb2 things have gone entirely wrong for White.

27 ... ♕xe5

If 27...♕g5+ 28 ♔h1 leaves Black the exchange down for a pawn with a wretched position. But it appears that the game move is a good fighting chance, as if 28 ♖xh4? then 28...♕g5+ regains the exchange and leaves White fighting for a draw.

However, Kramnik has prepared an insidious idea that destroys all resistance.

28 &d7!

In this game Kramnik demonstrates both a mastery of strategy and a sharp eye for tactics. By attacking the black rook he gains time to safely capture the bishop on h4.

28 ... ♖d8

Black's last hope is that White will play 29 ♗xe8?? when 29...♖xd4 keeps him alive. But after

29 ♖xh4 1-0

...the dust has settled and Black is a rook down. If now 29...♕g5+ then simply 30 ♖g4 – the response that was prepared by 28 ♗d7!

Therefore Svidler took the only course of action possible against one of the top three players in the world: he resigned.

Game Eighteen
V.Korchnoi - A.Karpov
World Championship,
Merano 1981
Queen's Gambit

1 c4

A very logical move which gains control of the d5 square.

1 ... e6

Black wants to set up a firm barrier of pawns on the light squares in the centre. If instead 1...d5 2 cxd5 ♕xd5 3 ♘c3 leads to a loss of time for Black as his queen must move again. Note that the very strength of the queen can be its weakness: it must always run away if attacked by an inferior piece. That is why early adventures with the queen in the opening are seldom a good idea.

2 ♘c3

White responds with a sound developing move which increases his influence over the d5 square.

2 ... d5

As planned: Black now has a fair chunk of the centre and already threatens to drive away the white knight with 3...d4.

Anatoly Karpov has always been more or less happy to draw as Black against another top class opponent, and so has a repertoire that stresses safety. However, as we shall see if given the chance he will pounce.

3 d4

Play now transposes from the English Opening into the Queen's

Gambit Declined, which normally begins 1 d4 d5 2 c4 e6 3 ♘c3. Both players have chosen to build a wall of pawns in the centre, behind which they can develop their forces.

3   ...   ♗e7

If instead 3...dxc4 then 4 e4 and White will soon regain his pawn with ♗xc4. Despite the opening being called the Queen's Gambit White isn't really offering a pawn – he is employing a strategic device to put pressure on d5.

In a classical opening like the Queen's Gambit it is normal to abide by rules such as 'develop knights before bishops!' However, after 3...♘f6 White can pin the knight with 4 ♗g5 and then develop his king's knight on e2 in the sequence e2-e3, ♗d3 and ♘ge2. The experience of master games has shown that the knight is more flexible on e2 than f3. Therefore Black waits a move before putting his knight on f6 so that White has to commit his knight to f3. In the Queen's Gambit Declined the best place for Black's king's bishop has long been established as e7, so it doesn't do any harm putting it there at this early stage.

4   ♘f3

Despite the observations above, this is by no means a bad square for the knight as it is engaged in the fight for the centre.

4   ...   ♘f6

Black needs to develop his kingside. In principle 4...♘h6 would be wrong as it decentralizes the knight: even worse White could break up Black's kingside with 5 ♗xh6 forcing 5...gxh6. Therefore

there can be no doubt that the knight belongs on f6.

5   ♗g5

Korchnoi meanwhile is more concerned with the development of his queenside. And rightly so: Black hasn't adopted an aggressive posture that forces him to think about quickly evacuating his king from the centre, and so he has the opportunity to choose carefully the best squares for his pieces. Thus he doesn't hurry to play the immediate 5 e3, even though this clears the way for his king's bishop to go to d3, as it would shut in his queen's bishop. First of all he gets his queen's bishop outside his pawn structure and only then thinks about playing e2-e3.

5   ...   h6

Black gives the bishop a little nudge, so that it cannot remain both controlling the diagonal c1-g5 and putting pressure along the g5-d8 diagonal. The pawn move may also become handy later on in the game in giving the black king a flight square which avoids back rank mates.

6   ♗h4

Naturally in choosing a retreat square White keeps up the pressure on the knight on f6 which in essence is an attack on the defender of the key d5 square.

6   ...   0-0

Black has developed his kingside pieces, castled and established his centre: and it has only taken six moves!

7   ♖c1

Again Korchnoi is happy to delay his kingside development in favour of mobilizing his queenside pieces. By putting the rook on c1 he aims to deter Black from playing b7-b6 and ♗b7, his natural queenside deployment, in view of the weakness created on c7.

7   ...   dxc4!

Karpov voluntarily concedes a space advantage as he sees this will enable him to neutralize any possible pressure by the white rook along the c file.

8   e3

White clears the way to recapture with the bishop on c4.

8   ...   c5

The point of Black's idea: he gets rid of the potentially weak pawn on c7 after which there will be no structural defects in his position.

9   ♗xc4

You will see that even allowing for his emphasis on queenside action it has only taken Korchnoi nine moves to develop all his minor pieces and a rook and be on the verge of castling.

9   ...   cxd4

Now if White wants to try to win he will be obliged to retake with the pawn, as after 10 ♘xd4 or 10 ♕xd4 the absence of any pawn beyond the third rank deadens the game and makes a draw likely.

10   exd4

We have reached an Isolated Queen's Pawn position – this is commonly referred to as an 'IQP position' in chess books. The big question is whether the pawn on d4 is strong or weak. The answer is – both! From a structural point of view it is weak, as it cannot be supported by other pawns and stands on an open file, where it can be assaulted from the front by the black rooks and queen. Furthermore, the square in front of the pawn, d5, would make a perfect base for a black knight as it can never be driven away by any white pawn.

On the other hand, a centre pawn is still a centre pawn, even if it is isolated. On d4 it provides a white knight with a supported outpost on e5, and in some circumstances c5. Behind the pawn the white pieces have more space to manoeuvre, and in some cases the pawn can even leap forwards to d5 with a powerful central breakthrough. Furthermore, if Black avails himself of the outpost square on d5 by playing ♘d5, then a direct attack on the pawn by his rooks is obstructed.

In the game Karpov makes the d4 pawn look like a liability with some wonderful positional play, but the pros and cons of the IQP are in fact finely balanced.

10   ...   ♘c6

An astute move: Black blocks the c file, attacks the d4 pawn and gets another piece involved in the action.

11   0-0

One good feature for White is that he has all his pieces deployed to decent squares, whereas Black still has to find a useful role for his queen's bishop.

11   ...   ♘h5!

Karpov takes the chance to force off a pair of bishops. With every exchange there will be one less white piece able to benefit from the dynamism that a space advantage confers and at the same time one

fewer black piece feeling oppressed by its cramped quarters. Therefore, the structural – or static – weakness of the d4 pawn will become more significant.

12   ♗xe7

There wasn't much choice as White didn't want to give Black the bishop pair after 12 ♗g3 ♘xg3 13 hxg3.

12   ...   ♘xe7

The correct recapture as Black strengthens his hold on the d5 square. If instead 12...♕xe7 13 d5! gives White the initiative in the centre – and no more IQP!

13   ♗b3

In a World Championship match the white pieces are precious, so Korchnoi had no wish to force dead equality with 13 d5 when the centre pawns are dissolved. But the game move is slow to say the least. More natural was 13 ♖e1.

13   ...   ♘f6

The knight returns to the centre and further consolidates Black's grip on d5.

14   ♘e5

Meanwhile White's knight utilizes the e5 square where it is excellently supported by the IQP. In effect this is an outpost square, as although the knight can be driven away by a pawn Black is unlikely ever to want to loosen his kingside with f7-f6.

14   ...   ♗d7!

Black develops without creating any weaknesses on the queenside. If instead he succumbs to temptation and puts the bishop on a beautiful diagonal after 14...b6 15 ♖e1 ♗b7, we see a sacrificial motif typical of IQP positions: 16 ♘xf7! when 16...♔xf7? 17 ♗xe6+ ♔e8 leaves the black king horribly placed, whilst 16...♖xf7 17 ♗xe6 will give White more than enough material after he takes on f7, besides having an initiative. IQP positions must be handled with great care!

15 ♕e2

It is almost always a healthy sign when a player succeeds in connecting his rooks – it means that he has got all his minor pieces off the back rank and castled.

15 ... ♖c8

Black must continue to play cautiously, for if 15...♗c6 he still has to reckon with the sacrifice 16 ♘xf7!? ♖xf7 17 ♗xe6.

16 ♘e4?

We already know that exchanges favour the defender in IQP positions, so White should have preferred simple development with 16 ♖fd1 and a balanced position.

16 ... ♘xe4

Black exchanges one piece...

17 ♕xe4

...and after White's recapture...

17 ... ♗c6!

...he gains time to offer another exchange by attacking the queen.

18 ♘xc6

White can hardly refuse to exchange as otherwise the bishop will control a fine diagonal.

18 ... ♖xc6

Offering yet another exchange, which this time White is wise to decline. Already the disappearance of his two knights has undermined any initiative he might develop to compensate for the isolated pawn.

19 ♖c3

If instead 19 ♖xc6 then White would equalize easily after 19...♘xc6 20 d5 getting rid of his isolated pawn: in fact he would have a slight edge as the bishop would prove more powerful than the knight – its long range power means that it can attack either b7 or f7 as appropriate.

However, Karpov intended to recapture with 19...bxc6! This one move is a whole lesson in positional play.

It looks odd to split up his own pawns, but the pawn on c6 wouldn't be as weak as the pawn on d4 which is now forever fixed by Black's vice like grip on the d5 square. Black would then have a ready plan to win the d4 pawn:

(a) put the queen on b6

(b) put the rook on d8

(c) if White has played ♖c1 and ♖c4 in the meantime, defending d4 and attacking c6, play ♖d6 so that the c6 pawn is defended again.

(d) play ♘f5 and win the d4 pawn, unless White tries ♗a4, attacking c6 again, when ♕xb2 picks up some queenside pawns.

19   ...   ♕d6

White would also have a rather fragile pawn structure after 19...♖xc3 20 bxc3 ♕c7 21 c4 when the c and d pawns are known as hanging pawns – but at least the pawns would have some dynamism. Karpov prefers to give White not the slightest hint of counterplay in the centre and instead continues his attack against the isolated pawn.

20   g3?

White makes an escape hole for his king in case the issue of back rank mates ever arises. But if he is looking for activity then taking away the g3 square from the rook doesn't make much sense. Instead 20 h4!? would be an interesting attacking gesture. White would follow up with ♗c2 when appropriate: if Black then blocked the mate threat on h7 with g7-g6, his kingside would be rammed with h4-h5. Or if the black knight blocked on f5 or g6, White could chase it away with g2-g4 or h4-h5 respectively. So Black would probably have to answer ♗c2 with f7-f5, though this weakens his kingside somewhat – in particular the e6 pawn.

Of course Karpov wouldn't have let himself lose in three moves after 20 h4 – in fact after 20...♖d8 the immediate 21 ♗c2? looks poor after 21...f5! so White would have to keep the idea of ♗c2 in reserve and play 21 ♖d1. But the important thing is that White would be *doing something*. Even if forcing f7-f5 doesn't do Black any great harm, it still creates a target on e6 – and targets mean counterplay.

20   ...   ♖d8

The rest of the game is a model of positional play from Karpov: with every move he wears down White's resistance. First of all he ties down a white rook to the defence of d4.

21   ♖d1

White has no choice but to defend dourly and hope for a slip up from his opponent.

21   ...   ♖b6!

For once Black avoids an exchange, as he wants to keep both rooks to besiege the d4 pawn. Therefore he

♦ prepares to triple rooks and queen against d4 with ♛d7 and ♖cd6. If immediately 21...♛d7? 22 ♗a4 wins the exchange.

♦ introduces the idea of ♖b4, with a lateral attack on d4 – the pawn being pinned against the white queen.

♦ ties down the white bishop, as if 22 ♗c2 f5 followed by ♖xb2 wins a pawn.

22 ♛e1

This is an awkward move that shows something has gone wrong with White's strategy. Still, at least 22...♖b4 can be met by 23 ♖c4.

22 ... ♛d7

Simple and strong: Black prepares to exert maximum pressure on the d4 pawn.

23 ♖cd3

It is a bad sign when pieces as powerful as rooks have to be used as baby sitters to defend a weak pawn.

23 ... ♖d6

The noose tightens on the IQP. In the words of Aron Nimzowitsch, an isolated pawn should be first restrained, then blockaded and finally destroyed!

24 ♛e4

The queen returns to the centre so that if 24...♘f5 White can get rid of the pesky pawn with 25 d5!

24 ... ♛c6!

Another unwelcome offer to exchange pieces.

25 ♛f4

The white queen must flee to a square where she defends d4 as after 25 ♛xc6 ♘xc6 26 d5 ♘b4 the d5 pawn drops.

25 ... ♘d5!

Not 25...♘f5 26 d5 and White escapes as if 26...exd5? 27 ♛xf5: that is why White put his queen on f4. At last Black has the d5 pawn blockaded, rather than just restrained: there is no longer the propensity for a sudden d4-d5! break out. The knight is an ideal blockader, as it can sit in front of the pawn without having its power in the slightest circumvented – whereas a rook finds its way forward blocked if the pawn is adequately defended.

26 ♕d2

Nevertheless, the IQP still has a lot of friends and will prove a tough nut to crack.

26 ... ♕b6

Now there is the threat of 27...♘b4, chasing away the rook from d3 followed by ♖xd4.

27 ♗xd5

A lesson in the art of exchanging unwisely. White decides to get rid of the strong knight, but now there is no imbalance at all in the position: everything is identical except that White has a terribly weak pawn on d4. Therefore a far better chance was to keep the bishop and play 27 a3 to rule out ♘b4: if Black had then pushed too hard in trying to exploit the IQP the bishop might have had the last laugh.

27 ... ♖xd5

Of course if 27...exd5 the players could have shaken hands and gone home. But now the threat is 28...e5, winning the pawn as the white pieces are defensively speaking in the wrong order after 29 dxe5? ♖xd3.

28 ♖b3

Instead of this pseudo active move Karpov suggests that White might have played 28 f4 immediately to rule out 28...e5.

28 ... ♕c6

Naturally Black has no intention of giving up his healthy b7 pawn for the weakling on d4 with 28...♕xd4 29 ♕xd4 ♖xd4 30 ♖xd4 ♖xd4 31 ♖xb7.

29 ♕c3

The white queen steps out of the looming pin on the d file and offers an exchange that would strengthen the d pawn: 29...♕xc3 30 bxc3!

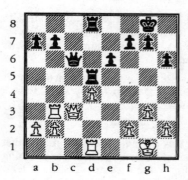

29 ... ♕d7!

Rather than becoming active the white queen and rook on b3 are now seen to be misplaced for the task of defending the IQP, which is now attacked three times.

30 f4

This is a desperate measure as it leaves wide open spaces around the white king which Karpov will later exploit to win the game. Nevertheless, it was the only way to prevent 30...e5, which would not only win the pawn but also create a passed pawn after 31...exd4.

30   ...   b6!

A quiet move but it introduces the threat of 31...♖xd4 as b7 is no longer hanging after the exchanges on d4.

31   ♖b4

The rook is reduced to a tortuous sideways defence of d4 – it would have been so much better to leave it on d3!

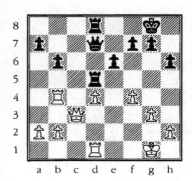

31   ...   b5!

This second pawn move confounds White's plan of 32 ♖c4! when the rook would suddenly find itself well placed on the open file. Now there is no good answer to prevent 32...a5 forcing the rook back, when 33...b4 and 34...♖xd4 will win the pawn.

32   a4

The weakness of d4 has already infected White's kingside – 30 f4 – and now it spreads to the queenside, where White sheds a pawn in a desperate bid for activity.

32   ...   bxa4

The first White pawn drops – and rather surprisingly it isn't the prime target on d4.

33   ♕a3

This is White's idea: he will counterattack on the wing with 34 ♖xa4 threatening 35 ♖xa7.

33   ...   a5!

Karpov wisely returns the pawn in order to leave the white queen and rook misplaced on the edge of the board.

34   ♖xa4

White is battling hard. Korchnoi has proved throughout his career that as long as material is equal there is always the chance of escaping from positional pressure, no matter how overwhelming it may seem.

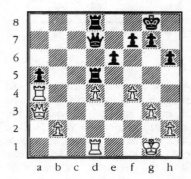

34   ...   ♕b5!

The queen prevents 35 ♖xa5 and leaves the white rook unpleasantly boxed in on a4 – it has no safe move. The white queen also finds herself paralyzed by the need to defend the rook. As well as this Black is threatening to invade

White's second rank with 35...♛e2, or perhaps even stronger 35...♜c8 and 36...♜c2. This is the first indication of the price White will have to pay for exposing his king with 30 f4.

35   ♜d2

The only hope was to free the white queen from the defence of the rook on a4 with 35 b3, though Karpov's intention of 35...♜b8 and 36...♛xb3 leads to a winning rook and pawn endgame for Black.

35   ...   e5!!

An unexpected breakthrough, but entirely logical. White's queen and rook on a4 are both far off on the queenside; meanwhile White's king is lacking pawn cover. So where should Black concentrate his attack? Is it on the queenside, or against d4 (which is defended three times)? No, the right place to hit White is where he has fewest defenders: the kingside. As so often, a pawn advance provides the decisive blow in wrenching open lines.

36   fxe5

Black cannot be allowed an extra passed pawn with 36...exd4.

36   ...   ♜xe5

Now the threat is mate in two: 37...♜e1+ 38 ♔g2 ♛f1, and if 37 dxe5 ♜xd2 leaves White unable to prevent disaster following with 38...♜d1+ or 38...♛e2, with a quick mate: such is the power of a rook on the seventh rank.

37   ♛a1

Korchnoi defends grimly, but there are simply too many holes in his position.

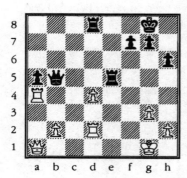

37   ...   ♛e8!

A beautiful retreat which compels his opponent to take the unwanted rook.

38   dxe5

There was no longer any choice as the lethal 38...♜e1+ was threatened.

38   ...   ♜xd2

So Black gets a rook on the seventh rank after all.

39   ♜xa5

Now White has even won a pawn, but it is irrelevant: disaster is bound to follow on his entirely undefended second rank.

| 39 | ... | ♛c6 |

The black queen has never wandered far from her starting square on d8, but she has brilliantly utilized the light square diagonal b5, c6, d7 and e8. Now she threatens mate on g2.

| 40 | ♖a8+ |

It might appear that White is attacking, but this is just an illusion. The white king can only dream of the kind of pawn cover that his black counterpart enjoys.

| 40 | ... | ♚h7 |

The black king finally uses the bolt hole made for him back at move five!

| 41 | ♛b1+ |

He has to check or resign at once after 41 ♛f1 ♛xa8.

| 41 | ... | g6 |

Now the checks are over and mate looms on the g2 square.

| 42 | ♛f1 |

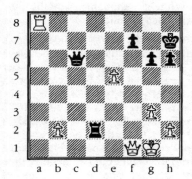

In contrast to the rampaging black queen, the white queen can only crawl along the back rank to defend the g2 square. Still, even with his

back to the wall Korchnoi has managed to stir up a mate threat of his own: 43 ♛xf7 mate.

| 42 | ... | ♛c5+ |

The queen wants to coordinate her action with the black rook and so wins time for the enterprise by ensuring that she goes to d5 with check.

| 43 | ♚h1 |

The only move, but now we see the power of a centralized queen in all her glory.

| 43 | ... | ♛d5+! |

0-1

The black queen radiates power in all directions on the light squares: she has influence over far flung corners of the board on a8 and h1, as well as two other crucial squares: f7 for defence, and d1 for attack.

White is mated after 44 ♛g2 ♖d1 or else loses his queen for a rook after 44 ♚g1 ♖d1. There was however one last pitfall for Black to avoid: after 44 ♚g1 Black mustn't snatch the rook with 44...♛xa8 as after 45 ♛xf7+ ♚h8 46 ♛f6+ Black finds to his horror that he must accept a perpetual check with

46...♔h7 47 ♕f7+ ♔h8 48 ♕f6+ ♔h7, as he would lose his own rook after 48...♔g8 49 ♕xg6+ ♔f8 50 ♕xh6+ and 51 ♕xd2, when he is suddenly four pawns down in a queen ending!

Naturally Korchnoi knew that Karpov would take the queen with 44...♖d1 and so he immediately resigned. However, I would recommend that lesser players play on just one more move with 44 ♔g1, just in case their opponents are ensnared by the trap above.

This was a beautiful positional display by Karpov.

Game Nineteen
B.Gelfand - V.Kramnik
Berlin 1996
Slav Defence

1   d4

Mirror, mirror on the wall,

is 1 e4 or 1 d4 best of all?

Let's look at the record of two of the greatest players of our era, who both gained World Championship titles of one form or another.

Anand was always a devoted 1 e4 player at the start of his career, and then he added 1 d4 to his repertoire. In contrast Kramnik began as an expert on 1 d4 openings – usually beginning with the flexible 1 ♘f3, but soon transposing to mainlines. Then he switched to 1 e4. The result? Anand won a lot of wonderful games with 1 d4, and Kramnik crushed all his opponents with 1 e4. So in other words, nothing changed. There is nothing

to choose between 1 e4 and 1 d4 – if you are a genius you can make either move look good.

In the present game Kramnik proves that ability is what matters by winning in 28 moves as Black.

1   ...   d5

An ancient and well respected response: Black refuses to allow his opponent a space advantage in the centre.

2   c4

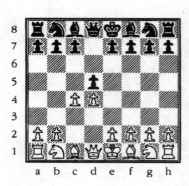

White's thoughts might be expressed as follows:

'I already have an idea for a strategy: I'll attack d5. If he plays 2...dxc4, I'll regain the pawn sooner or later, when the way is clear for an eventual e2-e4, when I have a nice pawn centre. If instead 2...♘f6 3 cxd5 and after either 3...♕xd5 4 ♘c3 or 3...♘xd5 4 e4 I have not only removed the pesky black pawn from the centre but I'm gaining time by attacking one of his big pieces with a lesser unit. So I reckon he'll defend the d5 pawn with either 2...e6 or 2...c6. If he plays 2...e6 I've made him shut in his queen's bishop – that doesn't sound like much but it's an advantage I can start to build on.'

2   ...   c6

Kramnik decides to stand his ground on d5 by adopting the Slav Defence.

3   ♘c3

White develops the knight now that it doesn't block his c pawn. As a further benefit of 2 c4 he has the option of ♕b3 to put pressure on d5 or possibly b7 once Black has developed his queen's bishop.

3   ...   ♘f6

In response, the black horse springs to its best square where it helps bolster d5.

4   ♘f3

If there is no penalty involved, a good player will take every opportunity to bring out his pieces for the middlegame struggle.

4   ...   e6

Here however there is a penalty if Black elects to develop with 4...♗f5, as 5 cxd5 cxd5 6 ♕b3 would cause him some anxiety over the b7 square. It is a pity to hem in the bishop on c8, but Black is eager to develop his kingside.

5   e3

White also decides it is best to shut in his queen's bishop. He could play 5 ♗g5, but now Black can snatch the c4 pawn and refuse to give it back: the variation 5...dxc4 6 e4 b5 7 e5 leads to mind bending complications – White doesn't win a piece as Black can play 7...h6 8 ♗h4 g5 etc. Even many top class players are keen to steer away from

this complex line as White. The game move is perfectly good as it defends c4 and stabilizes White's centre, but it gives up on any hope for a quick knockout blow based on rapid development.

5   ...   ♘bd7

Having been deprived of its best square on c6 the knight has to make do with the only other centre square available to it.

6   ♕c2

White has in mind a very interesting plan based on a pawn advance on the kingside. Therefore the queen moves out of the way to make possible queenside castling: a necessary preparation as White's own king would be both a target and a hindrance to his idea if situated on the kingside. In choosing a square the queen selects c2, where she controls e4, thus making it more difficult for Black to stir up any counterplay in the centre based on ♘e4.

6   ...   ♗d6

The bishop finds a suitable niche in Black's pawn structure: he keeps a watch on the dark squares c5 and e5 which aren't defended by the little triangle of pawns.

7   g4!?

The aforementioned idea. Gelfand intends 8 g5, evicting the knight from its centre post, followed by a well timed e3-e4, when the disruption caused to Black's piece coordination will give White the upper hand in the centre. The tactical justification is that after 7...♘xg4 8 ♖g1 the knight has to retreat, whereupon the rook invasion ♖xg7 is bound to prove awkward for the black king.

7   ...   ♗b4!?

Kramnik shows a blatant disregard for the rule that says you shouldn't move a piece twice in the opening. Why in the space of one move has b4 become a more attractive post for the bishop than d6?

The point is that White has burnt his boats with 7 g4: the pawn can never retreat back to g2 and so the white kingside is left permanently disjointed and can never be a safe haven for his king.

Note that if Black had played 6...♗b4 one move earlier White is

by no means obliged to play 7 g4: he can develop quietly with 7 ♗e2 and 8 0-0, followed by b2-b3 and ♗b2. At some point the bishop would have become restless on b4: either it would go back to d6 – a loss of time – or else capture the knight – when White would have the two bishops and superior dark square control. So the bishop move to b4 only becomes effective once White has committed himself to 7 g4.

The situation has therefore changed dramatically in the mere half move since Black played 6...♗d6. In these new circumstances, Black aims to take the sting out of the g4-g5 advance by eliminating the knight on c3, which would make it possible for the black knight to stay in the centre with ♘e4. If Black succeeds in his plan, then 7 g4 would begin to look like a needless weakening of White's kingside.

8   ♗d2

White breaks the pin on the knight and clears the way for queenside castling. If instead 8 g5 ♘e4 intending ♕a5 would give Black annoying pressure on c3.

8   ...   ♕e7

Very methodical; Kramnik defends the bishop on b4 and so prepares to develop his other bishop to b7, without being press ganged into an immediate exchange on c3 as would occur after 8...b6 9 ♕a4 – attacking c6 – 9...♗xc3 10 ♗xc3.

9   a3

All the same White wants to force the exchange on c3, but Kramnik thinks that 9 g5 was the better way to do it, with a balanced game after

9...♗xc3 10 ♗xc3 ♘e4 11 ♗d3. It
should be remembered that any
loosening of White's pawn structure
on the queenside – even the
apparently insignificant a2-a3 – is a
weakening of the future residence of
the white king.

9 ... ♗xc3

It's unpleasant to part with such a
fine bishop, but its value is
outweighed by the urgency of
winning e4 for the knight.

10 ♗xc3

Much better than 10 bxc3? as it
keeps the queenside structure intact
for the white king and introduces
the threat of 11 ♗b4, when Black
will pay dearly for giving up his
dark-squared bishop.

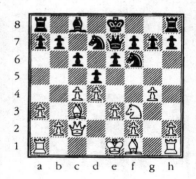

10 ... b6!

A tale of two bishops: Kramnik
prepares to develop his own bishop
and at the same time readies himself
to answer 11 ♗b4 with 11...c5
shutting out the white bishop.

11 ♗d3

White develops as he is loathe to
hand over the e4 square after 11
cxd5 exd5.

11 ... ♗a6!

A more active square for the
bishop than b7 as it immediately
attacks c4.

12 ♕a4

An awkward way to defend c4,
but Gelfand is still desperate to
avoid giving Black's knight access
to a wonderful centre post on e4
after 12 cxd5 ♗xd3 13 ♕xd3 exd5.
If that happened then the whole
point of White's strategy with 7 g4
would have failed.

12 ... dxc4

Black counterattacks against the
white bishop.

13 ♕xa6

It is best to accept the offer, as if
13 ♕xc6 ♖c8.

13 ... cxd3

Obviously there is no choice but
to regain the piece...

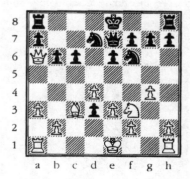

14 ♕xd3

...but this capture wasn't forced
for White. Kramnik suggests that he
should have fished in troubled
waters with 14 ♕b7 when 14...0-0
15 ♘e5 ♕e8 – breaking the pin on

the knight on d7-16 ♘xd3 ♖c8 17 ♕xa7 ♘xg4 is none too clear, though White has the headache of deciding where his king will be safe.

14   ...   0-0

Black's completes his development: his king is completely secure as any attempt by White to begin a pawn assault can be met with action in the centre.

15   g5

Despite his rather unsuccessful opening it is some consolation to White that he has kept the black knight out of the e4 square.

15   ...   ♘d5

Sometimes the best move can be found by eliminating all the alternatives. The knight must move, but it has no wish to be shut out of the game on h5; nor is e8 very inviting, as besides being a passive post it obstructs its own rooks. Therefore the horse goes boldly to d5.

16 ♗d2

With this quiet retreat Gelfand prepares to gain space with 17 e4 without allowing his opponent to

solve the problem of his harassed knight with ♘xc3. Unfortunately for him Kramnik finds a powerful preventive measure.

16   ...   f5!

If now 17 gxf6 ♕xf6 and disaster follows for White along the f file. Therefore Black has secured the knight on d5 from being driven away by e3-e4, which means it becomes undoubtedly the best minor piece on the board: a knight loves nothing better than to be placed on a good centre square where it can't be attacked by a pawn or easily exchanged.

17   0-0-0

The white king cannot remain permanently in the centre as Black is going to open lines with c6-c5, etc. Castling queenside appears the lesser evil, but the king will prove to be far from safe.

17   ...   c5!

After a fairly quiet opening phase during which he has dealt with all White's potential threats Kramnik decides it is the moment to go over to the offensive. From now on all his attention is focused on opening lines on the queenside to expose the white king.

18   ♔b1

The king decides to get off the c file as quickly as possible both to avoid being caught in the open and to vacate the c1 square for a rook and.

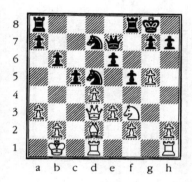

18   ...   b5!

We will all eventually pay for our sins, at least against a strong chess opponent. You may recall that way back in the opening White unnecessarily weakened his queenside with 9 a3. It didn't seem important then, but now the pawn on a3 provides Black with a 'hook' on which he can latch his queenside advance with b5-b4 – perhaps after the preparatory moves c5-c4 and a7-a5.

19   ♕xb5

Therefore White feels obliged to eliminate the advancing pawn before it reaches b4, but opening lines on the queenside is hardly going to make a king sitting on b1 feel more secure.

19   ...   ♖ab8

Now the b file becomes the perfect channel of attack for the black rooks.

20   ♕a5

The queen has to stay in the thick of the action on the queenside as after 20 ♕e2 cxd4 21 ♘xd4? ♕xa3 White would already be facing catastrophe.

20   ...   ♖b3

The rook is delighted to be stationed on a square deep in enemy territory that cannot be easily attacked by pawn or piece. Here it has maximum attacking potential and little defensive frailty.

21   ♔a2

Having been let down by his pieces the white king tries to oust the rook himself. Still, the king will be prove to be the hunted rather than the hunter on a2; so he should have submitted to 21 ♔a1! with chances for a successful defence.

21   ...   ♖fb8

The rook is immediately defended with the catastrophic threat of 22...♖xb2+.

22   ♖b1

The barrier on b2 must be held at all costs against the marauders on the b file.

22   ...   e5!

The black rooks are superbly placed, but few attacking plans can succeed without the help of the queen. Kramnik therefore clears the e6 square for his strongest piece, so that the a2 square will no longer feel like a sanctuary for the white king. At the same time the tearing away of the white centre pawns will increase the scope of the black knights.

23   ♖hc1

After 23 dxc5 ♘xc5 the white queen suddenly finds herself in danger of being trapped by 24...♖3b5. Meanwhile if 23 dxe5 ♘xe5 24 ♘xe5 ♕xe5 and the b2 square is attacked a third time.

23   ...   ♕e6

Now the threats include 24...♖3b5 when the white queen dare not move as if 25 ♕xa7 ♘c3+ is double discovered check and 26 ♔a1 ♕a2 is mate.

24   ♔a1

Here Gelfand must have wished fervently that he had put the king on a1 when he had the chance back at move 21!

24   ...   exd4

Not only is the white king in peril but his centre is crumbling away. Therefore desperate remedies are called for.

25   ♖xc5

White tries to escape from the growing pressure by sacrificing the exchange: a strategy that might well

have worked if Kramnik hadn't been so tactically alert. In any case White was in trouble as 25 exd4? just drops the knight to 25...♖xf3.

25   ...   ♘xc5

Black is by no means displeased to exchange off his only piece not involved in the attack for a rook.

26   ♕xc5

Now Black is the exchange up for a pawn, but he has to deal with the threat of 27 ♘xd4 forking his queen and rook. If 26...dxe3 then 27 ♘d4 looks no better than unclear for him.

But Black shouldn't be thinking of how to hold onto his paltry material gain. His sights should be much higher: how can he mate the white king? After all, he has two rooks putting pressure down the b file and the knight and queen both poised to help in the attack. The obvious move is 26...♘c3, threatening 27...♘xb1, when Black wins quickly after both 27 bxc3? ♖xb1 mate or 27 ♗xc3 dxc3 and 28...cxb2+ next move is slaughter. The apparent drawback is 27 ♘xd4, but Black nonetheless has a winning combination after this. It is a question of looking deeply into the position and trying out various sacrificial sequences until you find the bull's eye! Let's see how Kramnik found it in the game.

26   ...   ♞c3!

Before playing this move, Black had to have seen the mating finish. You can't rely on general principles when you have three pieces en prise!

27   ♞xd4

Gelfand had relied on this move to defeat the black attack: indeed although he is the exchange up Black has a rook, queen and knight all hanging, and the heroic 27...♖xa3+? fails to 28 ♛xa3 covering the a2 square against mate by 28 ♛a2. But the Russian GM was in for an unpleasant surprise.

27   ...   ♖xb2!!

Now would you have seen this move during the game? In fact it isn't too difficult to calculate. The trick is to let yourself think about various 'impossible' or 'ridiculous' sacrifices until you find one that works.

28   ♖xb2

There is no choice but to accept the rook as the a2 square must be

defended and if 28 ♞xe6 Black has a choice of mates on a2 or b1.

28   ...   ♛a2+!
0-1

The white rook is deflected to a2 allowing mate after 29 ♖xa2 ♖b1. A brilliant finish, but it wasn't magic: it was the logical culmination of Black's pressure along the b file.

Game Twenty
J.Timman - L.Ljubojevic
Hilversum 1987
Slav Defence

1   d4

On the very first move of a game it's impossible to devise a precise opening strategy: you have to wait and see what squares the opponent puts his pieces on first. Nonetheless you can't go far wrong if you clear the way for your queen and bishop.

1   ...   d5

White has got in the great move d2-d4, but his opponent isn't going to let him complete his centre with e2-e4, or at least not without some resistance.

2   c4

It has been known for hundreds of years that White does better to put pressure on d5 with this pawn move rather than develop with 2 ♞c3. If Black now responds 2...dxc4 then White will sooner or later regain the pawn and then have a slight space advantage, for example after 3 ♞f3 e6 4 e3 c5 5 ♝xc4.

2   ...   c6

Ljubojevic ensures that he can keep a pawn on d5 in the event of 3 cxd5. He avoids 2...e6 as he has no wish to block in his queen's bishop.

3   ♘f3

The f3 square has a magnetic effect on the king's knight: it is rare indeed in a game between strong players that it doesn't reach this square by move five at the latest.

3   ...   ♞f6

Black also wastes no time in bringing out his horse. He now has the e4 square covered twice – not bad after only three moves!

4   ♘c3

Timman continues to develop in fearless style, even though with each move Black has extra resources to grab and hold onto the pawn on c4.

4   ...   dxc4

A chessboard gambler like Ljubojevic cannot resist snatching the booty, despite the disappearance of the strong bulwark on d5.

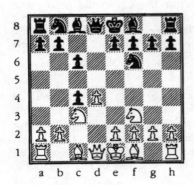

5   e3

White would like to play 5 e4 when he has a broad pawn centre,

but first things first! After 5 e4 b5 it would be difficult to regain the pawn: for example if 6 a4 b4 7 ♘a2 ♞xe4 and the beautiful white centre has been destroyed. So Timman makes do with a more restrained approach. He is planning 6 ♗xc4 and if 5...b5 6 a4 when he is bound to regain the pawn after 6...b4 7 ♘a2. Similarly if 6...a6 7 axb5 cxb5 8 ♘xb5 and again White gets the pawn back with an excellent position.

5   ...   ♗e6

An audacious move. Black thinks "I've found a way to defend c4 and at the same time develop my queen's bishop. It looks risky as I'm obstructing the development of my kingside with e7-e6. But I'm feeling lucky and a pawn is a pawn is a pawn!"

6   ♘g5!

The pace of the game suddenly increases after Black ambitious fifth move. Now is not the moment for conscientious development with 6 ♗e2 and 7 0-0 as Black has issued a direct challenge to White: if you don't do anything fast I am going to hold onto the extra pawn and complete my development. It is often the case that an unusual idea has to met with an equally unconventional response. Here Timman refuses to give his opponent time to develop his pieces quietly.

6   ...   ♗d5

The bishop runs away from the attentions of the knight as otherwise 7 ♘xe6 fxe6 would have left his kingside shattered. However, if the bishop wanted to flee then 6...♗g4 looked safer; or else the bishop might have been defended with 6...♕d6.

7   e4!

White is able to add momentum to his attack with the advance he has been aiming for ever since 1 d4.

7   ...   h6

A necessary counterattack, as Black can't contemplate 7...♗e6 7 ♘xe6 fxe6 8 ♗xc4, when he is left with a smashed pawn centre.

8   exd5

White's play is also forced as if he retreats the knight from g5 then the e4 pawn will drop.

8   ...   hxg5

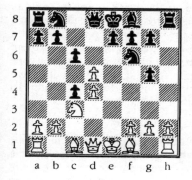

Ljubojevic recaptures his piece, leaving the game delicately balanced: he hopes that the white centre is going to crumble away, whereas Timman wants to prove it still has an attacking capacity.

9   dxc6!

At first glance this appears to play into Black's hands by helping him develop his queenside, but in reality the knight that appears on c6 will be a target.

9   ...   ♘xc6

The only reasonable reply as after 9...bxc6 10 ♗xc4 White would have regained his pawn and still be attacking g5.

10   d5

White saves his d pawn from capture in the best possible way by using it to dislodge the knight from c6.

10   ...   ♘e5

The knight is driven onto this insecure square by the need to defend c4.

11   ♗xg5

Timman recoups his pawn and can be be pleased at the return on his investment: the bishop pair, a space advantage and a ready target on c4. Already there is the tactical threat of 12 ♗xc4! ♘xc4 13 ♕a4+ ♕d7 14 ♕xc4 when he is a fairly safe pawn up.

11   ...   ♕b6

Ljubojevic decides to meet the threat to c4 by counterattacking against b2, or possibly against f2 if next move 12...♘fg4 proves apposite.

12   ♗e3!

A great move that exemplifies the golden rule of positional play in chess: the coordination of the pieces is of paramount importance. Rather than stoop to the mean task of defending the b2 pawn the Dutch Grandmaster brings his bishop to d4 where it is finely placed for both defensive and aggressive measures.

12   ...   ♕xb2

Many an unwary queen has perished after snatching the pawn on b2. For this reason such a pawn is often referred to as a Poisoned Pawn. Nevertheless, Black might as well grab the pawn, as if he retreats his queen he has a rotten position for no compensation.

13   ♗d4

The bishop reaches its ideal centre square. Here it:

♦ attacks the knight on e5

♦ defends the knight on c3

♦ guards f2 against possible attack by either black knight to g4

♦ has potential for a discovered attack on the black queen.

13   ...   ♘d3+

Here's what might have happened after 13...♘eg4: 14 ♕a4+! and Black is lost as after 14...♘d7 15 ♖b1 his queen has no safe square while if 14...b5 15 ♘xb5! there is the irresistible double threat of 15 ♗xb2 and 15 ♘c7+. Here we see another role for the bishop on d4 – it defends the rook on a1 through the black queen.

14   ♗xd3

The bishop only makes one move in the entire game, but what a move! He eliminates the black knight and clears the way for white to castle with no loss of time.

14   ...   cxd3

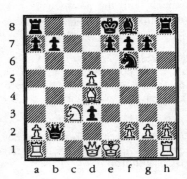

The pawn on d3 provides a life line to the black queen as he can fight on after 15 ♖b1 ♕c2. Meanwhile capturing the pawn with the queen drops the rook on a1 and there would be a mate that everyone apart from Timman would find amusing after 15 ♕a4+ b5! 16 ♘xb5? ♕e2 mate.

15   0-0!

White's strongest attacking move of the game is castling. Now the rooks are connected and there are no checks to aid the retreat of the black queen. Already White intends 16 ♕a4+ followed by ♖ab1 with a deadly attack down the b file.

15   ...   ♕b4

The queen does well to extricate herself while she can. After 15...♕c2 16 ♕f3! she cannot offer her king any help against the multiple threats which include 17 d6! opening the way for ♕xb7 as well as undermining the defences in front of the black king.

16   ♕xd3

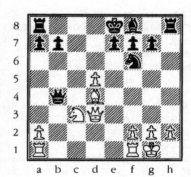

White regains his pawn. If we compare the relative activity of the white and black pieces, there might not seem much to choose between the queens, knights or rooks; but with the bishops it is quite another story. The white bishop is all powerful on d4 while the black bishop on f8 has no possible move. It isn't wholly useless, as it is defending e7, a vital shield for the black king: on the other hand, there is no square on the first three ranks where Black wouldn't prefer to have the bishop instead of f8. If it were on one of these other squares then Black would be able to castle: and g8 would be an incomparably safer square for the black king than

g8. Therefore it can be said that Black perishes for one reason only: his bishop on f8, which is not only a feeble piece in its own right but even worse a fatal obstacle to the king's safe redeployment.

There will be tactical variations and a hard fight ahead, but it is no wonder that they all turn out in White's favour when the positional outlook is so good for him.

16   ...   a6

Black is unable to improve the strategic situation on the kingside as if 16...g6. hoping to develop with ♗g7, White can open lines against the black king with 17 ♗xf6 exf6 18 ♖fe1+. Therefore Ljubojevic makes do with preventing the strong attacking move 17 ♘b5.

17   ♖fe1

Over the next few moves White concentrates his might against the e7 pawn. This makes much more sense than chasing the black queen as after 17 ♖ab1 there follows 17...♕d6 when 18 ♖xb7??? allows 18...♕xh2 mate.

17   ...   ♖c8

Black puts up maximum resistance as he now has every piece apart from the cocooned bishop involved in the struggle. Here on c8 the rook puts pressure on the white knight and in some cases is available to defend with ♖c7.

18   ♗xf6

White exchanges at the right moment. Of course he is loathe to part with his excellent bishop, but the black knight was an equally formidable defender. It should be remembered that as long as Black remains with a buried bishop every more or less 'equal' exchange of the other pieces is bound to increase the disparity in strength between the attackers and defenders.

18   ...   gxf6

Black recaptures and is suddenly menacing the white knight.

19   ♘e4

The knight skips away and introduces a threat of its own: 20 ♘xf6+. Already Black misses his own brave steed on f6.

19   ...   ♔d8

The king tries to save himself by stepping off the e file, which has begun to resemble a shooting gallery. If Black had met the attack on f6 with 19...♗g7 or 19...♖h6 then besides 20 d6 as in the game White can win tactically with 20 ♖ab1! forcing the black queen away from the defence of d6 whereupon 20...♕a5 21 ♘d6+ wins material at once.

20   d6!

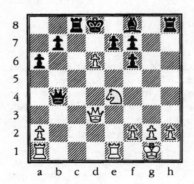

A pawn is a highly effective battering ram when it charges against a king's defences.

20   ...   e6

Black cannot allow his pawns to be split asunder with 20...exd6. when the following exciting finish was possible: 21 ♘xf6 ♕h4 – attacking both the knight and h2, but White can win the game with checks: 22 ♖e8+ ♔c7 23 ♕c3+ ♔b6 24 ♘d7+ here the dull 24 ♖xc8 leaves White a rook up, as it is only a harmless check on h2, but this is more forceful – 24...♔a7 25 ♕e3+ ♖c5 26 ♖a8+!! ♔xa8 27 ♕e8+ and mate will follow on b8. Note that White should only play 21 ♘xf6 if he has a forced win worked out. If not, then he should prefer a strong positional move such as 21 ♖ab1, which keeps a decisive advantage without any risk.

21   ♖ab1!

It is important not to be in a rush in a winning position. Black can do nothing to solve his king's predicament in the centre and so White simply develops his last inactive piece. Instead the impatient 21 ♘xf6? would give Black serious counterplay after 21...♕h4! hitting the knight and h2.

21   ...   ♕a5

Tricky until the end. The queen chooses this retreat square so that if 22 ♖xb7?? Black's fortunes change for the better after 22...♕xe1+.

22   ♕d4!

Very methodical: having compelled Black to rupture his pawn front with 20...e6 White now aims his queen at the secondary weakness on f6. There is also another sinister motive behind this move which soon becomes clear.

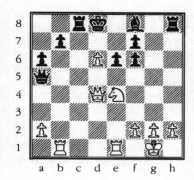

22   ...   ♗g7

At last Black puts the bishop to some use by defending f6 but it is all too late: nothing can save his king any longer.

After 22...♕e5 White can keep an enormous advantage with the straightforward 23 ♕xe5 fxe5 24 ♖xb7 when if 24...f5? 25 ♘g5 is crushing in view of 26 ♘f7+ or 26 ♘xe6+. But if White wants to finish the game most efficiently he should choose 23 ♕b6+ when there are two variations:

(a) 23...♔e8 24 d7+! ♔xd7 25 ♕xb7+ ♖c7 (Black is also obliterated after 25...♕c7 26 ♖ed1+ ♔e8 27 ♘xf6+ ♔e7 28 ♖d7+) 26 ♖ed1+ ♗d6 (or 26...♔e7 27 ♕b4+ ♔e8 28 ♕b8+ ♔e7 29 ♕d8 mate) 27 ♖xd6+ ♕xd6 28 ♘xd6 ♖xb7 29 ♘xb7 and White is a piece up in the endgame; or

(b) 23...♔d7 24 ♕xb7+ ♔d8 25 ♕xc8+!! forces mate: 25...♔xc8 26 ♖ec1+ ♔d7 (or 26...♔d8 27 ♖b8+) 27 ♖c7+ ♔d8 28 ♖b8 mate.

It is a matter of very fine judgment as to whether after 22...♕e5 White should choose 23 ♕xe5 or 23 ♕b6+. The latter move is a cast iron 100% win – but only if

it has been calculated correctly. On the other hand, 23 ♕xe5 is a simple way to maintain a huge advantage, but it doesn't finish off the game beyond all doubt – White would certainly win if he played even only fairly accurately, but where there is life there is hope for Black.

It all depends on how much you trust your powers of calculation. As a rule you should always try to play the best move, which in this case is 23 ♕b6+. Furthermore, calculating a forced win is one of the more delightful ways to improve your tactical ability!

23   ♖ed1!

Timman sticks to the rule 'do not hurry!' He removes the rook from e1 so 24 ♖xb7 becomes a threat.

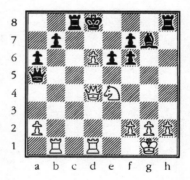

23   ...   ♖h5

An ingenious defensive attempt. If now 24 ♖xb7 ♖d5! would be awkward for White as if 25 ♕a1? ♖xd1+ 26 ♕xd1 ♕d5! attacks the white queen, knight and rook when it would be White who gets mated after 27 ♕xd5 ♖c1+ or 27 ♕b1 ♕xb7 28 ♕xb7 ♖c1 mate. Looking more closely, even this is only a bluff by Black as White can answer

24...♖d5 with 25 ♘xf6! when 25...♖xd4 allows 26 ♖d7 mate. Still, White has no need to live life dangerously like this as he has a road to a quick victory that entails no risk.

24   ♕a7!

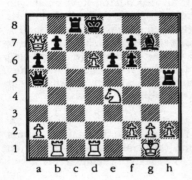

An unexpected winning method. The white queen goes to the edge of the board for two reasons: the first is to rampage along the seventh rank with the rook after 25 ♖xb7; the second threat is more pernicious – to take away the a8 square from the black rook!

24   ...   ♖b5

Black deals with the first of the threats, but is powerless against the second.

25   d7!   1-0

The black rook is crowded out from its defence of the first rank thanks to the white queen being on a7. If it moves anywhere safe along the c file then a queen check on a8 or b8 forces the passed pawn through.

5   The Art of Counterattack:
1 d4 ♘f6

'Chess is a terrible game. If you have no centre, then your opponent has a freer position. If you do have a centre, then you really have something to worry about!'

Tarrasch

In the olden days, right up until about 1920, it was *de rigueur* for games to begin 1 d4 d5 or 1 e4 e5. Then a new approach to the openings was discovered: the centre could be controlled by pieces from a distance without the necessity of packing it with pawns! This new, restrained method of play in the opening was a favourite of the so called hypermodern school of chess that had as its pioneers the old masters Reti and Nimzowitsch. Hypermodern ideas have had a particular impact on how Black begins a game: it is now fully accepted that Black doesn't have to answer 1 d4 with 1...d5: he can yield space with 1...♘f6 2 c4 g6 3 ♘c3 ♗g7 as in the King's Indian Defence or 1...♘f6 2 c4 e6 3 ♘f3 b6 4 g3 ♗b7 (Queen's Indian Defence). In neither case is he neglecting the centre: he is simply trying to control it without occupying it from the outset with pawns – which makes a lot of sense when you realize that after 1 d4 d5 Black has created an immediate target for a white attack with 2 c4.

Nowadays a compromise has been reached: putting pawns in the centre as soon as possible or the opposite – restraining the pawns to control the centre from a distance – are both recognized as fully acceptable strategies. In fact in most opening schemes it is essential to combine both methods of play. Every opening requires some early pawn moves, while in many schemes it is often better to fianchetto either on the queenside or kingside rather than put the bishop in the centre.

Note that it isn't being suggested that a player should permanently restrain his pawns – even in openings like the King's Indian Black usually advances e7-e5 within the eight moves, while d7-d5 often occurs in the Queen's Indian. It is a question of delaying pawn advances, not avoiding them. If Black (or White) never made any pawn moves he would be squashed sooner or later.

These dynamic openings deliberately hold back the black centre pawns and so coax White into building a pawn centre in order that it can be subjected to pressure from the wings. A key feature is the fianchetto of the king's bishop on g7.

White's advantage in moving first doesn't go away, in fact from an objective point of view he might have better chances of winning in these lines than after 1 d4 d5. A space advantage must mean something, or else all the laws governing strategy fall apart. Nevertheless, the struggle is made much more complicated by Black holding back his centre pawns, and it is very easy for White to go wrong. Furthermore, the punishment for error can be much more severe: it might not matter too much if White makes a second best move in a quiet position in the Queen's Gambit; but if he goes wrong in the King's Indian he could get mated! It is far more difficult to understand counterattacking openings, and therefore the risks – and opportunities – are much higher for both players.

In this chapter we'll look at some success stories for both White and Black.

Game Twenty-One
Y.Seirawan - V.Ivanchuk
Groningen 1997
King's Indian Attack

Although never quite in the super star status of his countrymen Morphy and Fischer, Yasser Seirawan has wins to his credit against all time giants of the chess world such as Karpov and Kasparov. Here he crushes Ivanchuk in a mere 22 moves!

1   d4

1 e4 or 1 d4, that is the question! In just one stroke, White takes a lump of the centre, frees his queen's

bishop and gives some air to his queen. As an added bonus compared to 1 e4, the d4 pawn is safely defended.

1   ...   ♘f6

On the other hand, devotees of 1 e4 might point out that Black is pleased to be able to put this knight on its 100% best square without being harassed as would occur after 1 e4 ♘f6 2 e5. Instead, the knight deters White's king's pawn from even reaching e4 – or at least for the moment.

2   c4

Having put one pawn on the fourth rank, White follows the time honoured recipe of putting another pawn alongside it. Now his pawns control the centre squares c5, d5 and e5 – not bad after only two moves!

2   ...   g6

Black could have advanced his own pawns to contest the centre immediately, but he prefers to adopt a more sophisticated approach. He invites White to build a pawn centre and then intends to undermine and eventually destroy it. As the first stage in this plan he will put his bishop on g7 where it will aim at the d4 pawn.

3   ♘c3

Meanwhile White develops his pieces in straightforward and fearless style: the knight will be needed to support the advance of the king's pawn.

3   ...   ♗g7

The bishop is excellently placed on g7 both for defensive and aggressive duties.

4   e4

White completes his pawn centre and now has an impressive space advantage: he has three clear ranks behind his pawns to develop his pieces.

4   ...   d6

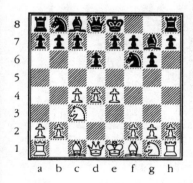

A useful all purpose move. Black

♦ deters White from playing e4-e5 to chase away the black knight

♦ opens the diagonal for his queen's bishop

♦ clears the d7 square for his knight

♦ prepares to strike at the white centre on his next move.

5   ♗d3

A very safe method of development. Seirawan plans ♘ge2, f2-f3 and ♗e3 when his centre is proof against any attempted attack. Therefore, although the bishop has no immediately active role on d3, it is a good idea to move it out before it gets blocked in by the knight on e2.

5   ...   e5

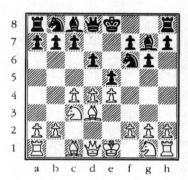

It might seem strange that Black goes to the trouble of putting his bishop on g7 to attack the white centre – and then promptly blocks its diagonal with 5...e5!

Of course the bishop himself is far from delighted by this; but imagine what would happen if Black avoided making any challenge to the white centre with his pawns and satisfied himself with moving his pieces around. Play could go something like 5...♘c6 6 ♘ge2 0-0 7 0-0 ♗d7 8 f4 and you will see that Black faces being pushed back with 9 e5 or 9 d5 when his pieces must retreat in disarray.

Modern, dynamic opening strategy hasn't dispensed with the idea of using pawns to fight for centre control – it has refined the strategy to a higher level.

In playing 5...e5 Black stakes his claim to an equal share of space on the kingside; this will define his strategy in the middlegame.

6   d5

Here 6 dxe5 dxe5 would be fine for Black: the white centre is split in two and misses the strong pawn on d4 which deprived the black pieces of squares. Furthermore, a so-called hole on d4 becomes accessible to a black knight: no white pawn can protect this square. In contrast the d5 square isn't as useful for White's knight as it can always be covered by c7-c6 if necessary.

Instead White keeps his centre intact and maintains a space advantage on the queenside. It is reasonable to suppose that his strategy will involve engineering the advance c4-c5, in keeping with the principle that you should try to put another pawn next to your furthest advanced pawn. Having achieved c4-c5, White could then capture on d6 and use the open c file for his rooks to infiltrate into the black queenside.

Of course, such an advance is way ahead in the future, but it is good to have the guiding light of a strategical plan, even if it is shining very dimly.

6   ...   a5

Ivanchuk takes measures against White's plan outlined above with this far sighted move. He realizes that the move b2-b4 will be very useful in supporting a c4-c5

advance and so immediately obstructs it.

7   ♘ge2

A higher strategic consideration overrules putting the knight on its favoured f3 square. Seirawan develops it on e2 so as not to obstruct the f pawn – as will be seen this is a wise decision, as this pawn will be both a good defender on f3 and a great attacker on f4!

7   ...   ♘a6

Meanwhile Ivanchuk increases his grip on both the b4 and c5 squares. It might seem trivial work for a knight, but if it holds up White's strategical plan then it is an excellent use of Black's resources.

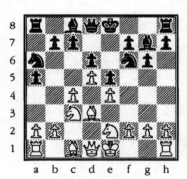

8   f3

A necessary precaution: White wants to put his bishop on the centre square e3 but after 8 ♗e3 he would be hit by 8...♘g4 9 ♗d2 f5 and Black has gained time to start his counterplay on the kingside. Note that the bishop *must* retreat from the knight in this sequence: if instead 9 0-0 then 9...♕h4! – forcing White to weaken his dark squares further by

threatening mate on h2 – 10 h3
♘xe3 11 fxe3 is a positional
disaster for White: Black's dark-
squared bishop has no rival and will
become dominant after say 11...
♗h6.

8   ...   ♘d7

Ivanchuk clears the way for the
pawn advance f7-f5: this method of
generating counterplay is one of the
most important strategical themes in
the King's Indian set up. Of course,
in this specific instance Black will
have to defend f5 again or White
would simply capture the pawn: this
can be done most efficiently with
0-0 bringing the rook to the f8
square.

9   ♗e3

White slots the bishop into a
perfect gap in his pawn structure
and is ready to support it with ♕d2.

Now Black could play 9...0-0
planning f7-f5 as outlined above;
this would lead to an unclear and
interesting position. Instead he came
up with a surprise move!

9   ...   ♗h6

Has Ivanchuk made a terrible
blunder?

10   ♕d2!

No, Black doesn't lose a piece as
after 10 ♗xh6 ♕h4+ followed by
11...♕xh6 he regains his bishop. In
this scenario the black queen ends
up sitting on h6 in command of an
excellent diagonal.

Therefore, if the bishops are to be
swapped Seirawan chooses a
method that ensures it is his queen
that benefits rather than the black
queen.

10   ...   ♗xe3

The only consistent move as now
the bishop was attacking twice.

11   ♕xe3

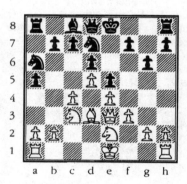

The white queen takes over
residence on e3 from the bishop.
Black's idea in exchanging bishops
was that all the white pawns in the
centre are on light squares, and the
bishop on d3 is little more than a big
pawn, as it can't attack anything;
therefore White is going to start
suffering from a dark square
sickness.

On the other hand, by exchanging
bishops Black has left holes in his
own position on f6, g7 and h6: the

dark squares in the vicinity of his king are looking underdefended. This means that his king is a potential target.

Overall Ivanchuk's decision therefore looks risky. Nevertheless, it creates an imbalanced position and Seirawan will have to play with accuracy, courage. and imagination to come out on top.

11   ...   c6

A very tempting move which opens up the b6 square for the black queen. Nevertheless, in view of White's strong reply Seirawan has suggested 11...♕h4+ 12 g3 ♕e7 13 h4 ♘dc5 as a better approach for Black – his queen should stay on e7 to aid the defence rather than go off hunting counterplay on the queenside.

Firstly, if 12 0-0? Black can exchange queens with 12...♕b6! when he will no longer have to worry about his vulnerable king and can exploit White's weak dark squares at his leisure.

Secondly, very natural was 12 0-0-0? which develops the rook and puts the king in an apparently safer position. Not so: there are more dangers to the white king on the queenside than on e1, where it is safely out of the range of the black knights. Black could reply 12...♘ac5 followed by a5-a4, etc. with an attack of his own.

In spurning these obvious moves Seirawan demonstrates a wonderful feel for the true needs of the position.

12   ...   ♘dc5

12   ♕h6!!

Like a menacing eagle, the white queen swoops into one of the dark square holes and prevents Black from castling.

Actually, this is a brilliant positional move as White avoids two errors that a routine player might well have fallen into.

Black continues his counterattack, but his kingside is losing the services of a powerful defender in the shape of the knight. If for example White had tried to attack down the f file with f3-f4 then after the pawn exchange e5xf4 and the recapture ♖xf4 the way would be clear for ♘e5, when the knight would be dominant. Therefore it was better to employ the other knight with 12...♘ac5.

13   ♖d1!

Again Seirawan avoids castling queenside. Here is a tragi-comedy that might have happened after 13 0-0-0: 13...♘b4 14 ♗b1 a4 15 a3?? – preventing the dangerous advance 15...a3, but 15...♘b3 is mate!

13   ...   ♛b6

Once you have decided on an incorrect plan it is very difficult to give it up and submit to passive defence. Nevertheless this is what Black should have done with 13...♛e7: the queen is needed to hold things together on the kingside.

14   ♗b1!

The bishop moves out of the way so that 14...♛xb2 can be answered by 15 dxc6 bxc6 16 ♖xd6 when Black is crumbling on the dark squares – the immediate threat is 17 ♛g7.

14   ...   ♚e7

It is ominous for Black's position that his king has to be pressed into service defending d6 but if instead 14...♗d7 15 dxc6 ♛xc6 16 ♘b5! attacking d6 is lethal, for example 16...0-0-0 17 ♖xd6 traps the black queen. Now at least 15 dxc6 can be answered by 15...bxc6 keeping control of the b5 and d5 squares.

15   f4!

At last the moment is ripe for a winning breakthrough in the centre.

15   ...   exf4

Black's centre crumbles as if 15...f6 16 ♛g7+ while otherwise the threat of 16 fxe5 dxe5 17 d6+ is intolerable.

16   ♖f1!

Rather than immediately recapture White brings his final reinforcements into the battle. This is the best, most flexible approach as the f4 pawn is indefensible.

White has been able to develop all his pieces to good, active squares without needing to castle. Meanwhile his king has been perfectly safe on e1.

16   ...   ♖f8

Meanwhile Black is hopelessly outgunned where it matters – in the centre. He has a rook on a8 and a knight on a6 completely out of the game, whilst his queen is barely in touch with events in the centre. Meanwhile White has both rooks and his queen in the thick of things. You don't need to be a Grandmaster to know something has gone horribly wrong for Black here. And it all began with the inspired 12 ♛h6!

17   ♛xf4

The queen returns to the centre to support the advance 18 e5 or give a check on f6.

17   ...   f6

This deals with White's two threats outlined above, but when a player has such an overwhelming advantage in firepower it is impossible to find a defence, no matter how ingenious, that doesn't buckle at some point or another.

18   dxc6

Sure enough, a collapse occurs along the d file. Now Black faces the double threat of 19 ♘d5+ winning the queen and 19 ♕xd6+.

18   ...   ♕xc6

He has to defend d6 but now the white knight on c3 has a dream square on d5...

19   ♘d4

...and the other knight reaches almost as fine a square with gain of time.

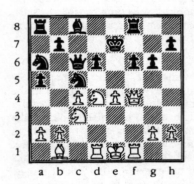

19   ...   ♕e8

A thoroughly ignominious retreat for a black queen. She has to hide behind her king as she would be lost to a fork on b6 or c7, whilst 19...♕d7 20 ♘d5+ ♔d8 21 ♘b6 costs a rook.

20   ♘d5+

The knight has been rooted on c3 since move three, so this is a great reward for patience.

20   ...   ♔d8

It has taken a lot of misplaced ingenuity to get the black queen and king to swap their starting squares.

21   ♕xd6+

The final collapse of Black's hold on the dark squares.

21   ...   ♗d7

Or 21...♘d7 22 ♘e6+.

22   ♘b5

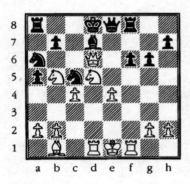

1-0

Ivanchuk resigned because the threat is 23 ♕b6+ ♔c8 24 ♘d6+ winning the black queen and if 22...♘xe4 23 ♗xe4 ♕xe4+ 24 ♔f2 ♕h4+ 25 ♔g1 Black has run out of checks leaving him defenceless against all the threats – 26 ♕xf8+, 26 ♘xf6, 26 ♘b6 or 26 ♕b6+, to name but four!

A wonderful positional display from Seirawan.

Game Twenty-Two
V.Korchnoi - G.Kasparov
Amsterdam 1991
King's Indian Defence

1   ♘f3

The most flexible move in the opening. As will be seen, Korchnoi is happy to take on Kasparov in the King's Indian, but is keen to avoid the Grunfeld as would occur after 1 d4 ♘f6 2 c4 g6 3 ♘c3 d5. With a bit of jiggery pokery with his move order he manages to get the opening line he wants.

1   ...   ♘f6

Black also keeps his options open with this first rate developing move. The knight will be excellent on f6 whether Black decides to swamp the centre with pawns later on or tries to control the centre with his pieces whilst holding back his foot soldiers.

2   c4

White begins to show his cards. This is evidently the first stage in the construction of a pawn centre stretching all the way from c4 to e4.

2   ...   g6

The defining moment in the opening. Black had two other options:

Contest White's plan to build a pawn centre with 2...c5. If then 3 d4 cxd4 4 ♘xd4 White has a shade more space in the centre which grants him a slight advantage, but he hasn't got a complete pawn centre.

Let White have his centre, but restrain its dynamism by blocking it. This can be done with 2...e6 followed by 3...d5. Black then has a very secure set up in the centre.

In the game Kasparov chooses a third option that is in keeping with his dynamic style: he lets White build his pawn centre unopposed as he intends to break it down with pressure from the wings. The first step in this plan is putting the bishop on g7, where it will aim at the d4 square.

3   ♘c3

Here the knight is on an ideal square to support a large pawn centre.

3   ...   ♗g7

For an ambitious player it can be deeply frustrating to be on the black side of a protracted positional struggle, as often occurs in the Queen's Gambit. The fianchetto on g7 indicates the desire to play a lively fighting game.

4   e4

If 4 d4 then 4...d5 is the Grunfeld Defence. By first advancing the pawn to e4 Korchnoi manages to build a broad pawn centre whilst ruling out this opening. Evidently that day the veteran Russian maestro was keen to take on the World Champion in a King's Indian.

4   ...   d6

The situation in the centre gradually unfolds. Black prevents any further expansion by his opponent with e4-e5 and forms the base of a pawn chain of his own.

5   d4

Now White has achieved everything that classical chess demands from the opening: he has both his knights on safe and active centre squares and an imposing pawn centre, behind which he can mobilize his other pieces.

5   ...   0-0

Whatever a player of the 19th century might have thought about Black's apparently inert approach to the centre so far, he couldn't have accused him of neglecting his development: after only five moves he has mobilized his kingside and castled.

6   ♗e2

White also prepares to castle. This is superior to 6 ♗d3 as the bishop on e2 takes the sting out of any pin with ♗g4 and the queen is able to maintain a protective eye on the d4 pawn.

6   ...   e5

At last Kasparov makes a challenge to the white centre. It is too late to prevent White maintaining a space advantage, but the black pieces get enough room to allow them to organize counterplay.

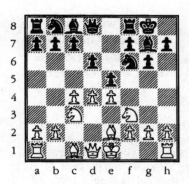

7   0-0

White would get into hot water if he tried to steal a pawn from right in front of the 'demon' bishop on g7: 7 dxe5 dxe5 8 ♕xd8 ♖xd8 9 ♘xe5?! – the restrained 9 ♗g5 offered some chances of a slight edge – 9...♘xe4! 10 ♘xe4 ♗xe5 and Black has regained his pawn with a pleasant game thanks to his liberated dark square bishop. Even worse would befall White if he tried 10 ♘xf7?? in this sequence, so that he has sold his knight as dearly as possible after 10...♔xf7? 11 ♘xe4, as Black also has a zwischenzug: 10...♗xc3+! 11 bxc3 ♔xf7 with an extra piece for Black.

Therefore Korchnoi simply castled.

7   ...   ♘c6

Black develops his knight and goads the white pawn forwards to d5, after which the centre becomes closed.

You might be wondering why Black didn't take the chance to break up White's pawn centre with 7...exd4. Such an idea is possible: indeed, when the King's Indian was first developed in the 1950s by David Bronstein and others it was usual to see a sequence such as 7...♘bd7 8 ♖e1 exd4 9 ♘xd4. The pawn barrier to the bishop on g7 is removed, and the e4 pawn can be targeted with ♘c5 and ♖e8, etc.

However, as the years went by and the King's Indian was scrutinized ever more deeply, an audacious alternative for Black was discovered to playing in the centre. Basically, Black keeps the pawn on e5 as the supporting pillar of an all out assault on the kingside beginning with f7-f5 and possibly culminating in the advance of all Black's kingside pawns. At first such a strategy seems reckless, as the white kingside is well defended and White's own attack on the queenside seems to flow much more easily; but years of trial and error have shaped Black's plan into a dangerous counterattacking system.

doomed to failure if White could counter-punch in the centre. Korchnoi is happy to oblige by closing the centre, as throughout his long career he has never been impressed by the King's Indian: he has triumphed many times with the white pieces by crushing the black offensive on the kingside and staging a breakthrough of his own on the queenside.

8   ...   ♘e7

This looks like a dismal location for a self-respecting knight, despite being a centre square, as it is now boxed in, with no safe move. It is true that a knight on e7 is often poorly placed in the King's Indian, but there was no better move, as retreating back to b8 would waste too much time. As will be seen, Kasparov plans to activate the knight on the g6 square once his kingside attack is under way.

9   ♘e1!

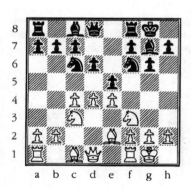

8   d5

By advancing the pawn to d5 White ensures that he keeps his centre pawn chain intact. Black's strategy outlined above depends on the centre being blocked, or at least stable, as a kingside attack would be

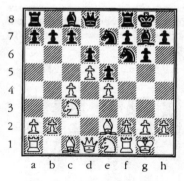

It looks distinctly odd to move the knight backwards, but even the strangest looking move can be valuable – or even essential – if it is part of a well thought out strategy.

In fact this is an excellent retreat from both a defensive and

aggressive point of view. In this type of fixed centre, with a white pawn on d5, White has a space advantage on the queenside; therefore his primary goal is to achieve the advance c4-c5 and open up lines of attack for his pieces on that side of the board. The actual implementation of his plan can take many forms, but c4-c5 is always a part of the strategy. Therefore White prepares to manoeuvre his knight to d3 where it can support the key pawn advance.

At the same time, White is anticipating his opponent's forthcoming counter attack on the kingside, which will include the pawn stab at e4 with f7-f5 (after the knight on f6 moves out of the way, of course). Therefore he clears the way for f2-f3 to buttress the e4 pawn. In turn, f2-f3 will clear a useful square for the queen's bishop, as will be seen. A final worthy point about the knight retreat is that Black might have intended ♘h5 to clear the way for f7-f5, followed perhaps by ♘f4; but now 9...♘h5 just loses a pawn to 10 ♗xh5.

9   ...   ♘d7

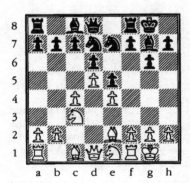

A race is about to begin between rival pawn attacks on the wings, so Kasparov wastes no time in clearing the way for his f pawn. At the same time his knight helps fortify the c5 square to slow down White's advance.

10   ♗e3

The bishop espies the diagonal a7-g1, where he can put pressure on both the a7 pawn and the important c5 square, and defensively speaking can help shield his king from f2 once this square is vacated by f2-f3. He goes there immediately, as the chance would be lost after 10 ♘d3 f5 11 f3 f4 when ♗e3 is prevented.

10   ...   f5

The first belligerent gesture of Kasparov's kingside attack. He plans to partially dismantle White's centre with 11...fxe4 when amongst other things the puny knight on e7 suddenly gains a strong post on f5.

11   f3

Korchnoi ensures that he can recapture on e4 with a pawn and clears f2 for his bishop.

11   ...   f4

Here we see that the decision to put the bishop on e3 was not without drawbacks as Black gains a useful tempo in his pawn charge by attacking it.

12   ♗f2

The bishop retires into the safety of the kingside fortress.

12   ...   g5

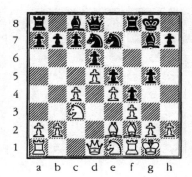

Kasparov would like to disturb the bishop again, this time by advancing a pawn to g3 where it would split open the kingside defences. Note that the black king is in no danger of facing a direct attack, despite its loss of pawn cover, as White's pieces are in no position to mount such an assault. Any danger to the black king is likely to come 'sideways' or diagonally via the queenside, if ever White breaks through there.

13   a4

Korchnoi is satisfied he has done enough to reinforce his kingside and so begins his own pawn raid on the queenside.

13   ...   ♘g6

The knight that was imprisoned on e7 is the first piece to benefit from the space created behind the advancing kingside pawns.

14   ♘d3

Now White is ready to forge ahead with 15 c5. It would make no sense for Black to try to slow his progress with 14...b6 as this just creates a fresh target that can be assaulted with 15 a5 followed by b2-b4 and c4-c5, etc. It is imperative that Black do nothing to aid the white advance.

14   ...   ♘f6

Unable to prevent White gaining ground on the queenside, Kasparov has to trust in the power of his counterattack. On f6 the knight will assist the next stage of his plan: namely the advance g5-g4.

15   c5

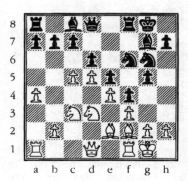

At last White has achieved his strategical objective. The battle has reached a very tense phase: just the loss or gain of one tempo could mean victory or defeat.

15   ...   h5

Meanwhile Black continues to charge forwards with his kingside pawns. Kasparov is in his element in this perilous position. He wants to win every game, even if it entails a lot of risk.

16   h3

White places another obstacle in the way of the g5-g4 advance, but in such a double-edged position every move is open to question. Is the pawn on h3 really a barrier, or is it a convenient hook on which Black can fasten his kingside attack? It was possible to make do without the pawn move, at least temporarily, and continue to press forwards on the queenside with 16 c6 or open lines with 16 cxd6.

16   ...   ♖f7!

Both players have to find the perfect balance between the execution of their own plan and the hindrance of the opponent's aims. Here Kasparov puts his rook on his second rank, where it defends the c7 square in case White decides to open the c file with c5xd6 and after the recapture c7xd6 tries for an invasion down the c file with ♖c1, etc. In such an eventuality it would also be handy that the f8 square had

been vacated so that Black could add to the defence of d6 with ♗f8 if necessary.

From a more positive viewpoint, once the bishop moves from g7 the rook will be ready to swing over to the h file to join the looming attack on the white king.

17   c6

As Black is well prepared for c5xd6 Korchnoi decides on a different plan of action on the queenside.

If now 17...bxc6 then after 18 dxc6 there are light squares in the centre which he can exploit with ♘b4, intending ♘bd5 as well as ♗c4, when the black rook is suddenly pinned against the king.

Of course Black is planning a kingside attack and wants to keep the centre closed, but if 17...b6 then 18 a5 is very strong-already there is the threat to create a passed pawn with 18 axb6 as 18...cxb6 would be forced.

As well as these line opening ideas White has a more insidious threat: 18 ♘b5!! attacking a7 when after 18...a6 (if 18...b6 19 a5! as above) 19 ♘a7 the knight is on a ridiculous square but next move it can be exchanged for Black's light-squared bishop with ♘xc8. This bishop is an essential piece as it is needed to support a break through on the kingside with g5-g4. Therefore under no circumstances should Black allow this exchange to take place.

You will see from the above that White has very real threats and it is only thanks to Kasparov's great play that it appears to be an easy victory for Black: Korchnoi would have beaten most Grandmasters as White from this position.

17   ...   a5!

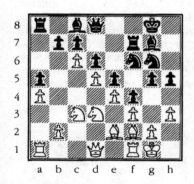

Tony Miles once described playing Kasparov as like facing a thousand eyed monster – indeed Kasparov's eyes are all over the position – queenside, kingside and centre.

One of the unwritten rules of chess is that if there is a battle going on between attacks on opposite wings, then you should avoid pawn moves on your weaker side. But Kasparov knows that such rules are only guides which should never interfere with making the best move. By evacuating the pawn from

a7 and ruling out a4-a5! by White he squashes the plan of 18 ♘b5, as it can be answered by 18...b6 when 19 ♘a7 is no longer possible.

18   cxb7

Korchnoi has to switch to another plan: the creation of a passed pawn. The question will be whether he can exploit it before Black's attack on the kingside becomes overwhelming.

18   ...   ♗xb7

The light-squared bishop is deflected from its role in supporting g5-g4, but it won't be for long.

19   b4

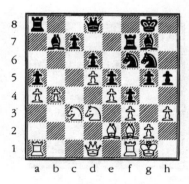

Now things begin to get hot for Black on the queenside as the barrier on a5 is about to crumble. He needs counterplay at all costs or else the newly minted outside passed pawn will win the game for White.

19   ...   ♗c8!

Sometimes a piece is best developed on its starting square! Black needs the bishop back on c8 to add vital oomph to his kingside assault. If the World Champion isn't afraid to look silly by retreating his pieces then neither should we be fussy: the key thing is to play the best moves and win.

Note that Kasparov has been doing his best to prevent White from exploiting the hole on c6 with ♘b4 and ♘c6 both with 17...a5 and here by avoiding 19...axb4 20 ♘xb4 when after 20...♗c8 21 ♘c6 the white knight is excellently placed.

20   bxa5

The passed pawn appears. Now Black does best to leave well alone on a5 as if 20...♖xa5 21 ♘b4 threatens to win a whole rook with 22 ♘c6.

20   ...   ♗h6

The situation on the queenside is dire for Black whether or not he is a pawn down, so all his efforts have to go into a do or die mission on the kingside. To this end he clears the way for his rook to swing over either to g7 or to h7, in either case to support a frontal attack on the white king. Once the g5-g4 advance has occurred the bishop will be able to edge forwards to h4 via g5 and offer its exchange for White's dark-squared bishop: his best defensive piece.

21   ♘b4

At last the knight is on its way to c6 but it will soon become clear that this manoeuvre is too insipid – White needs to play very energetically to distract Black from his kingside onslaught. This can be done with 21 a6! – a move that Black would be unwise to ignore in the style of the game with 21...g4 as after 22 fxg4 hxg4 23 hxg4 there is as yet no strong blow on the kingside and meanwhile White threatens 24 a7 when the passed pawn is defended and can be shepherded to a8 after ♖b1 and ♖b8. So instead he should prefer 21...♗xa6 when 22 ♘b4! (only now) 22...♗c8 23 a5 is unclear. Note that Black wants to keep his bishop for the attack and so avoids the exchange on e2. Black still has his potential attack against the white king, but the well supported passed pawn isn't to be underestimated.

21   ...   g4!

Here is the long trumpeted pawn advance. Black gives up a pawn to clear the lines for his pieces.

22   ♘c6

The knight takes up an excellent post with gain of time by attacking the black queen. Nevertheless, all White's queenside trumps will mean nothing if he is mated on the kingside.

22 ... ♛f8

The black queen is actually happy to be chased to f8 as she can join in the onslaught on the h file once the h6 square is vacated for her by the bishop.

23 fxg4

Of course he cannot ignore the g4 pawn as allowing 23...hxg3 smashing his kingside would be intolerable.

Normally capturing towards the centre is recommended, but White must capture this way to get his bishop on e2 involved in the defence. If 23 hxg4 Black can decline to recapture and simply play 23...♝g5! when after 24 gxh5 ♘xh5 he can win quickly with a build up such as ♛h6, ♜h7 and ♘g3.

23 ... hxg4

Black recaptures and menaces the h3 pawn.

24 hxg4

There is little choice as the defences on the h file collapse after 24 h4 g3 25 ♝e1 ♘xh4.

24 ... ♝g5!

The bishop makes way for the queen and rook to infiltrate along the h file. It is also well placed in its own right to pierce the enemy defences via h4.

25 ♝f3

Things have grown so alarming on the h file that Korchnoi clears the e2 square in the hope that his king might eventually be able to flee there.

25 ... ♛h6

The arrival of the black queen on h6 is a dreadful omen for the white king. Now he is already in danger of being struck down by 26...♜h7 and 27...♛h1 mate.

26 ♜e1

The rook vacates f1 as a possible escape hatch for the white king.

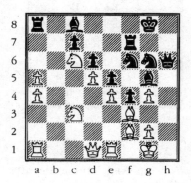

26 ... ♘h4!

Only thus. It was tempting to offer the exchange of dark-squared bishops with 26...♗h4, but as Kasparov points out in *Informator* this allows the white king to escape into the comparative safety of the centre after 27 ♔f1 ♗xf2 28 ♔xf2 ♘xg4+ 29 ♔e2! (but not 29 ♗xg4? ♕h4+ 30 ♔e2 ♗xg4+ and White drops his queen.

27   ♗xh4

Positionally speaking it is horrible to give up the dark-squared bishop, but Black intended 27...♖h7 followed by taking on f3 with check and then mating on h1.

If the king tries to slip out now with 27 ♔f1 then Kasparov intended 27...♘xf3 28 gxf3 ♗xg4! – a purely temporary sacrifice – 29 fxg4 ♕h3+ 30 ♔e2 ♕xc3, when with e4 and g4 both hanging the centre has ceased to be a refuge for the king.

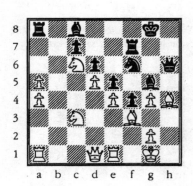

27   ...   ♗xh4!

The white king runs again after 27...♕xh4 28 ♔f1 ♘xg4 29 ♔e2.

28   g5

A despairing move, but if 28 ♔f1 Black has the pleasant choice between continuing his attack or simply 28...♗xe1 winning the exchange.

28   ...   ♕xg5

The black queen has been distracted from the h file, but it is only temporary, as White has nothing constructive to do. In fact it could be said that it isn't the weaknesses on the kingside that have destroyed White – these were in fact inevitable – but rather his complete lack of counterplay on the queenside.

29   ♖e2

Putting his pieces on light squares won't save White as the dark squares around his king are fatally weak.

29   ...   ♘g4

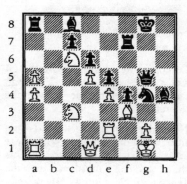

One by one the black pieces move in for the kill. Now Black has a rook, knight, two bishops and his queen all awaiting the order to mate the white king. In contrast, only the white bishop on f3 is performing any noticeable role in resisting the attack: the white knights are way too far off. The white queen and the rooks would like to help, but there is simply no means to get them over to the h file.

30   ♖b1

Such moves are futile here, but White's position is already way beyond hope. On the queenside he stands excellently, but there is about to be a fearful massacre on the other wing.

31   ...   ♗g3

The bishop steps nimbly aside to open the h file for Black's queen and rooks.

31   ♕d3

There was no longer any way for White to mend the holes in his position. Black has control of all the important dark squares on the kingside: as well as h4, g3 and h2, which are in his uncontested possession, he has deadly influence over e3 and f2. It is no wonder that he can finish the struggle with his next move.

31   ...   ♕h4

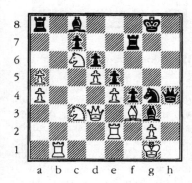

White can only avert mate in two with 32...♕h2+ 33 ♔f1 ♕h1 by vacating the e2 square, but after 32 ♖eb2 there follows 32...♘e3 cutting

off the white king's flight to f1. Then unless White gives up his queen with 33 ♕xe3 it will be mate on h2.

Therefore Korchnoi simply resigned.

Game Twenty-Three
A.Karpov - G.Kasparov
World Championship,
London/Leningrad 1986
Grunfeld Defence

1   d4!

A case of know thy enemy. The debate over whether 1 e4 and 1 d4 is the best opening move will go on for as long as chess is played, but here pushing the d pawn gets the nod: in their World Championship matches Karpov made many fruitless attempts to beat Kasparov in the Sicilian Defence, until finally out of exasperation he switched to 1 d4.

1   ...   ♘f6

If there was a prize for flexibility this would win it. It keeps White guessing as play can transpose to virtually any opening system: the only significant idea prevented is the Dutch Defence which requires 1...f5.

2   c4

Just so: it is White's privilege and duty to try to exploit the advantage of the first move by marching his pawns into the centre. Much less effective would be 2 ♘c3 as after 2...d5 White is lacking his main idea: pressure on d5 with c2-c4 as his own knight is in the way.

2	...	g6

Kasparov begins to reveal his hand. The power of the kingside fianchetto first became widely understood in the 1940s and 1950s. It was a wonderful discovery that reinvigorated chess as it has since become Black's best weapon against 1 d4.

3	♘c3	

Now that his pawn is on c4, White strengthens his hold on d5.

3	...	d5

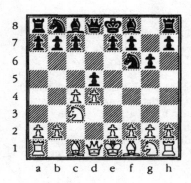

This immediate challenge to the white centre constitutes the Grunfeld Defence. In contrast to the King's Indian Defence Black doesn't allow his opponent to build a pawn centre undisturbed after 3...♗g7 4 e4.

4	♗f4	

Karpov refuses to be drawn into the mainline with 4 cxd5 ♘xd5 5 e4 ♘xc3 6 bxc3. Karpov and Kasparov have contested many games from that position, but here the 12th World Champion decided to try a less ambitious approach that involves straightforward develop-

ment. Therefore he gets the bishop out to a good centre square before he plays e2-e3, when it would be shut in.

4	...	♗g7

All according to plan. The placement of the bishop on g7 signifies that Kasparov intends to attack the white centre.

5	e3	

Safety first: this little pawn move clears the way for the development of the king's bishop and strengthens the d4 pawn in anticipation of Black's next move.

5	...	c5

Black does everything possible to empower his bishop on g7 as it is the key piece in his opening strategy. He therefore attacks the d4 pawn in similar vein to White's assault on d5 in the Queen's Gambit after 1 d4 d5 2 c4. He reasons that firstly, if White ignores the challenge then c5xd4 will soften up the d4 point; and secondly, if d4xc5 then sooner or later he will regain his pawn, when the bishop is free of the barrier on d4.

6	dxc5	

Karpov snatches the material, after which a tense tactical battle begins: the question is whether Black will get back his pawn with a good game, or will suffer punishment for playing too actively at the start of the game.

6 ... ♛a5

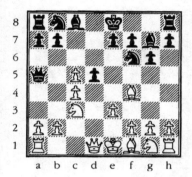

The only way to continue the counterattack is to put further pressure on c3 with the queen. Now the threat is 7...♘e4! when the power of the queen, bishop and knight all converge on the pinned white knight.

7 ♖c1

Simple and safe: White bolsters the knight against the coming attack.

It was tempting to capture on d5, when the following sharp forcing variation is possible: 7 cxd5 ♘xd5! 8 ♛xd5 ♗xc3+ 9 bxc3 ♛xc3+ 10 ♔e2 ♛xa1. It looks like Black is winning, but 11 ♗e5! unexpectedly forks the black queen and rook. However, Black has at least a quick draw if he wants it with 11...♛c1 12 ♗xh8 ♗e6! 13 ♛xb7 – if he doesn't attack the rook then 13...♗c4+ will pick up his bishop – 13...♛c2+ and

now after 14 ♔e1 ♛c1+ the game ends in perpetual check. Here 14 ♔f3 is just an unnecessary risk, as 14...♛f5+ forces the king back to e2, or else Black checks on g5 and h5 as appropriate. As back on move 14 Black can also play to win with the sharp 11...♛b1, it is clear White does best to avoid this. A draw against Kasparov might not be too bad a result for you or me, but not for Karpov with the precious White pieces in game 5 of a World Championship match.

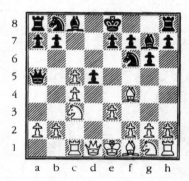

7 ... ♘e4

Kasparov presses on eagerly with his attack on c3. Once bitten is twice shy, and in games 9 and 11 of the same match he settled for the less ambitious 7...dxc4 8 ♗xc4 0-0 (the c5 pawn won't run away) 9 ♘f3 ♛xc5 10 ♗b3 ♘c6 11 0-0 ♛a5. The disappearance of the centre pawns and balanced pawn structure make it look drawish, but White has a continuing small plus as he has a rook already in play on c1 whilst Black's queen's bishop is as yet undeveloped. That is the way it is in the middlegame, if White has played the opening correctly: the advantage of the first move continues to make itself felt, whether in giving him the slight initiative in a quiet looking position or in the superior chances in a tactical melee. Kasparov held the draw in the other two games, though not without enduring some tricky moments in the second of them.

8   cxd5

Karpov decides it is the right moment to accept the booty. Remember Steinitz's motto that a pawn ahead is worth a little trouble? Well now White has two extra centre pawns, so Kasparov had better have some serious trouble lined up for him!

8   ...   ♘xc3

The only way to disrupt White's game as giving up the bishop would make no sense: 8...♗xc3+? 9 bxc3 ♘xc3?? 10 ♕d2 and already Black can resign. This variation gives us a useful clue as to the best reply for White to the game move.

9   ♕d2!

Exactly! The knight can't run away as it is pinned, so this is much better than the automatic 9 bxc3 when 9...♗xc3+, forcing 10 ♔e2, is excellent for Black.

9   ...   ♕xa2

Black has little choice but to snatch back some material. This is the most disruptive way to do it as 9...♕xc5 10 bxc3 leaves White with a far more solid pawn structure.

10   bxc3

Only now does White regain his piece.

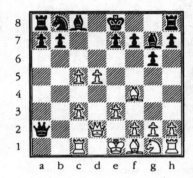

10   ...   ♕xd2+

The plan behind this exchange is interesting, ambitious, very hard for the opponent to answer properly ...and wrong.

Instead 10...♕a5 would allow Black to restore material equality after say 11 ♘f3 ♘d7 12 ♗c4 ♕xc5 13 ♗a2, but White's extra centre pawn would still give him the preferable chances as he can castle and then prepare the advance e3-e4-e5, etc. Still, with precise play this would have been far preferable to the debacle Black suffers in the present game.

Incidentally the opening line with 7...♘e4 is something of a graveyard for great players, as it was here in 1971 that the great Bobby Fischer's famous run of 14 consecutive wins came to an end against Petrosian in the 10...♛a5 variation above.

11 ♔xd2

Kasparov's idea is that the exchange of queens has forced the white king to a square where he is a potential target as well as interfering with White's own plans for centre expansion. As for the c5 pawn, well that can be regained later as it is too sickly to defend!

11 ... ♘d7

Already Black intends 11...♘xc5, when the white king is harassed with the threat of 12...♘b3+ winning the exchange or 12...♘e4+. If 12 c6 bxc6 13 dxc6 ♘c5 looks horrible for White as the c6 pawn is doomed in any case.

12 ♗b5!

Karpov prepares to eliminate the knight. Tarrasch condemned giving up a bishop for a knight as 'losing the minor exchange'. However, every position has to be judged on its specific merits and here the knight would have been so menacing after 12...♘xc5 that it is well worth 'sacrificing' the bishop for it. It should be noted that the

transaction is part of a plan by Karpov to remove the energy from Black's position by restricting his bishops, and isn't just a small minded attempt to hold onto the c5 pawn for as long as possible: if that were the case then Tarrasch would be right!

12 ... 0-0

Black breaks the pin, develops his king's rook and forces White's hand over the capture on d7.

13 ♗xd7

There is no turning back – the knight has to be removed before it causes havoc with 13...♘xc5.

13 ... ♗xd7

At a superficial level things don't look at all bad for Black – he has the two bishops, an outside passed pawn on a7 and can regain his pawn sooner or later with ♖c8 and ♖xc5.

14 e4!

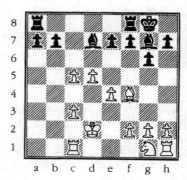

Nonetheless, Karpov has a great asset in his massive clump of centre pawns. He has judged correctly that they can be used to shut in at least one of the enemy bishops, besides creating a passed pawn. It took a lot of imagination and courage, besides strategical skill, for Karpov to play like this. After all, he would have been aware that Kasparov, the greatest theoretician of all time, must have analyzed this variation at home before the game and reached the conclusion that Black can break any bonds that White tries to impose on him and emerge with at least an equal game. To prove the 13th World Champion wrong in a theoretical duel is no mean achievement!

14   ...   f5

If immediately 14...♖fc8 then 15 ♗e3 holds onto the pawn.

15   e5

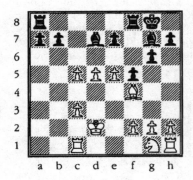

Now White's plan begins to take shape as the e5 pawn encloses the bishop on g7. However, it still looks as though White's centre might crumble away under the pressure from Black's pieces.

15   ...   e6

Kasparov gives the edifice of pawns another shake in the hope that it will collapse. If now 16 d6 then 16...♖dc8 intending ♖xc5, ♗c6 etc. would be terrible for White. He couldn't even answer 17 ♗e3 as 17...♗xe5 would bring the king's bishop to life – that is why Kasparov cajoled him into 15 e5.

16   c4!

Fortunately there is one more supporting column available for the d5 pawn.

16   ...   ♖fc8

At last Black is ready to regain his pawn with 17...♖xc5, when his rook will put intolerable pressure on both d5 and c4 – strengthened as necessary with ♖ac8. In that case White's centre would disintegrate, his entire opening strategy would be proved wrong and he would be struggling for a draw. But Karpov has other ideas!

17   c6!!

The pawn is doomed anyway so Karpov gives it up in the most disagreeable way for his opponent.

17   ...   bxc6

Of course Black must regain his pawn, but it is a far poorer meal than he had hoped for.

18   d6

Now we can see the damage inflicted on Black's position by 17 c6!

♦ his queenside pawns are split

♦ the bishop on d7 is blocked in

♦ the rook on c8 can no longer attack c4 or d5.

18 ... c5

Having been frustrated in his bid to dismantle the white centre, Kasparov tries to restore some energy to his position by reopening a diagonal for his bishop on d7. However, it is at a serious cost as not only is the pawn terribly weak on c5 but even worse the bishop on g7 becomes permanently entombed. It was essential to activate the other bishop with 18...g5! 19 ♗xg5 ♗xe5, even though after 20 c5 White firmly protects his passed pawn and leaves the black queen's bishop shut in on d7.

19 h4!

Karpov isn't going to let the bishop on g7 see any daylight! He hinders Black's plan of breaking out by g6-g5 by putting an extra guard on the g5 square.

19 ... h6

Hope springs eternal. Kasparov reintroduces the freeing idea: 20...g5 21 hxg5 hxg5 22 ♗xg5 ♗xe5.

20 ♘h3!!

White wants to achieve two positional ends:

♦ firstly, to keep the bishop on g7 under lock and key by maintaining a firm grip on g5

♦ secondly, to attack and win the c5 pawn by putting the knight on d3 and his bishop on e3.

The natural move was 20 ♘f3, which controls g5 and prepares to win the c5 pawn with ♘e1, ♘d3 and ♗e3. Unfortunately for White after 20 ♘f3 Black can respond 20...♗c6! when 21 ♘e1, planning ♘d3, allows the familiar break out with 21...g5, whilst otherwise Black can take the knight with 21...♗xf3, when again White's hold on the g5 square is broken and g6-g5 follows.

So after the alternative 20 ♘f3 White's two aims – keeping control of g5 and playing ♘d3 and ♗e3 – would be mutually incompatible.

But we shall soon see that things are very different after Karpov's brilliant decision to put the knight on h3, which at first glance appears an inferior square to f3.

Whereas we can play 2 ♘f3 or 3 ♘f3 in the opening phase and justify it as a natural developing move, once the middlegame has begun every move has to be judged according to whether it fits in with a player's plan, and not whether it 'looks right'.

20   ...   a5

Black utilizes his passed pawn without any delay as it is his best chance to save the game. It isn't yet time to despair as White's knight is a long way from d3, and if it ever heads there then he has the by now familiar g6-g5! freeing move.

21   f3!

Nonetheless Karpov prepares the way for his knight to reach d3.

21   ...   a4

The passed pawn continues its headlong rush in an attempt to distract White from his logical plan.

22   ♖he1!

But this simple move dashes all Black's hopes as by defending e5

with his rook Karpov rules out ♗xe5, and so renders the idea of g6-g5 useless. This means that his knight is freed from the necessity of guarding g5 and so can head off for d3.

This essential intermediate move would have been impossible if White had chosen ♘f3 and ♘e1 instead of the brilliant 20 ♘h3!!

22   ...   a3

The advance continues, but it is rather forlorn now that the pawn can never hope for any help from the bishop on g7.

23   ♘f2

The knight continues steadfastly on his journey.

23   ...   a2

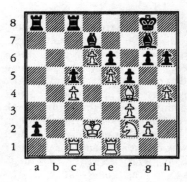

So near and yet so far. White is winning rather than losing for one reason only – he has restrained the black bishop on g7.

Try a little experiment: remove the white pawn from e5 and the black pawn from e6. Now you will see that Black is suddenly winning, as the bishop on g7 controls the queening square of the passed pawn. The pawn threatens to advance at once, and useless is 1 ♗e5 ♗xe5 2 ♖xe5 a1=♕, so White would have to give up the exchange immediately with 1 ♖a1 ♗xa1 2 ♖xa1 with a hopeless position.

Now let's go back to the game, with pawns on e6 and e5. The passed pawn still makes an impressive visual picture on a2 where it is tantalizingly close to queening, but without the support of the bishop it is a weakness rather than a strength.

Chess strategy is as much about preventing your opponent's pieces functioning properly as improving the action of your own pieces.

24   ♘d3

The culmination of a splendid manoeuvre than began with 20 ♘h3. Here the knight

♦ defends b2 against any invasion by ♖b8 and ♖b2+

♦ attacks c5 in preparation of ♗e3 and ♘xc5

♦ guards e5 again so that ♗e3 won't allow ♗xe5

♦ is available for operations against the a2 pawn.

24   ...   ♖a3

Kasparov strains his utmost to generate counterplay by setting a devilish trap.

25   ♖a1!

Safety first: if 25 ♗e3 Black can break out of the bind with 25...♖xd3+! 26 ♔xd3 ♗xe5.

Karpov decides to keep ♗e3 as a latent threat to hamper the black pieces, as a simpler winning plan has emerged: he will attack and capture the impetuous passed pawn.

25   ...   g5

Rather than await a slow death Black makes a desperate lunge.

26   hxg5

The bind on the g5 square does its duty.

26   ...   hxg5

Black has to recapture and hope that deflecting the bishop from the defence of e5 gives him some counterplay.

27   ♗xg5

The first material gain for Karpov's well executed strategy.

27   ...   ♔f7

This rather purposeless move is an admission that his attempt at a break out was all bluff. Still, as will be seen Kasparov still has one or two tactical tricks up his sleeve which might have fooled a less wary opponent.

28   ♗f4

Karpov is in no hurry to exploit his advantage. After all, if he is vigilant Black can do nothing, so why should he be in any rush?

Therefore first of all he restores the absolute bind on the e5 square.

28   ...   ♖b8

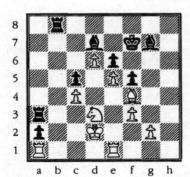

If White is now tempted by 29 ♘xc5? then Black escapes with 29...♖b2+ 30 ♔c1 ♖xg2! when it is perpetual check after 31 ♘xd7 ♖c3+ 32 ♔d1 ♖d3+ 33 ♔c1 ♖c3+ etc.

29   ♖ec1!

Karpov however isn't to be distracted from his methodical strategy. The basic idea is to feast on the passed pawn with ♖c2, ♘c1 and then either rook takes on a2. To add to Black's woes 30 ♘xc5 ♖b2+ 31 ♖c2 is also on the cards.

29   ...   ♗c6

This is the last attempt to create some confusion after 30 ♘xc5 ♗xf3!? 31 gxf3 ♖xf3.

30   ♖c3!

...but once again Karpov refuses to give his opponent even the ghost of counterplay. The rook is forced to give up its vantage point on a3 as the exchange of rooks after 30...♖xc3 31 ♔xc3 or 30...♖b1 31 ♖xa3 ♖xa1 32 ♘c2, winning the a2 pawn, is entirely hopeless for Black.

30   ...   ♖a5

Black's activity fades as the rook is reduced to defensive duty of a2 and c5.

31   ♖c2

Having ousted the rook from a3 Karpov turns his attention to his real target – the a2 pawn.

31   ...   ♖ba8

Now the other black rook is compelled into a passive role.

32   ♘c1   1-0

There is now no answer to the threat of 32 ♖cxa2, when White has two extra pawns and can target a third pawn on c5. Therefore it is no surprise that Black gave up.

A beautiful display of preventive chess from Karpov. The knight on c1 did a lot of work in this game, but the real star of the show was the pawn on e5. There are few pawns that have succeeded in so effectively holding Kasparov's army at bay!

The Big Three

Three players have dominated the chess rating list since the late 1990s – Anand, Kramnik and Kasparov. Indeed at the time of writing (2004) Kasparov has been top of the rating list for 20 years!

Their dominance can be compared to that of the big three of the 1920s and early 1930s: Lasker, Capablanca and Alekhine.

Kramnik has a style akin to that of Capablanca: he excells in semi simplified positions – especially in heavyweight middlegames without queens. Suffice to say that once the queens are exchanged Kramnik is well nigh invincible, as he proved in wresting the crown from Kasparov in 2000.

Anand's style is like that of Lasker: an arch tactician who shows amazing resourcefulness, especially in defence. Anand has beaten Kasparov twice with Black by defeating impetuous attacks. It is seldom a good idea to sacrifice material against Anand: he won't be mated and you won't get the material back!

Kasparov's advantage in theoretical preparation can be compared to that of Alekhine, who in his day was streets ahead of his opponents in the openings. They both play aggressive mainlines and are willing to take risks with Black: gradually outplaying the opponent with Black isn't to their taste. In Game Eight we see Kasparov winning thanks to his superior opening preparation: Anand had no chance to show his tenacity.

Here we see an example of Kramnik's clinical positional play once the queens have been exchanged.

Game Twenty-Four
V.Kramnik - L.Van Wely
Wijk aan Zee 2001
Grunfeld Defence

1   d4

Two small steps for a pawn, but a giant leap for White's strategy! This is an excellent move that shows Kramnik means business:

♦ the c5 and e5 squares are controlled

♦ the queen's bishop and queen are released

♦ the d4 pawn is a stronghold in the centre – and defended!

1   ...   ♘f6

It can be deduced logically that this is the best move as follows:

There were three ways to prevent White achieving the goal of his opening, which is the establishment a pawn centre with 2 e4

Firstly, 1...d5 which helps Black's development but leaves the pawn open to attack with 2 c4;

Secondly 1...f5 which leaves no pawn as a target, but does little for Black's development;

And thirdly, the game move 1...♘f6 which not only develops a piece but doesn't leave any pawn open to attack.

2   c4

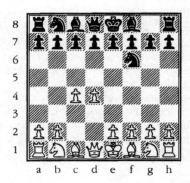

'The d and e pawns are the only pawns that should be moved in the early part of the game' wrote Steinitz. A noble exception to this rule is the c pawn: thwarted in his plan to seize the e4 square, White finds another way to enlarge his pawn centre and control d5.

2   ...   g6

Should you aim for safety or counterattack with Black? This is a crucial question as a player must always try to choose openings that suit his or her style.

If you want to challenge your opponent in a tough positional battle, without giving an inch, then play openings in which the main theme is restraint.

Here the move 2...e6 would suit that method of play, so that if 3 ♘c3 Black can choose between 3...d5 – the Queen's Gambit – and 3...♗b4, the Nimzo-Indian Defence. The first of these options restrains White by refusing to allow him a space advantage; the second restrains him by pinning his knight and not falling behind in development.

In either case, Black would be solidly placed though still slightly worse: there is less danger facing him than after 2...g6 but also less opportunity for aggressive action.

In contrast, the Dutchman Van Wely has a vigorous style of play and so is willing to concede space and time in order to arrange a counterattack against d4 with a kingside fianchetto. This is a dynamic, enterprising but also risky approach – especially when facing a player such as Kramnik!

3   ♘c3

This move is all the better for being delayed: the knight has been wise enough to let the pawn go to c4 before taking up its regulation post in the centre.

3   ...   d5

Van Wely takes the fight immediately to his opponent with the Grunfeld Defence.

4   cxd5

As the whole point of the Queen's Gambit is to remove the black pawn from d5 by force or persuasion, it is no wonder that here White jumps at the chance to liquidate the obstacle to e2-e4.

4   ...   ♘xd5

The knight recaptures and clears the diagonal for the bishop which will shortly appear on g7.

5   e4

The perfect move: White seizes the e4 square and clears the way for the development of his king's bishop with gain of time by attacking the black knight.

5   ...   ♘xc3

Black decides not to waste any more time with his knight by exchanging it forthwith.

6   bxc3

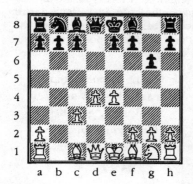

White can be pleased to have built an impressive centre with pawns on both d4 and e4. However, it will only prove an asset if it stands firm against the pressure that Black can now exert against it from the wings. If it crumbles under the strain then White will be ruined: therefore absolute precision and vigilance is demanded of him in the moves ahead.

6 ... ♗g7

Already the black bishop on g7 glares balefully at the d4 pawn.

7 ♘f3

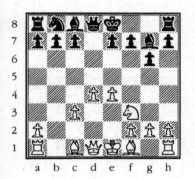

Over the next few moves there is an arms race: White rushes all his forces into action to staunch up his centre, whilst Black tries to hit the d4 point as hard as possible. Putting the knight on f3 is a doubly blessed move as it fulfils the requirements of both development and strategy.

7 ... c5!

Even in a counterattacking opening a player neglects his pawns at his peril. Here the c pawn is a vital part of Black's attacking apparatus. Far inferior would be 7...♘c6. as not only is the c pawn itself obstructed, but also the black queen is blocked from entering the fray via a5 or c7.

8 ♗e3

Kramnik further strengthens his d4 pawn and clears the c1 square for his rook.

8 ... ♛a5

The requirements of strategy overrule general principles. We are always warned against moving the queen too early in the game, but it was impossible to resist using such a strong piece to attack the c3 pawn, the chief defender of d4. Besides, there is no white piece that can harass her on the a5 square.

9 ♕d2

White must also utilize his queen, as if 9 ♖c1 his centre is broken up after 9...cxd4 as he can't recapture on d4 with the c pawn.

9 ... ♘c6

More reinforcements arrive to pummel the d4 pawn.

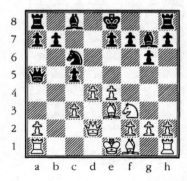

10 ♖c1

A great square for the rook. On c1 it defends c3, the supporting beam of the d4 pawn; is out of the range of the black bishop on g7; and finally will be well placed once the c file becomes open.

An embarrassing way to lose would be 10 d5?? when the separate powers of the black queen and bishop suddenly converge on the c3 square with 10...♗xc3! winning the white queen.

10   ...   cxd4

Thanks to Kramnik's careful play Black hasn't been able to destroy White's centre, but he still finds a way to use his pressure on d4 to cause the white king some discomfort.

11   cxd4

The only logical recapture as the pawn centre must be kept intact.

11   ...   ♕xd2+

Black exchanges immediately in order to compel the white king to renounce castling.

12   ♔xd2

The only way to recapture, as 12 ♘xd2 or 12 ♗xd2 both drop the d4 pawn to 12...♘xd4. As queens have been exchanged the white king isn't in mortal danger on d2. On the other hand, his situation is far from being ideal for White, despite the dictum that the king is best placed in the

centre in the endgame. This is because there are still a lot of other pieces on the board – in fact the position would be better described as a complex middlegame without queens rather than as an endgame.

12   ...   0-0

Meanwhile Van Wely has no illusions that his king is best whisked away from the centre.

13   d5

Finally White has succeeded in evacuating all his pieces and pawns from the deadly diagonal a1-h8. However, Black hasn't given up on the fundamental aim of his opening: to destroy the white centre.

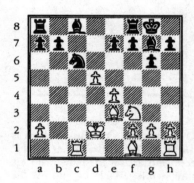

13   ...   ♖d8!

Rather than move his knight Black exploits the awkward situation of the white king. Now the threat is 14...e6 when the d5 point crumbles.

14   ♔e1

The white king retreats to safety after which the threat to the black knight is renewed.

14   ...   ♘a5

The knight is driven from its optimum centre post, but as consolation Black has coerced the white king back to e1, where it blocks in his rook on h1.

15 ♗g5!

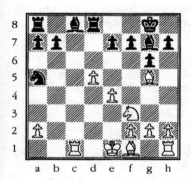

A major part of strategy is preventing your opponent playing good moves. Here White avoids a routine developing move such as 15 ♗d3 in order to stop Black attacking his centre with 15...e6.

15 ... ♗d7!

The most efficient response – far better than 15...f6 which is met by 16 ♗d2, when Black has shut in his king's bishop and damaged his kingside. Instead Van Wely ignores the threat to e7 and prepares to challenge for control of the c file.

16 ♗d3

White hurries to develop so that he can connect his rooks and not be outgunned on the c file.

If 16 ♗xe7? ♖e8 17 d6 ♘c6 forces the bishop to retreat, when 18...♖xe4+ regains the pawn with advantage. But no matter: the bishop on g5 has done its job in

restraining e7-e6 even if it can't actually capture the pawn.

16 ... ♖dc8

Van Wely tries to wrest control of what is a unique avenue of attack for the rooks, whether white or black: the only open file on the board. At the same time he breaks the pin on e7 and so reintroduces the idea of e7-e6.

17 ♔e2!

It is vital that the rook on h1 make its presence felt and so the king continues his short range journeys: e1-d2-e1-e2!

Embarrassing would be 17 ♖xc8+ ♖xc8 18 ♗xe7?? ♖c1+ when Black wins a rook.

17 ... e6

Frustrated in his bid to acquire the c file, Black switches back to his original plan: the attack on White's centre.

18 ♗e3

So the bishop didn't prevent Black playing e7-e6 but it certainly lessened its effect by coaxing the black rook away from the d file: the pawn on d5 is now much safer.

Having done its duty on g5, the bishop is redeployed to a square where it indirectly fights for control of the c file.

18   ...   exd5

Black exchanges in order to isolate forever the passed pawn from the other white kingside pawns.

19   exd5

It is a matter of very subtle judgment as to whether the pawn on d5 is strong or weak. On the plus side, besides its potential to advance and become a queen, it interferes with the coordination of Black's pieces by depriving the knight of the c6 square and the bishop of a post on e6 – where it could attack the a2 pawn.

On the other hand, it is set adrift from the other white pawns and cannot be supported by them; nor at the moment can it be defended in any direct way by the white pieces.

But notice that although the pawn isn't defended in any 'direct' way, from an 'indirect' point of view it is being given a lot of help by the other pieces. Thus the black rooks would like to attack the pawn, but

they are pinned down by the need to contest the c file; and meanwhile the black knight is prevented from leaving a5 and therefore cannot harass the pawn. In what follows Kramnik manages to highlight all the good points about having the passed pawn, whilst nullifying all the negative features. Let's see step by step how he does it.

19   ...   b6

Black meets the threat of 20 ♖xc8+ when he must either undevelop his bishop with 20...♗xc8 or lose a pawn after 20...♖xc8 21 ♗xa7.

20   ♗a6!

The bishop immediately seizes on the chance to use the a6 square to help White win control of the contested file.

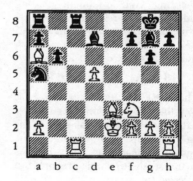

20   ...   ♖d8

Black has to relinquish control of the c file and in doing so is wise to keep both pairs of rooks on the board. Here is what might have happened if after 20...♖xc1 21 ♖xc1 Black targeted the d5 pawn with 21...♖d8: 22 ♖c7! – the familiar and wonderful rook on the seventh rank! – 22...♗g4 23 ♖xa7 ♖xd5 Black has captured the dangerous pawn, but alas after 24 ♖a8+ ♗f8 25 ♗h6 he is suddenly mated!

Always keep your eyes open for back rank mates, even if your opponent has moved one of his pawns in front of his king. Back rank mates are the most common of all mates.

21 ♖hd1

The king's rook finally enters the game in support of the passed pawn.

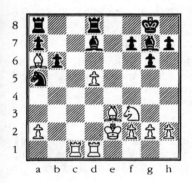

21 ... ♗c8

Black is eager to regain control of the c file, but the passed pawn on d5 soon becomes menacing as there are fewer obstacles in its way.

Chess never stands still, and as soon as he lost this game Van Wely must have started planning his revenge. The fruits of his efforts were seen when he reached the position after 21 ♖hd1 again, this time against fellow Dutch GM Jeroen Piket: 21...♗a4! – an aggressive counterthrust with the bishop instead of the limp defensive move versus Kramnik. The game continued 22 ♖d3 b5! – creating an outpost on c4 for his knight as well

as cutting off the retreat of the white bishop on a6 – 23 ♗f4. White threatens to trap the rook on a8 with his next move, but Van Wely shows that sometimes the best way to meet a threat is to ignore it! 23...♘c4! 24 ♗b7 ♗b2! 25 ♗xa8 White cannot win the exchange by first moving his rook to safety from c1, as this allows ♗b2! when the rook on d3 is trapped! 25...♗xc1 26 ♗xc1 ♖xa8 27 d6 f6 and Black's active pieces mean that the passed pawn on d6 is a liability rather than a strength.

Of course, Kramnik is very likely to have revealed a better way to handle the position for White if Van Wely had played 21...♗a4 against him. Nevertheless, it was a much better fighting chance for Black.

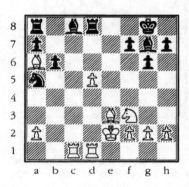

22 ♗xc8!

It is vital to be willing to give up one advantage for an even greater one. Kramnik realizes that the game will be won by advancing the passed pawn, not by utilizing the c file. Therefore with his next couple of moves he hands it over to Black in order to remove obstacles from the path of the passed pawn.

22 ... ♖axc8

Naturally Black recaptures with his last undeveloped piece.

23 ♖xc8

The multiple exchange of pieces emphasizes White's advantage in the centre as the black knight remains stranded on the wing.

23 ... ♖xc8

At last Black has control of the c file, but can he restrain the passed pawn? If he is given time the answer is 'yes' as he will play ♘b7 and ♘d6 when the knight will prove an excellent blockader.

24 ♘d4!

A tremendous centralization. The idea is to put the knight on b5, where it not only attacks a7 but also supports the advance of the passed pawn. At the same time the black knight is paralyzed, as 24...♘b7 can be answered by 25 ♘c6! threatening both 26 ♘e7+ winning the rook and 26 ♘xa7, as well as controlling the queening square of the passed pawn.

As an incidental benefit the knight move also prevents 24...♖c2+. What more could you ask for from a move?

24 ... ♗f8

To exchange or not to exchange? The eternal dilemma of the chess player! Every Grunfeld or King's Indian player is loathe to give up his beautiful dark square bishop for a mere knight. Nevertheless, it is no ordinary knight sitting on d4: as will be seen it has been imbued with magic by Kramnik. Therefore 24...♗xd4! was in order, no matter how painful. After 25 ♗xd4 f5 the black king could then join in the fight against the passed pawn. This was Black's last chance to defend successfully.

25 ♘b5!

The white knight will prove far more adept at driving the passed pawn forwards than the black bishop at restraining it.

25 ... a6

Black saves his pawn and hopes to gain time by attacking the knight, but a nasty surprise awaits him.

26 d6!

Passed pawns must be pushed! After 26...axb5 27 d7 ♖d8 – if 27...♖c2+ 28 ♔d3! wins the rook or queens – 28 ♗xb6 ♘c6 29 ♗xd8 ♘xd8 30 ♖d5! contains a double threat of 31 ♖xb5 and 31 ♖e5! followed by 32 ♖e8 when the passed pawn will cost Black his knight, if he can stop it at all. Black must deal with the second of these threats by say 30...♗e7 intending 31...♔f8, but after 31 ♖xb5 White has a decisive advantage. Materially speaking, it doesn't seem too bad for Black to have a bishop and knight versus a rook and two pawns, but his minor pieces are tied down by the passed pawn on d7, which allows the other pawn on a2 to quickly march forwards.

That wasn't such a hard calculation, as the play was of a so called forcing nature – after 27 d7 the black rook must move to d8 to block the pawn, then on the next move the rook has to be defended, and the move after that the black knight has to recapture the rook: all these moves are forced. When the opponent has no choice about his moves it makes it much easier to look ahead.

The difficulty of the combination was the need to assess the position after 31 ♖xb5 in view of the unusual material balance. Kramnik's fine judgment told him that dealing with both passed pawns would cost Black a piece, when the exchange up he should win the endgame.

26   ...   ♖c2+

Black rests his hopes on counterattack against the white queenside pawns.

27   ♔d3!

The only move: White must attack the black rook with his king

or else snatching the knight becomes feasible for Black.

27   ...   ♖xa2

Black acquires two connected passed pawns, but they are too far back to cause White any problems at the moment. Still, Van Wely hopes that he can give up his bishop or knight for White's passed pawn and then trust in his queenside pawns to give him long term counterplay.

28   d7!

'The passed pawn' wrote Nimzowitsch, 'is a criminal who should be kept under lock and key. Mild measures, such as police surveillance, are not sufficient'.

28   ...   ♘b7

It seems that only a disaster as big as his opponent queening was sufficient to make the knight awake from its slumber on a5.

29   ♘c3!

In contrast to its sluggish black counterpart the white knight leaps nimbly over the whole board. Here it gains time by attacking the black rook to reach the d5 square.

29   ...   ♖b2

There wasn't much choice as after
29...♖a3 30 ♔c2 the white king has
slipped away from the d file and the
pawn is ready to promote.

30   ♘d5

Here the knight surveys the whole
board. Amongst other threats Black
has to reckon with 31 ♗xb6
followed by queening the pawn.

30   ...   ♖b5

The rook does its best to dislodge
the white knight.

31   ♔c2

The king deftly retreats after
which the white rook not only
guards the knight, but looks through
it towards the d7 and d8 squares.

31   ...   ♗c5

Van Wely battles hard. If he can
exchange bishops his queenside
passed pawns will give him some
survival chances, even if the pawn
on d7 costs a knight.

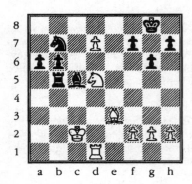

32   ♗h6!

A vital part of Kramnik's winning
plan. On h6 the bishop:

♦ prevents the black king from
approaching the passed pawn via f8

♦ forces a weakening of Black's
kingside by introducing mating
threats.

32   ...   f6

Black has to make a hole for his
king as he is mated after 32...♘d8
33 ♘f6+ ♔h8 34 ♖e1 when there is
no answer to 35 ♖e8+ or after
32...a5 33 ♘f6+ ♔h8, either by 34
d8=♕ ♘xd8 35 ♖xd8+ and mate
next move, or if White wishes to
show off then 34 d8=♘ with
unstoppable mate on f7: 34...♘d6
35 ♖xd6 ♗xd6 36 ♘xf7 mate.

33   ♘c7

1-0

The knight attacks the black rook
and clears the way for White's own
rook to support the queening of the
passed pawn. Now a possible finish
is 33...♖a5 34 d8=♕+ ♘xd8 35
♖xd8+ ♔f7 36 ♖d7+! and Black has
no chance to get his queenside
pawns moving before disaster
strikes:

(a) 36...♔g8 37 ♘e8! when there
is no good answer to 38 ♘xf6+ ♔g8
39 ♖xh7 mate, or more prosaically

(b) 36...♗e7 37 ♗e3! and as
37...b5 38 ♗c5 wins the bishop

Black has to allow 38 ♗xb6 taking one of the queenside pawns and at the same time removing all of his swindle hopes. Therefore the Dutch GM resigned.

Game Twenty-Five
A.Shirov - V.Ivanchuk
Manila Olympiad 1992
Dutch Defence

1   d4

'Help your pieces so that they can help you!' said Paul Morphy more than 150 years ago. And what more can White do to help his pieces than clear the way for his queen and queen's bishop?

1   ...   e6

Ivanchuk keeps his opponent guessing: whatever form the black centre eventually takes this little pawn move will be a useful building block in its construction.

2   c4

White stays in Queen's Pawn territory by declining the offer to enter the French Defence with 2 e4 d5. Now 2...d5 gives us the Queen's Gambit, whilst 2...♘f6 could lead to the Nimzo-Indian after 3 ♘c3 ♗b4. Alternatively, 2...b6 is the English Defence.

2   ...   f5

Black decides to play the Dutch Defence. The good feature of this opening is that it gives him influence over the e4 square without exposing a pawn to immediate attack, as would be the case after 2...d5. Furthermore, he can dream of using the f pawn to spearhead a kingside assault. The drawback is

that Black's kingside pawn structure is slightly weakened and the move contributes nothing directly to the mobilization of his pieces.

3   g3

A kingside fianchetto is a good response to the Dutch Defence. From a purely defensive point of view the bishop will be a powerful guardian sitting in front of the king on g2 and so shielding him from harm; whereas the pawn on g3 puts an obstacle in the path of future attack based on f5-f4.

3   ...   ♘f6

Black consolidates his hold on the e4 square with this natural developing move.

4   ♗g2

Here the bishop not only supports an eventual space gaining advance in the centre with e2-e4 but also puts pressure on b7, which makes it hard for Black to develop his queen's bishop: after all, this bishop is already boxed in by its own pawns on e6 and f5, and so would like to enter the game via b7 after b7-b6.

4   ...   c6

Ivanchuk intends to solve the problem of developing his queen's bishop by putting a pawn on d5, which cuts out the pressure of the white bishop along the diagonal and so makes possible b7-b6 followed by ♗b7. Another good point about playing d7-d5 is that it makes it much harder for White to arrange e2-e4.

That is Black's basic idea, but rather than commit himself to it he engages in a bit of sharp practice with the move order. For the moment the black pawn on c6 supports the ghost of a pawn on d5, as if immediately 4...d5 then White could develop his king's knight to h3: 4...d5 5 ♘h3! when the knight would have an excellent centre square waiting for it on f4. So Ivanchuk waits a move to play d7-d5...

5   ♘f3

...until White puts his knight on f3. If instead 5 ♘h3, then Black still has the chance to change his mind with 5...d6! when the f4 square is no longer looking pretty for the white knight, as it can be driven back with e6-e5. Therefore the white knight would be left looking rather silly on h3.

It would also be ineffective for White to block Black's plan of d7-d5 by playing 5 d5 himself, as Black emerges with a good centre after all following 5...cxd5 6 cxd5 e5!

5   ...   d5

Only now. Black has a formidable clump of pawns on light squares and is ready to develop his queen's bishop. But as we know everything comes at a price for Black in the opening: the advantage of the first move remains until White squanders it in an 'accident' and so far Shirov has done nothing wrong.

The downside of Black's light square strategy is that he has neglected the dark squares f4 and e5. In particular the e5 square is a hole which can no longer be protected by a pawn. Therefore he has to be very careful that these squares don't fall into White's hands.

6   0-0

If you have a choice of moves in the opening, the golden rule is: play the move you definitely want to play first. Here there is no question that the white king belongs on g1 where he is safe behind his defences; therefore it makes sense to put him there before committing the queen's knight or bishop to any task.

Note that there is nothing to fear in 6...dxc4? as dismantling his own centre is no part of Black's thoughts. In any case White could regain the pawn immediately with 7 ♘e5 intending ♘xc4, as if 7...b5 8 ♘xc6.

6   ...   ♗d6

Having built a solid wall of pawns on the light squares Black places his bishop on sentry duty to guard the vulnerable e5 square. This is a more active post than e7 – besides, as will be seen that square is reserved for the black queen.

7   b3

Naturally the hole on e5 hasn't escaped the notice of White either. He prepares 8 ♗a3! when the exchange of bishops will deprive the square of its best defender.

7   ...   ♕e7!

Unlucky White. The queen takes her seat at the nerve centre of the Black position where she:

♦ prevents White from playing ♗a3

♦ is well placed to support an e6-e5 advance, if the dissolution of the centre is in Black's favour

♦ gets off the first rank and so makes way for the eventual development of the queen's rook.

8   ♘e5

White perseveres in his attempt to extract maximum benefit from the hole on e5. A knight is always delighted to be placed on a centre square where he can't be attacked by a pawn.

8   ...   0-0

Although there was no immediate danger, Ivanchuk wants his king out of the way before he proceeds with his development. Besides, the rook on f8 is now well placed to support action in the centre.

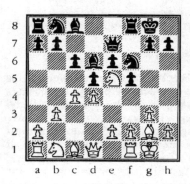

9   ♘d2

Very logical: the other white knight rushes over to f3 to support his brother in arms on e5. Here we see why it was worth White keeping his options open with the deployment of this knight: it would have been all too easy to have mindlessly developed the knight to its 'normal' square on c3 a couple of moves ago.

9   ...   ♘bd7

As the c6 square is denied it, the queen's knight chooses its second best deployment. Here it joins the king's bishop in the fight for e5.

10   ♘df3

The knight arrives just in time to keep a grip on the hotly contested centre point.

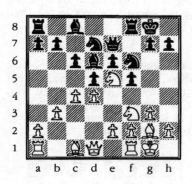

10   ...   ♘e4

Black wants to complete his development by putting the queen's bishop on b7. But if he plays 10...b6 then 11 ♘xc6 wins a pawn. Therefore he needs to exchange off the pesky knight on e5. But if 10...♘xe5?? 11 dxe5 is a fatal fork, whilst 10...♗xe5, giving up the dark-squared bishop, leaves Black uncomfortable after 11 dxe5 ♘e4. Therefore Ivanchuk first of all moves the knight from f6 so that he can initiate an exchange with ♘xe5 without falling into a fork.

From a point of view of pawn structure the e4 square isn't as good a post for the black knight as e5 is

for the white knight, as White can drive it back at some point with f2-f3; whereas Black cannot ever play f5-f6: pawns, like time, can only go forwards and never backwards! On the other hand, it will cost White some of the cohesion of his pawn structure to advance f2-f3. And in the meantime the black knight is enjoying life on an excellent centre square.

11   ♘d3

The knight voluntarily retreats to make room for the other knight to go to e5, which in turn by vacating f3 clears the way for White to begin active operations with his pawns: either f2-f3 (to evict the black knight from e4) or both f2-f3 and e2-e4, to attack the black centre. As will be seen, the latter idea involving e2-e4 is problematical to say the least.

If instead 11 ♗b2 ♘xe5 12 dxe5 ♗c5 looks sound enough for Black, or here 12 ♘xe5 ♗xe5!? 13 dxe5 b6 and although Black misses his dark-squared bishop he has a solid centre and is ready to develop his queen's bishop – perhaps to the a6 square, where it attacks c4.

Note that this last variation is a superior version for Black to the line considered on his previous move with 10...♗xe5 11 dxe5 ♘e4. This is because firstly he has succeeded in exchanging off two minor pieces, not just one, which eases his rather congested camp; and secondly in the latter scenario Black's move ♘e4 is more useful than White's ♗b2.

11 ...   b6

With the pressure temporarily off the c6 pawn, Ivanchuk takes the chance to develop his queen's bishop.

12   ♘fe5

All as planned: a new knight takes up residence on e5 with a direct threat to c6.

12 ...   ♗b7

The bishop is content to take over the defensive duty of c6. It might not look like an auspicious start to the bishop's career to be developed to a blocked diagonal, but a path may open in the future after a well timed c7-c5; and at the very least on b7 the bishop doesn't get in the way of his rooks.

13   ♘xd7

White exchanges knights as a prelude to an encroachment on the centre with his pawns.

13 ...   ♛xd7

Now the black queen has been deflected from e7 where it helped to control the c5 square. This becomes significant over the next two moves.

14   f3

Finally Shirov has the chance to use his pawns in a bid to gain more space. First of all he drives back the enemy knight.

14 ...   ♘f6

The knight must retreat, but at least White's centre has been softened up by his last move.

15   c5

An anti-bishop move. White

♦ stops Black ever playing c6-c5, which would activate his queen's bishop and liquidate the white d4 pawn

♦ aims to eliminate Black's good dark-squared bishop, either as in the game or after 15...♗c7 16 ♗f4! ♗xf4 17 gxf4, when his grip on the dark squares outweighs any superficial damage to his kingside. If 15 ♗f4 immediately Black can break out after 15 ♗f4 ♗xf4 16 gxf4?! c5! etc.

15   ...   bxc5

Black is prepared to yield the bishop pair in return for getting rid of the hole on e5.

16   ♘xc5

The consistent move as White has no compensation for Black's superior centre after 16 dxc5 ♗c7, intending ♕e7 and e6-e5.

16   ...   ♗xc5

Naturally the white knight couldn't be tolerated on c5 where it dominates the centre.

17   dxc5

As required, but the pawn has now been deflected from d4 where it performed a useful role in keeping control of the e5 square. Still, the elimination of Black's so-called good bishop in return for his knight is no small positional achievement for White.

17   ...   e5

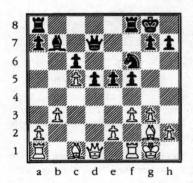

Now Black not only has an extra pawn in the centre − four against

three − but he also has a space advantage due to his wall of pawns on his fourth rank.

18   e4??

A horrible mistake. White is eager to open lines for his two bishops and no doubt assumed that the way to do it was to strike immediately at d5. But this reasoning is entirely wrong and leads to a quick defeat. He had to play in a restrained style with 18 e3! followed if possible by ♗b2 and then f3-f4, when he really does force open a long diagonal for the dark square bishop. Ivanchuk intended to cut across this plan with 18...♗a6 19 ♖e1 d4! 20 exd4 exd4, with balanced chances − White's bishop pair are useful in this fragmented pawn structure, but Black's passed pawn isn't to be underestimated. Whatever the verdict on this variation, White had to try it as in the game he is reduced to absolute paralysis.

18   ...   ♗a6

This bishop gets far more benefit from White's last move than the bishop on g2. Could it be that Shirov, wrapped up in his own plans, had simply forgotten that the bishop can enter the game via a6?

19 ♖e1

The rook is loathe to give up the fight for the f file which is about to be opened, but a possible disaster after 19 ♖f2 was 19...fxe4 20 fxe4 ♘xe4! 21 ♖xf8+ ♖xf8 22 ♗xe4 ♖f1+ when Black will pick up White's queen for a rook and bishop.

19 ... fxe4

This capture wins both the f file for the black rooks and the g4 square for the knight.

20 fxe4

Opening the f file proves grim but White can't afford to be a centre pawn down for nothing.

20 ... d4!

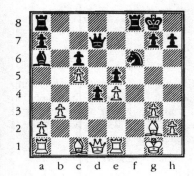

There goes all White's dreams of counterplay. The protected passed pawn isn't so much strong in itself, as in the fact that it obstructs the white pieces – its baleful glance seems almost to paralyze them.

21 ♕d2

White is no material down and there are no immediate tactical threats, but he is totally lost as he cannot contest the f file.

21 ... ♘g4

Ivanchuk has gained the initiative from the manoeuvring phase but now needs to strike hard to exploit his advantage. The key to victory will be the f file: every black piece must be brought to bear against it.

♦ the bishop already controls f1

♦ the knight eyes f2 to support an invasion with ♖f2

♦ the rook on f8 already looks down the file

♦ the queen's rook and queen will converge on the f7 and f6 squares

22 ♗h3

He must prevent 22...♖f2, which can now be answered by 23 ♕xf2! winning the rook.

22 ... h5!

Black defends the knight and so frees the queen to go to the f file.

23 ♗a3

Shirov desperately tries to find an active role for this bishop, but Ivanchuk can just ignore it.

23 ... ♕f7

Chess is an easy game when you have a clear plan that your opponent can't oppose.

24   ♗b4

The bishop continues on its useless expedition. Seldom has Shirov been reduced to such helplessness.

24   ...   ♖ae8

It's all too simple: the rook heads for the f file by the quickest route via e6.

25   ♗a5

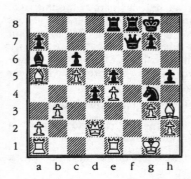

The bishops on a6 and a5 form a beautiful contrast. White's bishop does nothing at all; it neither attacks anything nor slows down Black's attack by reducing his options. It might as well be off the board. On the other hand, Black's bishop, though also isolated from the main body of pieces, is right in the thick of the action. Because it controls f1 it prevents a white rook from contesting the f file and so interferes with White's defences.

25   ...   ♖e6

It is often the case that the arrival of reinforcements in the shape of the queen's rook is enough to decide an attack. Now Black threatens ♖f6 and ♖f2, when White's king will be massacred on his second rank.

26   ♗f1

This leads to a quick defeat, but White has no constructive way to meet the threat outlined above, as demonstrated by his three pointless moves with the other bishop.

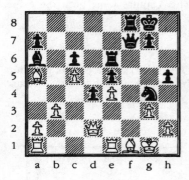

26   ...   ♘f2!

Shirov had gambled everything on Black responding passively to his challenge to the bishop on a6: if 26...♗xf1? 27 ♖xf1 gives White a fighting chance.

27   ♗xa6

White has revenge on the bishop which has so oppressed him, but it brings little joy as his king is about to die.

27   ...   ♕f3

0-1

The game ends abruptly as there is no good way to prevent 28...♕h1 mate or 28...♘h3 mate. The two white bishops stand magnificently and uselessly on the queenside as monuments to an incorrect plan.

6 Delayed Dynamism: The Flank Openings

Chess is a matter of subtle judgement – knowing when to punch and when to duck.

Bobby Fischer

In essence there are two ways for White to try to exploit the advantage of moving first. He can bring out all his pieces as rapidly as possible and try to strike a deadly blow before his opponent can mobilize his own forces; or more modestly he can aim to achieve a superior pawn structure or layout of his pieces and use this as a basis for outplaying his opponent later on in the middlegame. In reality, most opening systems are a mixture of these two approaches: after all, a crude attacking scheme is unlikely to succeed against an experienced opponent, whilst on the other hand White's advantage in moving first is likely to dwindle to nothing if he is content merely to bring out his pieces without trying to set his opponent any problems. As we have already seen in this book, Kasparov and other top players know when the moment is right to play aggressively and when to be content with nurturing a tiny positional advantage.

In this chapter we look at games in which White avoids the mainlines after 1 e4 or 1 d4 in favour of one of the so-called flank openings. Here the accent is very much on manoeuvring to enter the middlegame with a positional advantage rather than overt aggression, but as will be seen when Tal and Kasparov are playing White careless play by Black is punished in dramatic style.

Game Twenty-Six
A.Miles - U.Andersson
Las Palmas 1980
Fianchetto Opening

1   g3

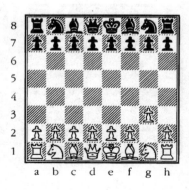

Instead of immediately putting pawns in the centre White prepares to develop his king's bishop where it controls the centre from a distance.

Generally speaking the kingside fianchetto is less popular for White than it is for Black, as he can boldly play 1 e4 or 1 d4 in the knowledge that if the position remains symmetrical he is bound to have the better chances for the simple reason that he moves first. The present game illustrates both modern and classical opening ideas.

1   ...   c5

Black seizes space in the centre before White can change his mind with 2 d4.

2   &g2

The bishop points at the d5 square which has been slightly weakened by Black's last move: he can no longer set up a pawn chain with c7-c6 and d7-d5.

2   ...   ♘c6

Black continues to concentrate his attention on the d4 square.

3   ♘f3

Despite his irregular opening Miles isn't neglecting his development. After only three moves he is on the point of castling – though without wishing to spoil the story I should mention that the

white king will find a far better home than g1.

3   ...   g6

Andersson also decides to fianchetto. After all, why should he develop his bishop to e7 after say 3...e6 where it will be obstructed by the pawn on c5, when there is a long open diagonal beckoning it on g7?

4   c3!

White switches from hypermodern to classical strategy. He decides it is time to gain some space and so prepares to put a pawn on d4

4   ...   &g7

It is too late for Black to change his mind: having played 3...g6 the only logical continuation is to fianchetto.

5   d4

A pawn move for all seasons, which

♦ introduces a tactical threat: 6 dxc5 winning a pawn

♦ contains a positional threat: 6 d5 driving the black knight from its post

♦ takes possession of d4, which was becoming a strong point for Black in the centre

♦ curtails the activity of the bishop on g7

♦ increases White's influence over e5, another important centre square

♦ clears the way for the development of the queen's bishop.

5 ... cxd4

The black pawn decides to eat his opponent before he is eaten himself.

6 cxd4

Completely anti-positional would be 6 ♘xd4 as White wants to maintain a pawn in the centre. With the game move he also clears c3 for his knight.

6 ... d5

Andersson realizes he also has to put a pawn in the centre in classical style or else White will disrupt his game with 7 d5.

7 ♘c3

The knight jumps to an active square and challenges Black to keep on copying him with 7...♘f6. But in that case 8 ♘e5! would break the

symmetry in powerful fashion: it threatens to give Black a weak backward pawn on an open file after 9 ♘xc6 bxc6 and if Black replies 8...♘xe5 then 9 dxe5 ♘g4 10 ♕xd5 gives White a dangerous initiative in the centre, even though Black can regain his pawn. Generally speaking it is a risky business for Black to keep on copying his opponent's moves, as sooner or later the advantage of moving first is going to be significant – possibly even decisive.

7 ... e6

Black sensibly avoids the variation above and defends his d5 pawn in a different manner. However, this is an important little victory for White as now the bishop on c8 is shut inside Black's pawn structure.

8 ♗f4!

In contrast White's queen's bishop is developed outside his pawn structure. A small difference? Perhaps, but games are often won and lost through the accumulation of advantages which in themselves seem of little significance.

8 ... ♘ge7

After 8...♘f6 White could still have tried 9 ♘e5 – whereas the game move makes this idea worthless, as Black can simply recapture ♘xc6 if necessary and avoid a weak pawn.

Nevertheless e7 is the 'second best' square for the knight compared to f6 which means White has acquired another small advantage.

9   ♕d2!

...which Miles uses in incisive style. He prepares to exchange off Black's fianchettoed bishop, which is the guardian of the important kingside dark squares f6, g7 and h6. If Black's knight had been on its best square, f6, then he could have met this with the annoying reply 9...♘e4! attacking the queen and so completely ruining White's plan.

9   ...   0-0

The knight on e7 can't redeem itself with 9...♘f5, hoping to force 10 e3 when the white queen no longer supports ♗h6, as 10 ♘b5! – threatening a fork on c7 – 10...0-0 11 g4 drives back the knight and then exchanges bishops with ♗h6 in similar fashion to the game. So

Black must be content simply to castle.

10   ♗h6

All as planned: White weakens the black kingside and leaves his opponent with a mouldy bishop on c8 which is shut in by its own pawn centre.

10   ...   ♗xh6

Normally it is a bad idea to invite an enemy queen onto your king's doorstep, but here she can be driven away with gain of time by a black knight.

11   ♕xh6

Now Black has to act fast or 12 ♘g5 will lead to mate in just a couple of moves: a queen and knight are well known to be a murderous force against an undefended king, partly because between them they combine the power of all the pieces on the board.

11   ...   ♘f5

The cavalry comes to the rescue: now the white queen has the more mundane task of saving herself and keeping d4 defended.

12   ♕d2

The queen goes all the way back as 12 ♕f4 ♕d6! offers an unwanted queen exchange. Nevertheless, she can be proud at having helped weaken the black kingside.

12   ...   b6

The centre being blocked, Andersson has to find an alternative way to activate his feeble bishop – or failing that, to at least get it out of the way of his other pieces.

13   ♖d1

White anticipates ♕f6 by Black and so overprotects the d4 pawn.

13   ...   ♗a6

Not a particularly glamorous square for the bishop, but at least it forces White to take the pressure on e2 into consideration when he devises his plan.

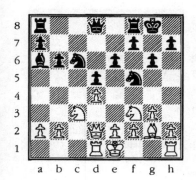

14   h4!

'Castle because you want to or because you have to, not just because you can' said the American chess genius Pillsbury.

In this position many club players would play the routine 14 0-0 after which White has no advantage. In fact, Black would have marginally

the better of it as all the action switches to the queenside when the bishop on a6, which I have previously maligned, suddenly looks superior to the bishop on g2 which is boxed in.

Instead after the game move White has a constructive plan which will utilise the bishop on g2 and the rook on h1, which would both have languished in passivity after 14 0-0. The h pawn will be used as a battering ram to force a structural weakness in Black's kingside.

14   ...   ♘a5?

White's restrained opening has succeeded in dulling the normally brilliant sense of danger of Ulf Andersson. Black wants to gain time for operations on the c file with ♘c4, but things move so fast on the kingside that this never materializes. Therefore the knight is simply left out on a limb on a5. As Tarrasch once said 'If one piece is badly placed, the whole game is bad' or in more colloquial terms 'a knight on the rim is dim'.

The obvious riposte to White's last move was 14...h5 to curtail the further advance of White's rook's pawn. Then White could try 15 ♕f4 to support a second wave of the attack with g2-g4, which gives him some advantage.

15   g4!

White is justified in starting a wing attack as the situation in the centre is quiet: Black can hardly hope to arrange a counter attack with e6-e5.

15   ...   ♘d6

After 15...♘c4 16 ♕c1 – a simple reply recommended by Speelman –

followed by 17 b3 etc. allows White to continue his kingside attack all the same. In retreating the other knight Andersson chooses a centre square where it doesn't prevent the queen coming to the defence on f6. If instead 15...♘e7 16 h5! already looks like an irresistible direct attack.

16   h5

It is remarkable that Miles has managed to develop a sharp attack from such a modest beginning.

16   ...   ♕f6

The queen rushes to the aid of her king...

17   hxg6

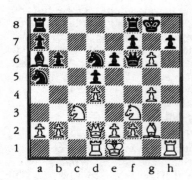

...but already Black faces a dilemma: should he allow the opening of the h file or recapture with the f pawn, when his centre pawn structure is weakened?

17   ...   fxg6

Here's what might have happened after 17...hxg6: 18 g5 ♕g7 19 ♘e5 with the devilish threat of retreating the knight with 20 ♘g4 and then 21 ♘f6+, when the vibrant knight forces Black to give up his queen.

To meet this threat Black would have to play 19...f6 when after 20 gxf6 his centre has been weakened in any case.

18   ♕h6

Of course White would like to put his knight on the wonderful, magnificent e5 square, but if 18 ♘e5? ♕xf2 mate! You always have to watch out for these tactics, even if you see a very good move. So Miles first of all has to deflect the black queen from the f file.

18   ...   ♖f7

Mate in one on h7 has to be stopped, and if 18...♕g7 then after 19 ♕xg7+ ♔xg7 20 ♘g5 there is the very, very ugly double threat of 20 ♘xe6+ and 20 ♖xh7+.

19   g5!

The value of a pawn move should be carefully considered, as there is no going back!

White allows Black's knight to get to f5 and blocks his own idea of ♘g5, but look at the good points of this move. In one stroke White

♦ drives the black queen from the f file where she is preventing ♘e5

♦ gains control of f6 and so establishes an outpost there for a knight

♦ clears the way for ♗h3 to activate the bishop by attacking the weak pawn on e6.

19 ... ♛g7

If 19...♛e7 20 ♘e5! At last the knight is freed and disaster strikes immediately for Black after 20...♖g7 21 ♘xd5! exd5 22 ♗xd5+ ♚f8 (also hopeless is 22...♚h8 23 ♗xa8) 23 ♘xg6+! hxg6 24 ♕h8+ ♖g8 25 ♕xg8 mate.

20 ♘e5

This is a dream square for the knight – but it will find an even better one!

20 ... ♛xh6

Black has little choice but to try to stem the attacking flood by exchanging queens. Unfortunately for him he will have little respite from the positional pressure in the endgame.

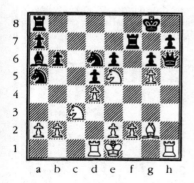

21 ♖xh6

The correct recapture as 21 gxh6? would not only block the attack on h7 but also remove the g5 pawn

which will soon prove a strong support for a white knight.

Weak points or holes in the opponent's position must be occupied by pieces, not by pawns – Tarrasch.

21 ... ♖ff8

A forlorn retreat, but he must defend his rook on a8. We have already seen the type of combination that could occur after 21...♖f5: 22 ♘xd5! exd5 23 ♗xd5+ ♚g7 24 ♗xa8 when White has won the exchange and two pawns.

Remember that if White had played 14 0-0 the bishop on g2 which supports this devastating sequence would have been a worse piece than the bishop on a6 which here is doing nothing at all. Such is the power of a well thought out plan in the early stages of the game.

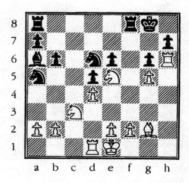

22 ♘d7!

One of the golden rules of chess strategy is: if you have a piece on a good square, find an even better square for it! The knight may look marvellous on e5 but Miles has correctly judged that it will be more useful on f6 where it not only looks pretty but can also take part in a coordinated attack on the h file. The most important thing in chess is to have all the pieces working together, not individual pieces on impressive squares. Though I should add the proviso that a piece on an aesthetically pleasing square is often excellently placed: truth is beauty and beauty truth!

22 ... ♖f7

The rook must be heartily sick of being pushed around by the white knight, but at least it defends the second rank again.

23 ♘f6+

White's strategy of exchanging off Black's dark-squared bishop has been a hearty success as now he has two pieces entrenched on squares that a black bishop on g7 should be defending.

23 ... ♔h8

The king is now trapped on a square which will eventually prove its tomb.

24 ♗h3!

'Haste is the great enemy' wrote Eugene Znosko-Borovsky. When you think you are winning try not to rush things!

Here White would like to checkmate Black as follows: ♔d2, ♖dh1, ♖xh7+ and after ♖(f7)xh7, ♖xh7 mates. Unfortunately Black can ruin this plan by answering 24 ♔d2 with 24...♘e8! when he either exchanges off knights or forces an ignominious retreat from f6.

So before embarking on this plan Miles uses what is called a *zwischenzug*—an in between move – to prevent Black from exchanging off knights. It may seem that White is making the winning plan harder by blocking the h file with his bishop, but sometimes preventing the opponent's plan is more important than carrying out your own idea as quickly as possible.

24 ... ♗c8

If instead 24....♖e7 25 ♗xe6! wins a pawn as the rook dare not touch the bishop in view of mate on h7. Therefore the black bishop is forced by the attack on e6 to move to a defensive square where it obstructs the challenge on the white knight with ♘d6-e8.

25 ♔d2!

Only now does the white king move out of the way of the rook on d1.

25 ... ♖g7

A crafty move with the threat of 26...♘f7 27 ♖h4 ♘xg5, winning the key pawn.

26 f4!

Miles is alert and defends the g5 pawn, after which all active resistance on the kingside comes to an end.

26 ... ♖b8

All Black can do is prepare to bolster his second rank with ♖bb7 and hope that his opponent loses the thread – but Miles is totally relentless.

27 ♖h1

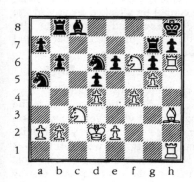

The arrival of the other white rook on the h file is a terrible omen for the black king. If the white bishop on h3 vanished into thin air then White would already be threatening mate in two moves beginning with ♖xh7+: such is the strength of the knight on f6.

27 ... ♘ac4+

This offside knight has been the ruination of Black's position, as in effect he has been fighting the whole game a piece down. The attempt to counterattack comes too late to change anything.

28 ♔d3!

The king is a strong piece: use it! urged Reuben Fine. Here the automatic move would be 28 ♔c1, which both defends b2 and keeps the king safe from checks. But then after 28...♖bb7 Black would be ready to bring his queen's knight to the defence of his kingside with 29...♘e3 and 30...♘f5! By putting the king on d3 White keeps this square defended and so rules out the mercy dash by the black knight.

28 ... ♖bb7

Black could take on b2, but after 28...♘xb2+ 29 ♔c2 ♘bc4 30 ♗xe6! the threat of mate in two moves on h7 is decisive. So he has to bring the other rook to the defence of h7.

29 b3

Now the ignominious black knight is sent back into exile on the rook's file.

29   ...   ♞a3

If Black is given a free move he can exchange off his bad knight with 30...♞ab5, so it is time for White to act fast.

30   e4!

This opens a second front in the centre which completely over-stretches Black's defence.

30   ...   dxe4+

White wins a pawn as a start after 30...♞ab5 31 ♞xb5 ♞xb5 32 exd5.

31   ♞cxe4

White recaptures and clears the way for his king.

31   ...   ♞xe4

Also hopeless is 31...♞f5 32 ♗xf5 exf5 33 ♞d6 ♖bc7 34 ♞xc8 when Black is mated in two moves if he retakes on c8.

32   ♚xe4

In contrast to the black king who is trapped on h8 the white king is able to advance fearlessly.

32   ...   ♞b5

The errant knight makes another attempt to get to the kingside to help

its beleaguered king, this time via the d6 square; but once again this idea is circumvented by the bold white monarch.

33   ♚e5!

The white king now has a grandstand view of the battle field. He cannot be attacked by any of the black pieces and is ready to slip further into the enemy camp and wreak havoc.

33   ...   ♖be7

Black has an apparently firm blockade on the light squares on the kingside, but when you are weak on squares of one colour you usually cannot help but be weak on squares of *both* colours. Here Black has lost control of the dark squares on the kingside. But how is White to make a breakthrough?

The secret is: when you have a bind on squares of one colour look for a breakthrough on a square of the opposite colour.

34   ♗f1!   1-0

This does the trick. The black knight is attacked and after 34...♞c7 35 ♗d3 White will mate with 36

♗xg6!! ♖xg6 37 ♖xh7+ ♖xh7 38 ♖xh7 mate!

You can be mated even after the exchange of queens.

Ulf Andersson is one of the greatest positional players of the modern era. He was under no illusions about his chances and simply resigned. It can't be often that a player resigns straightaway when his opponent plays ♗f1.

This was a positional masterpiece by the great Tony Miles, all the way from 1 g3 to 34 ♗f1.

Game Twenty-Seven
G.Kasparov - V.Ivanchuk
USSR Championship 1988
English Opening

The USSR Championship in 1988 featured a tremendous fight for first place between Karpov and the man who had deposed him as World Champion a couple of years before in 1986.

The final scores were Kasparov and Karpov 11½/17 a full 1½ points ahead of Yusupov and Salov who shared third and fourth prize. Both the Ks were undefeated. The battle between the two Ks has been the greatest struggle of the modern chess age – perhaps in any age.

Their struggle for supremacy has pushed chess to new heights.

1   c4

The main theme of White's strategy throughout this game is to gain absolute control of the d5 square. His first move is the perfect way to begin the task.

1   ...   ♘f6

A bishop can control events in the centre from a distance and so is perfectly satisfied when he is fianchettoed. In contrast the knight has a shorter range and so wants to be in the thick of things. On f6 the knight is ideally placed to fight for the d5 square and control e4 – it wouldn't be the same on h6.

2   ♘c3

White increases his influence on the d5 square with this sensible developing move.

2   ...   e5

Ivanchuk claims an equal share of the centre and frees his king's bishop. At the same time he deters White from playing 3 d4 as this loses time after 3...exd4 4 ♕xd4 ♘c6 when Black speeds up his development by hitting the white queen.

3   ♘f3

If there is any piece deployment in the opening guaranteed to be good for White then it is putting the king's knight on f3.

3   ...   ♘c6

Ivanchuk contents himself with defending his king's pawn in the most economical way. Less good are 3...d6 or 3...♛e7, as they block in his king's bishop. Being provoked into 3...e4 would be reckless as after 4 ♘g5 the impetuous pawn is in trouble: it is attacked for a third time after 4...♛e7 5 ♛c2.

4 g3

As White has played 1 c4, his king's bishop has been deprived of the option of an active development on b5 or c4. But never mind: the fianchetto on g2 accords well with White's plan of putting pressure on d5.

4 ... ♝b4

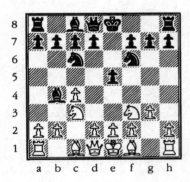

The big weakness of a bishop is that it remains bound to squares of just one colour which means that the other 32 squares on the board remain forever out of touch. Nevertheless, this doesn't mean that the bishop is unable to influence events on the squares that he can never directly control. Here for example the dark-squared bishop attacks the white knight and so joins in the fight for the d5 and e4 squares – both light squares.

5 ♝g2

White's bishop will also get involved in the struggle over the e4 and d5 squares, but in a direct manner.

5 ... 0-0

Before embarking on his bold advance in the centre Black wisely evacuates his king and brings his king's rook into the struggle.

6 0-0

White responds with the same excellent preparatory move, as immediate action in the centre with 6 d4 would leave the knight on c3 in a pin.

6 ... e4

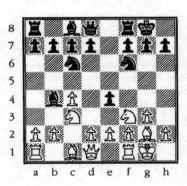

A very bold move: Black seizes the e4 square and so causes disruption to White's pieces – the knight is driven from its natural post on f3 and the bishop on g2 is blocked in. On the other hand the pawn will be subjected to enormous pressure and can hardly be maintained indefinitely on e4; but Black hopes that while White is engaged in disposing of the pawn he will get the chance to activate his pieces and achieve a good game.

7   ♘g5

Suddenly the pawn on e4 is attacked no less than three ways.

7   ...   ♗xc3

The only way to save the impetuous pawn is to concede the bishop pair. As long as the position remains fairly closed this won't be a serious issue, so it is reasonable to expect that Kasparov will strain to the utmost to open the arteries of the position.

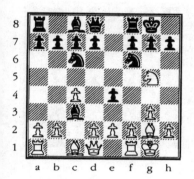

8   bxc3

If in doubt you should always recapture with a pawn towards the centre — 8 bxc3 — rather than away from it — 8 dxc3. Whilst it is true that after 8 dxc3 a central diagonal is opened up for the dark-squared bishop, it is more important to keep a pawn on d2 to challenge in the centre with d2-d3 or d2-d4.

8   ...   ♖e8

Black defends his advanced pawn in the most economical manner by centralizing his rook.

9   f3

Having failed to win the pawn, White must eliminate it by exchange if he is to loosen Black's grip on the centre.

9   ...   exf3

This looks forced, but in fact Black had the amazing pawn sacrifice 9...e3!? at his disposal, which was first played by Karpov against Kasparov in a World Championship match. After the reply 10 dxe3 Black could continue 10...b6 followed by ♗a6 and ♘a5, attacking the c4 pawn. It would be very hard for White to hold onto his extra pawn, which is doubled and sickly.

10   ♘xf3

In contrast to the position after 9...e3 above, White has his knight safely back on the f3 square and the open f file for his rook. He can therefore begin to play aggressively in the centre.

10   ...   d5

Ivanchuk clears the way for the development of his queen's bishop and forces White to attend to the threat of 11...dxc4 – or so he hopes!

11   d4!

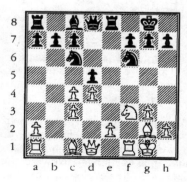

A fine pawn sacrifice to assert control of the centre. Now after

11...dxc4 there would follow 12 ♗g5 with a strong pin on the black knight – for example if 12...h6 13 ♗xf6 ♛xf6 14 ♘e5 and the f7 pawn is sure to drop next move.

11   ...   ♘e4

Black gets his knight out of the way of the ♗g5 pin and counter-attacks against c3.

12   ♛c2

White combines defence with attack: he saves the c3 pawn and brings his strongest piece to bear against the e4 square, which is still the focus of the opening struggle.

12   ...   dxc4

At last Ivanchuk accepts the pawn offer. He has little choice as 13 cxd5 was about to undermine his centre and if 12...♗f5 then 13 ♘h4 drives away the bishop.

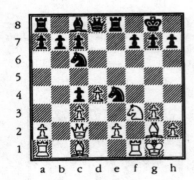

13   ♖b1!

Despite being a pawn down, Kasparov is in no hurry to do anything dramatic. The quiet rook move makes things awkward for Black, as if he develops his queen's bishop then b7 will drop leaving White with equal material and a much better pawn structure.

13   ...   f5

Again any attempt to embarrass the white queen with a discovered attack by the bishop fails after 13...♗f5 14 ♘h4!

Ivanchuk therefore supports the knight with his pawn. The moment of truth has arrived: has Black secured his grip on the light squares in the centre?

14   g4!

Kasparov answers this question with an emphatic 'No!' The second pawn offer will allow him to drive away the black knight and conquer the e4 square.

14   ...   ♛e7

The attempt to reinforce the knight backfires as it allows an opening of lines on the kingside that proves fatal for Black. He had to accept the sacrifice with 14...fxg4 and after 15 ♘e5 retreat with 15...♘f6 (as if 15...♘xe5 16 ♗xe4 leaves both the knight on e5 and h7 under threat). Then following 16 ♘xc6 bxc6 White would be foolish to snatch back material with 17 ♗xc6 as 17...♗e6! 18 ♗xa8 ♛xa8 leaves Black with wonderful light square control in return for the exchange. Far superior would be 16 e4! as pointed out by Kasparov, when White has tremendous compensation for the two pawns: he has achieved a broad pawn centre with absolute control over the e4 square, whereas Black's pawn structure is completely ruined. Nonetheless, this is the path that Black should have chosen as two pawns are a lot of comfort in a miserable position!

15 gxf5

Now Black's hold on e4 crumbles for if 15...♗xf5 16 ♘g5! ♘xg5 17 ♕xf5 is too strong. Even if he found a defence to the kingside and centre threats he would still have to reckon with ♖xb7, smashing his queenside pawns: here we see again the strategic value of the quiet 13 ♖b1

15 ... ♘d6

Perhaps Ivanchuk thought he was doing OK here as he has the double threat of 16...♗xf5 and 16...♕xe4. If so, he must have been quickly disabused by White's next move.

16 ♘g5!

Suddenly all the preconditions for an attack on the black king are in place as the knight is on a

formidable attacking square, the bishop on g2 is unleashed and the battering ram on f5 is defended by the rook. This is one of the wonders of a well conceived plan: all sorts of tactical opportunities arise for the player who has won the strategical battle.

16 ... ♕xe2

Black has little choice but to accept the latest pawn offer, as besides the immediate tactical threats he was faced with 17 e4, when White has a marvellous centre.

17 ♗d5+

The bishop finds an excellent station where in combination with the knight it can keep the black king under constant threat.

17 ... ♔h8

The only move as if 17...♔f8 18 ♘xh7+ (much simpler than the flashy 18 ♘e6+! ♗xe6 19 fxe6+) 18...♔e7 19 ♕xe2+ and White has won the queen.

18 ♕xe2

The golden rule when defending against an attack on the king is to exchange queens, but it won't save

Black here as the pressure from the other white pieces is overwhelming.

18   ...   Ξxe2

Having a rook on the seventh rank is usually a wonderful thing, but here the unhappy rook has no support whatever from the other black pieces.

19   ♗f4

At last the dark-squared bishop joins in the game. As well as introducing ideas of ♗xd6 followed by ♘f7+, when the black king is forced into a discovered check, it clears the way for an exchange of rooks with Ξbe1 which is most unwelcome for Black.

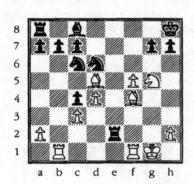

19   ...   ♘d8

It's usually a sure sign that something has gone wrong when a minor piece has to retreat to the first rank. However, Black needed to add a defender to the f7 square as he would drop a piece to a discovered check if he tried developing his bishop: 19...♗d7 20 ♗xd6 cxd6 21 ♘f7+ ♔g8 22 ♘e5+ and 23 ♘xd7.

20   ♗xd6

Kasparov is intent on eliminating any black piece that can oppose his plan to seize total control of the open e file. Speaking in the abstract, a bishop in an open position tends to be more valuable than a knight, but it is their function in their respective armies which is what truly matters – and here the exchange does a lot of harm to Black's position.

20   ...   cxd6

Now Ivanchuk could put up a stout resistance after 21 ♗xc4 Ξe8! but the World Champion is after far bigger game than the c4 pawn: his target is the black king himself.

21   Ξbe1

A wise man once compared happiness to an aery spirit who was liable to vanish as soon as you spoke her name. The same can be said about checkmate. If you make a clumsy, single minded lunge at your opponent's king then checkmate tends to hide herself; whereas if you content yourself with the gradual, methodical improvement of your position she will often appear of her own free will. Kasparov applies himself to the task of gaining the e file and this leads almost magically to an appearance by checkmate.

21   ...   Ξxe1

Moving the rook sideways allows mate on e8, so Black has no choice but to submit to the exchange of his last active piece.

22 ℤxe1

Now Black can only avert 23 ℤe8 mate by ceding his second rank to the white rook with gain of time.

22 ... ♝d7

This is a very belated attempt to mobilize the queenside and offer some sort of challenge to White's bishop.

23 ℤe7

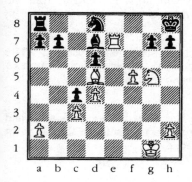

In ancient times the number seven was regarded as a magical number. There are the seven wonders of the world, the seven sisters and the seven seas, and in chess there is the seventh rank – a magical place whenever a rook gets there.

Now the black bishop has to run away to save itself.

23 ... ♝c6

Black still has a rook and a knight passively placed. Only his bishop is putting up a fight, but even he is overloaded in having to defend the back rank and oppose the white bishop.

Meanwhile White has all three of his pieces on beautiful attacking squares. But a little extra nudge is needed to push the black position into the precipice. Can we find it? We look around, knowing it is there somewhere and – yes!

24 f6!!

It is all too easy to forget about pawn power when we are attacking with the big pieces. But Kasparov is aware of all his attacking resources. Ivanchuk resigned here. The threat is 25 fxg7 mate. If 24...gxf6 25 ℤxh7 is mate – the rook proves its value on the seventh rank. Instead after 24...♝xd5 there is a glorious denouement on the eighth rank: 24...♝xd5 25 ℤe8+ ♝g8 26 f7! ♞xf7 – what else? 27 ♞xf7 mate!

A wonderful quartet of rook, bishop, knight and pawn.

Game Twenty-Eight
V.Korchnoi - L.Portisch
Bad Kissingen 1983
English Opening

1 c4

Throughout his long career Korchnoi has won many excellent

games with the English Opening. The idea is simple: control of d5.

1   ...   c5

A logical reply which prevents White from building a broad centre with 2 d4.

2   ♘f3

Even though he cannot maintain a pawn on d4, White is still keen to advance d2-d4 as it will consolidate his space advantage. If immediately 2 d4? cxd4 3 ♕xd4 ♘c6 loses time with the queen, so he prepares to recapture on d4 with the knight.

2   ...   ♘f6

A mirror image move, with a mirror image idea: if allowed Black would consider playing d7-d5 himself to seize terrain in the centre.

3   ♘c3

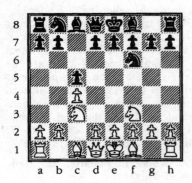

White has developed his knights first in good classical style – there is little doubt that they will prove to be well placed on c3 and f3 as they are centralized and unlikely to be harassed by the black pieces and pawns.

3   ...   ♘c6

Portisch continues to copy his opponent and why not, as he is playing good moves! Also possible was 3...d5 4 cxd5 ♘xd5, when Black has freed his game but he is a little vulnerable as lines have become open and he is slightly behind in development.

4   d4

After his careful opening, Korchnoi finally decides to exploit the advantage of moving first to gain the upper hand in the centre.

4   ...   cxd4

It is necessary to capture or else 5 d5 will drive his knight from the centre.

5   ♘xd4

Now positionally speaking White is slightly better as the pawn on c4 has no rival in the centre.

5   ...   e6

This frees the king's bishop and prepares to challenge the c4 pawn with d7-d5.

6   ♘db5

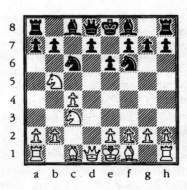

It is very important to learn the art of converting one advantage into another. Korchnoi sees that he cannot prevent Black from playing d7-d5 which will neutralize his spatial superiority; therefore he seeks to use his initiative – which in this case amounts to his better development – to gain another more durable advantage.

6 ... d5

The consistent move, which at the same time deals with the threat of 7 ♘d6+ ♗xd6 8 ♕xd6 when White has acquired the two bishops.

7 ♗f4

White continues his vigorous build up. Now he threatens to win a rook with 8 ♘c7+.

7 ... e5

A tough riposte which blocks the fork on c7 and counterattacks against the bishop.

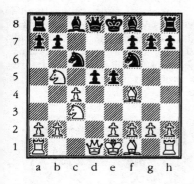

8 cxd5

No time is to be lost: if White had retreated his bishop then Black would have had an excellent game with his big centre. Instead Korchnoi uses his initiative to break up the black pawns and open lines for his more active pieces.

8 ... exf4

A necessary capture, as if the knight retreats to c6 then 9 ♗xe5 just leaves White two pawns up.

9 dxc6

White regains his piece. After the slow opening an energetic fight has stripped the d and e files of pawns and left the queens glaring at each other down the open file.

9 ... bxc6

The only move, as after 9...♕xd1+ 10 ♖xd1 Black cannot play 10...bxc6 because of 11 ♘c7+ winning the rook.

10 ♕xd8+

This is another essential move as from now on White's whole strategy will revolve around causing problems for the displaced black king.

10 ... ♔xd8

But all is by no means lost for Black as he has potentially the best minor piece on the board in the shape of the dark-squared bishop.

11 ♘d4

The knight must retreat and in doing so gains time by hitting the pawn on c6.

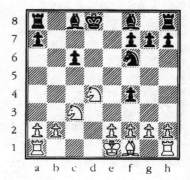

11 ... ♔c7?!

Black tries to kill two birds with one stone: he defends his isolated pawn by sheltering his exposed king behind it. Unfortunately the king doesn't prove to be safe on the c file. A better approach was 11...♗b7 when after 12 g3 – how else to develop the bishop? – 12...c5 13 ♘f3-the only move – 13...♗d6 14 ♗g2 ♖b8 Black has succeeded in activating most of his pieces.

12 g3!

In contrast to the variation given in the note above, here White succeeds in putting his bishop on g2 without any opposition from ♗b7. As a result his knight gets to stay on d4, where it is able to terrorize the c6 pawn.

12 ... ♗c5?

This attempt to chase the white knight from the centre rebounds spectacularly. Better was 12...♗b4 pinning the other knight when if 13 gxf4 ♘d5 will regain the pawn with 14...♘xf4 because of the threat to c3.

13 ♖c1!

There is an old saying that the best answer to a threat is to ignore

it! Here White plays the move he wants to play – bringing his rook to the open file – as 13...♗xd4 fails to 14 ♘b5+ ♔b6 15 ♘xd4, when the weak pawn remains on c6 and Black has lost by exchange his dark-squared bishop.

13 ... fxg3

It is of some consolation to Black that he can be rid of at least one of his weak pawns.

14 hxg3

As usual it is best to recapture with a pawn towards the centre. The rook on h1 suddenly enjoys an open file and can be brought into the attack with for example ♖h4 at some point.

14 ... ♗a6?

The opening hasn't gone well for Portisch and perhaps because of this he makes a poor move which overlooks White's strong reply. He had to evacuate the rook from a8 with 14...♖b8 when a satisfactory defence was still possible, despite the problems facing him on the c file.

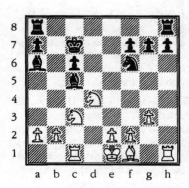

15 ♘xc6!

White's pressure along the c file has reached crisis point and now a tactical blow is not only possible but also necessary or else Black will escape.

15 ...   ♗b7

After 15...♔xc6 one simple continuation for White is 16 ♘a4 ♘d7 17 b4, when he regains his piece and remains a pawn up. So Portisch instigates a pin of his own – the knight on c6 dare not move or else the rook on h1 is lost. Does this mean that Korchnoi has miscalculated?

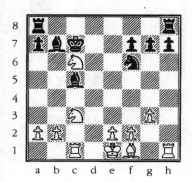

16   ♘a4

Not at all! White's pin on the c file is always going to be the more deadly as a pin on a king is absolute: any piece trapped in front of their monarch is completely paralyzed. Thus if 16...♗xc6 17 ♖xc5 the black bishop on c6 attacks two pieces but can do nothing.

16 ...   ♗xf2+

Rather than lose this bishop for nothing after 16...♗xc6 17 ♖xc5, Black decides he might as well sell it as dearly as possible by grabbing a pawn: a so-called 'Desperado' move.

17   ♔xf2

Now it all seems over as after 17...♗xc6 18 ♗g2 wins a piece, but Portisch finds the only way to battle on.

17 ...   ♘e4+

It is necessary to block the diagonal with this *zwischenzug* or in-between move before recapturing on c6.

18   ♔g1

A strange form of artificial castling, but as will be seen from White's next two moves the king doesn't get in the way of the development of the kingside pieces.

18 ...   ♗xc6

After some delaying tactics Black finally captures the knight. He has managed to stave off material losses so far but White's pressure along the c file is by no means quelled.

19   ♗g2

White improves the layout of his pieces with gain of time by attacking the knight.

19 ...   ♖ae8

Here's what would have happened if Black had decided to break the pin with 19...♔d6: 20 ♖xc6+! ♔xc6 21 ♗xe4+ ♔b5 22 ♗xa8 and White will emerge with an extra piece.

20   ♖h4

White's plan is to put such intense pressure on the knight on e4 that it will either:

♦ stand its ground alone and be lost

♦ be forced to retreat and allow a disaster on c6

♦ be supported by f7-f5, when Black's kingside falls apart.

20   ...   f5

Now White has all his pieces on useful squares whereas the black rook on h8 is still out of the game. Still, Korchnoi had better make something of his advantage quickly or else Black will complete his development with ♖e7, g7-g6 and ♖he8, when all his pieces will be acting together in support of the knight on e4.

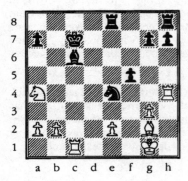

21   g4!

A nasty surprise for Mr. Portisch. In the middle of an attack with the pieces you should never forget the value of the pawns: if you think you have every piece on a good square,

look around and see if there is any pawn move that will provide the little bit of extra impetus that your strategy requires.

21   ...   f4

The ideal set up for Black requires the maintenance of a pawn on f5 to protect the knight and so restrain the pressure from the bishop on g2. Alas, this is impossible as after the natural 21...g6 22 gxf5 gxf5 catastrophe strikes from another direction: 23 ♖h6! wins a piece.

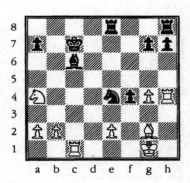

22   ♖xc6+!

Now that the black pawn has been dislodged from f5 White is able to carry out a combination to win material.

22   ...   ♔xc6

The unhappy black king is obliged to exchange a pin on the c file for one on the a8-h1 diagonal.

23   ♘c3

The knight returns from the edge of the board and wins the knight on e4 – evidently not every knight on the rim is dim, nor is every knight in the centre blessed! As always, what really matters is whether a piece is well co-ordinated with the rest of its army. Here the white knight and bishop are working together whilst the black king is paralyzing its own knight.

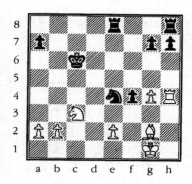

23 ... ♔c5

Portisch decides to make a fight of it. It makes sense both positionally and psychologically to advance his king forwards into the enemy camp: Black is way down on material so he needs to make use of all his resources, including the king – if he gets mated, it is tough luck, but at least there is a chance White could get confused by the king charging towards him, whereas if the king headed backwards to c7 then Korchnoi's technique would undoubtedly prevail sooner or later.

24 ♗xe4

The correct capture: after 24 ♘xe4 ♔d4 White has nothing better than 25 ♘c3, whereas now he can retreat his bishop to a square superior to g2 if it is attacked.

24 ... ♔d4

The black king continues his advance. The white rook is temporarily out of play so Portisch hopes to win material or stage a

breakthrough before it can join its comrades.

25 ♗f3

The bishop solidifies White's kingside by defending both the e2 and g4 pawns.

25 ... ♖b8

Black tries to puncture a hole in the white queenside before the white rook arrives on the scene.

26 ♘a4!

A beautifully calculated move. The knight goes to the edge of the board once again as believe it or not Korchnoi has seen that this is the best way to get his pieces working together.

26 ... ♖b4

A rook is seldom a match for two minor pieces, especially in situations where there are few open lines and no weak pawns to pick off. Portisch hopes to entice White into 27 b3, when after 27...h6 followed by ♖c8 and ♖c2 he will generate counterplay against the a2 pawn.

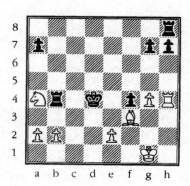

27 ♖h5!!

A superb move. Most of us would have played the lazy 27 b3,

especially as it preserves a huge advantage; but Korchnoi as always shows considerable tactical acumen. Here is the evidence: if 27...♖xa4 28 ♖d5+ ♔e3 29 ♖d3 mate! or more prosaically if 28...♔c4 29 b3+ wins the rook.

27 ... ♖d8

The rook finally emerges from its slumber on h8 but it is still in the role of a passive defender as it must guard d5.

28 b3

Only now does White take time out to defend his knight.

28 ... h6

He cannot afford to drop even more material by allowing 29 ♖xh7.

29 ♔f2

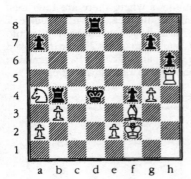

The brave black king now finds himself stalemated by the white pieces in the centre of the board.

29 ... ♖d6

By defending h6 with the rook Black hopes to shut out the white rook with 30...g5, but Korchnoi is on his guard.

30 ♖f5

The rook attacks the f4 pawn and thereby gains time to reach the seventh rank.

30 ... g5

The only move for if 30...♖f6 31 ♖d5 is mate.

31 ♖f7

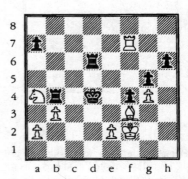

Now besides the attack on a7 there are direct threats to the black king for example if 31...a5 32 ♖e7! when 33 ♖e4+ will force the king onto d5 where it suffers a killer discovered check.

31 ... ♔e5

Portisch has no choice but to retreat his king and jettison the a7 pawn, though this is hopeless in the long run.

32 ♖xa7

Now that connected passed pawns have appeared it can only be a matter of time before Black has to resign.

32 ... ♖d2

This is a final desperate attempt to generate counterplay along the seventh rank.

33   ♘c5

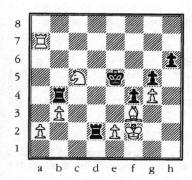

The black pieces are tripping over each other as 34 ♘d3+ with a fork is threatened.

33   ...   ♖bd4

Hoping against hope that White will blunder with 34 ♘d3+?? when 34...♖4xd3 wins a piece.

34   ♖a6

Of course Korchnoi isn't so easily tricked. Now there is the threat of 35 ♖e6 mate.

34   ...   ♖d6

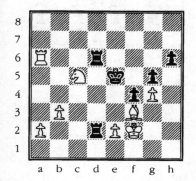

Portisch hopes to labour on after 35 ♖xd6 ♖xd6 but White's reply puts him out of his misery.

35   ♖a5!   1-0

The threat of 36 ♘e4, whether or not it comes with check, is decisive. This was a masterly display of the precise exploitation of a material advantage by Korchnoi.

Game Twenty-Nine
M.Tal - J.Van der Wiel
Moscow 1982
English Opening

Even though it is more than 40 years since Mikhail Tal was World Champion his reputation lives on. An imaginative and stylish sacrifice is still referred to as a Tal-like sacrifice.

Tal wrote quite possibly the best book of all time on chess: *The Life and Games of Mikhail Tal*. It is full of wonderful games and has a detailed, witty and thoroughly fascinating autobiography in the form of an interview between Tal and an imaginary journalist.

It is no wonder that Korchnoi said of Tal that he could have been a great writer if he hadn't become obsessed with chess. Literature's loss is chess's gain as he has left us a whole series of thrilling games played with gusto and panache.

Here is an example of Tal's flair for the attack. Tal himself once said that he wasn't a particularly calculative player; as we shall see, tactical brilliance is underpinned by his deep knowledge of chess strategy.

1   c4

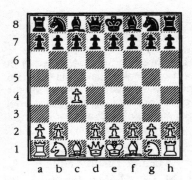

The English Opening was much favoured by Howard Staunton who was the best player in the World until the arrival of Paul Morphy in the 1850s. It is an eminently playable system which immediately exerts influence on the d5 square.

1 ... ♘f6

The development of the knight to f6 by the third move is a sound and sensible reply to virtually any opening system White might choose.

2 ♘c3

Every player brings his own style to the openings. Tal hasn't chosen the English because he is looking to outplay his opponent in a game of delicate manoeuvring. As will be seen he soon finds a way to introduce violence to the proceedings.

2 ... e6

A solid response that opens the diagonal for his king's bishop and also contests the d5 square.

3 ♘f3

The most flexible reply. Instead after 3 d4 d5 we would have the mainline of the Queen's Gambit Declined or after 3...♗b4 the

Nimzo-Indian. Grandmaster Van der Wiel is a theoretical expert so no doubt Tal wished to direct play away from more familiar lines.

3 ... b6

Black decides to develop his queen's bishop and try to control the e4 point from a distance rather than fight for it directly with 3...d5 or 3...♗b4.

4 e4

The boldest answer to Black's idea. The pawn will be a target for the black bishop, but on the other hand a pawn on the fourth rank means more space for the white pieces behind it.

4 ... ♗b7

This bishop is often Black's problem piece in Queenside openings. Therefore it is a delight for him to develop it to a square where it is safe from all possible attack and still has influence on the centre.

5 ♗d3

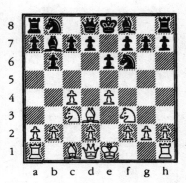

An ingenious idea that was popularized by the Ukrainian Grandmaster Oleg Romanishin. It looks odd to block the d2 pawn, but

the e4 pawn is under attack and if 5 d3 then the king's bishop has little scope. So White puts his bishop on d3 to defend the e4 pawn and then drops it back to c2 to clear the way for a space-gaining d2-d4 advance. That at least was Romanishin's basic idea. But as will be seen Tal is going to give it his own personal twist – the bishop will not go back to c2 but forwards to e4.

5 ... c5

An eminently sensible reply. By advancing c2-c4 and e2-e4 White has left a hole on d4 that can no longer be protected by a pawn; he has compounded his neglect of the centre square by putting his bishop on d3, where it obstructs the advance d2-d4 which would liquidate the hole.

Van der Wiel strives to bring the d4 square under Black's control, or at least force White to make some concessions to reassert his authority over it.

6 0-0

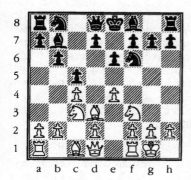

Despite the placid reputation of the English Opening and the eccentric 5 ♗d3, White has still managed to complete his kingside development in only six moves.

6 ... ♘c6

The knight adds to Black's ascendancy over the d4 square. Because of White's avoidance of d2-d4, a secondary dark square weakness is gradually appearing on e5: if left undisturbed Black will develop with ♗e7, 0-0, a7-a6, ♕c7 and ♘g4 when the two squares have merged into a weak dark square *complex* in the centre.

7 e5!?

Tal cuts across Black's plans, even though it will commit him to a pawn sacrifice if he wishes to keep the initiative.

7 ... ♘g4

Now the e5 pawn is attacked twice and can only be defended by pieces, not pawns.

8 ♗e4

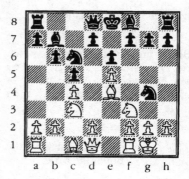

White wants to drum up a direct attack and so needs to clear the way for his d pawn to advance in order to free his queenside pieces.

Incidentally, this is much better than the routine 8 ♖e1. In such positions players often put the rook on e1 only to discover in a couple of moves that it would have been better left on f1 where it supports a pawn advance down the f file.

8 ... ♛c8

Not 8...♞gxe5 9 ♞xe5 ♞xe5 10 ♝xb7 when Black has lost a piece.

9 d3

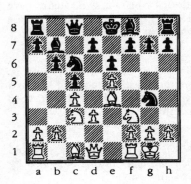

As so often during his long career, Tal sacrifices a pawn to inject dynamism into the situation.

9 ... ♞gxe5

Black bravely accepts the pawn offer. As Steinitz once remarked when he grabbed a hot e pawn 'a centre pawn is worth a little trouble'.

10 ♞xe5

This exchange facilitates the coming attack down the f file.

10 ... ♞xe5

Black recaptures and opens the way for an exchange of bishops as well. As a general rule, when there is an all out attack every diminution of material favours the defender.

11 f4

The main point of White's sacrifice is that he can gain time to

use the f pawn as a battering ram by attacking the black knight.

11 ... ♞c6

A sensible retreat as after 11...♞g6 White could have harassed the knight again with 12 f5.

12 f5

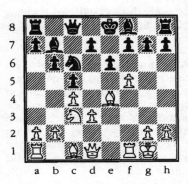

The onslaught gathers pace. Its strategical basis is that Black has a problem in deciding what to do with his king. The black pawn centre is highly resilient, but in the long term it is unlikely to provide a safe residence for its monarch. An even worse option would be the kingside, as White would have a ready made attack if Black opted to castle there. That leaves the queenside, where the king would enjoy a lot of pawn cover, but it is by no means easy to arrange queenside castling as if 12...♛c7 13 ♞b5! is highly awkward.

12 ... g6

An interesting defensive concept. After 12...♝e7 13 ♛g4 White's attack would continue unabated, so Black challenges the f5 pawn. His idea is firstly that after 13 fxg6 hxg6 the f file is open – which was of course inevitable in any case – but he has the defensive move ♖h7 available to fortify the f7 square. Secondly, if 13 fxe6 dxe6 gives the queen the d7 square, which facilitates castling queenside after ♛d7. Thirdly, if 13 f6 the f file is blocked; and fourthly 13 g4 gxf5 14 gxf5 ♖g8+ allows Black ample counterplay against the white king.

It appears that Black has found the perfect answer to White's sacrifice, but unfortunately for him there is a fifth option of the kind which Tal is not going to miss.

13   ♗g5!

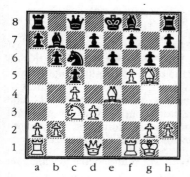

White develops his last minor piece in spectacular style. The bishop takes control of the dark squares around the black king – but has Tal forgotten about the light squares?

13   ...   gxf5

Black eliminates the only pawn that can trouble him. Therefore, if White wants to breakthrough and try to win he will have to sacrifice a piece, as there are no more pawns suitable to use as cannon fodder. Generally speaking, this gives the defender a chance in all but the most hopeless of cases, as there is

always an element of risk involved in a big sacrifice.

14   ♗xf5!

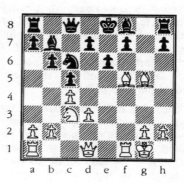

Nevertheless, this sacrifice is the logical consequence of White's plan: it is too late to retreat as after 14 ♗f3 he would be left two pawns down with a lost position.

Once you have committed yourself to an all out attack there is no place for half measures: you have to press forwards and win or else suffer defeat. Therefore, you should never embark on an aggressive venture unless you are fully convinced that you have the resources to finish off the game. Here the situation looks excellent for White as despite giving up the piece he will have superior firepower where it really matters – in the centre. Black's major pieces – his queen and rooks – are ill prepared to help the defence.

14   ...   ♗e7

What would have happened if Black had accepted the sacrifice with 14...exf5?

A seafaring analogy might help. Imagine that Black is a giant sea turtle, protected by the heavy armour of its shell; whilst White is a hungry shark with teeth as long and sharp as steak knifes looking for its next meal. The shark breaks one of its teeth but succeeds in prising open a large part of the turtle's shell. Losing a tooth is a painful business, but not as painful as it is for the turtle to lose its protection: there are a lot of other razor sharp teeth in the jaws of the shark!

After 14...exf5 the black king finds its pawn shell is split open: there is nowhere to run as the white bishop on g5 is stopping him from escaping to the left, whilst his own bishop is blocking his flight in the other direction. So all Black can do is fling the bodies of his minor pieces in the way if his king is checked down the e file. This is hardly a recipe for the harmonious coordination of the pieces.

Meanwhile White can concentrate all his efforts along the two open files with 15 ♕e2+ ♘e7 (even worse is 15...♗e7 as White has 16 ♘d5 without Black having the option of snapping off the knight with the bishop on b7) 16 ♖ae1. Now he has succeeded in mobilizing his last undeveloped piece, the queen's rook, with the terrible threat of 17 ♗xe7 ♗xe7 18 ♕xe7 mate. If Black plays 16...♕d8 to bring his queen to the defence, Black has his king, queen, king's bishop and both his rooks all on their starting squares – an almost ridiculous state of undevelopment. In contrast White has all his pieces ready for action and working together, to say nothing of the king safely tucked away on g1.

Taking the variation further, White could continue very simply

with 17 ♖xf5, removing another piece of the shell.

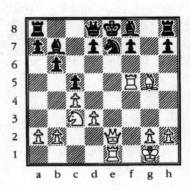

(analysis diagram)

Then he has the double threat of 18 ♖fe5 when his pieces are tripled on the e file and so the knight on e7 drops off; or with 18 ♕h5! he can launch a sudden attack on f7, the weakest point in Black's position. Black is so paralyzed he cannot hope to fend off both threats.

Well we didn't need to calculate umpteen moves deep like a computer to work out that White has a strong attack for the piece. In fact we didn't really need to calculate at all: the variation given above was merely illustrative of White's attacking chances which are self-evident once we have noticed the positional factors at work.

After all, we don't need to calculate to realize that our slightly maimed shark is going to rip apart the tortoise once it has lost its shell. In the same way it is enough to realize that once lines of attack are opened against the black king the catastrophic state of Black's development is going to prove fatal.

Of course all this presupposes that the defensive shell collapses. In reality sharks don't often attack sea turtles, as they are likely to damage their teeth without breaking through the shell. But Tal of course is no ordinary shark!

15   ♕h5

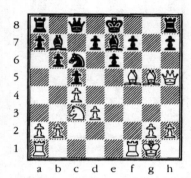

A dramatic entrance. The rules to chess were changed more than 500 years ago to make the queen the most powerful piece on the board, and it is no mere coincidence that from then onwards the f7 square has been the scene of greatest tragedy.

15   ...   ♗xg5

Disaster is inevitable after 15...exf5 16 ♖ae1 intending ♘d5, etc. White in effect would have a material advantage of two rooks for a bishop, rather than a bishop deficit, as his own rooks are very active whilst the black rooks cannot join in the game.

The game move deflects the white queen from the attack on f7 but leaves her in possession of key dark squares. Furthermore, the d6 square becomes available to the white knight who can prepare a big check there with ♘b5 or ♘e4.

16   ♕xg5

White's queen suddenly has control of a whole complex of dark squares around the black king – f6. g7 and h6.

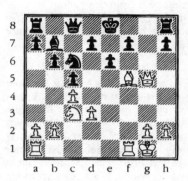

16   ...   ♘e7

Again Black decides to leave the bishop well alone. And rightly so, as after 16...exf5 17 ♖ae1+ the black king is at the mercy of an all out attack by the white pieces. The rooks thrive on open lines and here White has the e file and the f file for his rooks to exploit. After 17...♔f8 18 ♕h6+ ♔g8 White can choose between the simple and excellent 19 ♖xf5 when Black has no good way to fend off 20 ♖g5 mate, or the spectacular 19 ♘d5 ♕d8 – to stop 20 ♘f6 mate – 20 ♖e8+! ♕xe8 21 ♘f6 mate!

17   ♗e4

After offering itself for capture three times on f5, the bishop finally retreats. Now the way is open for White to put pressure with his rooks along the f file.

17   ...   ♗xe4

Black tries to free his game by exchanging pieces. This is normally a good idea, but the new resident on e4 proves even more deadly than the white bishop.

18   ♘xe4

The knight takes over a fine central post from the bishop and has a most ignoble threat: 19 ♘d6+ when the black king and queen are forked.

18   ...   ♛c6

The queen rushes to plug the hole on d6. It appears that Black has survived all the fireworks from the white pieces as 19 ♘f6+ ♚d8 leaves him a pawn up, when his king is solidly defended behind its barrier of pawns. But Tal has foreseen a way to drive the black king from his defences.

19   ♖xf7!

Another brilliant sacrifice. It is well known that at the start of a game the f7 square is the weakest point in Black's position – just as the f2 square is the weakest point in White's position. It is not uncommon for White to sacrifice a bishop or a knight to win control of the square, but Tal goes one step further in offering a rook.

19   ...   ♚xf7

The white rook cannot be allowed to remain alive on f7, but now the black king is forced out into the open.

20   ♛f6+

A very awkward check for Black. The queen and knight are a ferocious attacking force as they complement each other – between them they span the whole range of the powers of the pieces. Black now has to give up either his knight or rook.

20   ...   ♚g8

Black's only chance is to hold onto his booty and hope that White over reaches in his attack. If instead 20...♚e8 21 ♛xh8+ ♚f7 22 ♛xh7+ leaves the black king facing a deadly attack without even the consolation of extra material. Of course Tal isn't likely to go wrong.

21   ♛xe7

Now there is the terrible threat of 22 ♘f6 mate.

21   ...   ♖f8

The rook rushes over to prevent the deadly check but White also has reinforcements that he can bring into the attack.

22 ♖f1 1-0

White brings up the final reserves into the attack. Black now resigned as after 22...♖xf1+ 23 ♔xf1 his king is boxed in and facing a renewed threat of 23 ♘f6 mate, which this time can only be averted by giving up his queen.

You will see that despite Black having more 'points' on the board, White's army is much stronger as the rook on h8 is playing no part in the game.

Game Thirty
C.McNab - M.Adams
Dublin 1993
English Opening

1 ♘f3

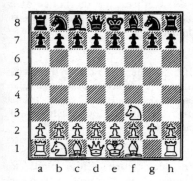

A flexible move that is a favourite of Vladimir Kramnik. The knight is almost always developed on f3 no matter what opening White adopts,

so why not play it there straightaway?

White can play the English Opening after 1...c5 with 2 c4, or if he is feeling more aggressive transpose to the Sicilian with 2 e4. Against other first moves by Black White has the option of transposing to 1 d4 openings, but only ones he is comfortable at facing.

1 ... ♘f6

Black responds in the same non-committal way by putting his knight on the tested and approved square.

2 c4

True to his style, the Scottish Grandmaster declines the chance to play 2 d4 and keeps play in the territory of the English Opening.

2 ... b6

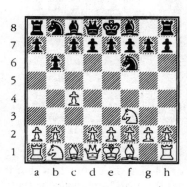

Black plans to set up a mini fortress in the centre by edging his two centre pawns one square forward. This is a respectable idea, but the drawback is that after e7-e6 the bishop on c8 is deprived of the diagonal leading out to f5 or g4. So Black begins by opening another avenue of development for the queen's bishop. He does this straightaway before White has time to play g2-g3 and ♗g2, when White's pressure along the diagonal pointing at a8 would make it awkward to begin weakening his pawns with b7-b6.

3   g3

White puts his bishop on g2, where the bishop is excellently placed both defensively in sheltering the white king and aggressively in aiming at Black's queenside.

3   ...   c5

Black refuses to give his opponent a freehand in the centre with 4 d4.

4   ♗g2

The bishop doesn't strike out to b5 or c4 as it does after 1 e4, but it is transformed from being a mere obstruction on f1 to the proud possessor of an important diagonal where it supports action in the centre. Such is the power of centralization.

4   ...   ♗b7

It is essential for Black to oppose bishops along the diagonal.

5   d3

After his restrained opening play White decides it is time to build a pawn centre.

5   ...   e6

Black now threatens to seize a large lump of the centre with 6...d5, which obliges White to act fast.

6   e4

Mission accomplished: the white triangle of pawns control a lot of centre squares. Nevertheless, the rigidity of this structure and the hole on d4 won't escape the notice of a master of positional play such as Adams.

6   ...   d6

If 6...d5 then 7 e5 drives the black knight away from its best square, so Adams settles for a quiet move which maintains the elasticity of Black's centre.

7   ♘c3

In due course White plans to advance d3-d4, in order to increase his space advantage. On c3 the knight helps make this possible by defending the e4 pawn again.

7   ...   ♗e7

In contrast Black is in no hurry to play 7...♘c6. even though it is the best square for the knight. This is because he wants to delay d3-d4 by White for at least a couple of moves by keeping the bishop on b7 aimed directly at e4.

8   0-0

The genius who changed the rules of chess to make the queen the strongest piece was quick to realize that if games weren't to be decided quickly and brutally in the opening the king needed to be given a special power to run away from the attack. Thus it was that castling was invented: the oddest move in chess, but also one of the most essential!

8   ...   0-0

The black king also retires into safety behind the wall of pawns on the kingside.

9   b3

As White is planning an eventual d3-d4, it is useful to defend the c4 pawn in anticipation of a future attack by ♖c8 or ♕c7 after the opening of the c file with c5xd4.

9   ...   a6

A useful semi-waiting move that prevents White ever targeting the black queen if she goes to c7 or the black pawn on d6 with ♘b5. At the same time it supports a possible expansion on the queenside with b6-b5.

10   ♗b2

Another point of White's previous move is that the bishop can be deployed to a post where it can support operations with d3-d4.

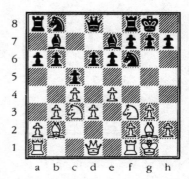

10   ...   ♕c7

Again Black delays developing his queen's knight as 10...♘c6 11 d4 allows White to carry out his plan immediately without worrying about the e4 pawn dropping off. The queen is well placed on c7 where she helps defend the b6 and d6 pawns and has influence over both the c file and the e5 square – these will prove valuable powers once White opens the centre with d3-d4. Furthermore, the queen doesn't get in the way of any other piece on c7 and has cleared the first rank to allow the rooks to work together.

11   ♕e2

McNab continues his methodical plan to enforce d3-d4. He defends e4 again to rule out the reply ♘xe4 and vacates the d1 square for his queen's rook.

11 ... ♘c6

Only now does Adams develop his knight – it is exactly the right time as it stops 12 d4.

12 ♖ad1

Now at last everything is ready for d3-d4. Black cannot prevent it without making concessions, as if 12...e5 White could reply 13 ♘d5 followed in due course by ♘h4 and f2-f4, putting more pressure on Black's centre. Equally if 12...♘d4 13 ♘xd4 cxd4 14 ♘b1 e5 – to defend d4 – 15 f4 leaves White with a pleasant initiative: he can build up along the f file whilst Black has no counterplay.

12 ... ♘d7!

Adams meets his opponent halfway: he allows him to play the advance he has so laboriously prepared as he hopes that the black pieces will profit the most from the struggle for the d4 square.

13 d4

There was no time to be wasted as Black intended to get control of d4 with 13...♗f6.

13 ... ♗f6

This is Black's idea. He is attacking d4 three ways which forces White to make an important decision: should he capture on c5 or advance his pawn to d5?

14 dxc5?

A strategical mistake. It is tempting to open the d file, especially as White has been the first to get a rook to the centre, but a far better approach was 14 d5! maintaining a space advantage. Then 14...♘d4 15 ♘xd4 cxd4 16 ♘b1 e5 would have been unclear: Black has a protected passed pawn in the centre but White can build up on the kingside with f2-f4 etc.

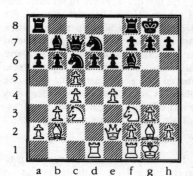

14 ... bxc5!

Black recaptures towards the centre, but isn't he leaving himself with a weak pawn on d6?

We should take a moment to look at the black pawn structure and consider how it is affected by the exchange of various pieces. A pawn structure is weak or strong according to the number, type and deployment of the pieces on the board, not just according to whether there are features such as doubled, isolated or back ward pawns.

Here we see that Black has a pawn on d6 that cannot be supported by its fellow pawns unless it advances to d5, which is highly unlikely to be feasible as White has this square in a pincer grip. So the pawn remains backward on d6 on the open d file. Structurally speaking this is a bad state of affairs for Black and if all the minor pieces were exchanged off, leaving only rooks and the queens on the board, the d6 pawn would be a serious liability: White could simply double or triple his major pieces – rooks and queens – against the vulnerable pawn and win it.

If we imagine a scenario with bishops as well as rooks and queens on the board, but no knights, the pawn would still be weak, but Black would have more defensive options: the pawn could be defended by ♝e7 or the e4 pawn counterattacked by the other bishop. With the presence of knights, however, things take a drastic turn in Black's favour: Black can get a grip on the d4 square with e6-e5 when ♘d4 leaves a knight wonderfully centralized – and the pawn on d6 provided with total shelter. A weakness is only a weakness if it can be attacked.

15 ♕d2

The battle along the d file begins in earnest with an immediate threat to the d6 pawn.

15 ... ♘d4

...but Adams has worked out that his possession of the d4 square will safeguard the d6 pawn against any attack.

16 ♖fe1

White has no active continuation and so quietly completes his development and adds further protection to the e4 pawn.

16 ... ♖ad8

Black anticipates the forthcoming attack on d4 and so prepares to defend the d6 pawn in a most clever way.

17 ♘e2

Suddenly White is hitting the black knight on d4 with no less than queen, rook, two knights and a bishop! Black's reply is critical.

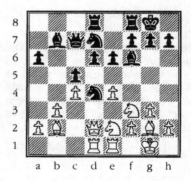

17 ... ♘c6!

'Discretion is the better part of valour' said Shakespeare. Let's look at White's alternatives.

Support the knight with 17...e5. A good idea, but the time isn't right! As quick as a flash White would play 18 ♘c3 returning the knight to c3 where it suddenly has access to the d5 square. Then the black knights have been deprived of access to e5 and the black bishop on f6 is shut out of the long diagonal. Black wants to play e6-e5 on his own terms – notably when he has exchanged off dark-squared bishops so that he isn't turning his bishop into a feeble piece.

Capture the e4 pawn. A definite no-no, as Black finds to his embarrassment that he loses a piece after 18 ♘exd4!

Exchange off by capturing the white knight either on e2 or f3. After 17...♘xf3+ 18 ♗xf3 or 17...♘xe2+ 18 ♖xe2 White is able to exchange off bishops with ♗xf6. With two minor pieces each less on the board, and no Black piece in a position to occupy d4, White's game has been eased by the exchanges.

18   ♘f4

The d6 pawn is immune for if 18 ♕xd6 ♕xd6 19 ♖xd6 ♗xb2 and Black has won a piece, while if 18 ♗xf6 ♘xf6 then the d6 pawn is safely guarded. White has clearly run out of ideas as the knight sheepishly returns to e2 in two moves time.

18   ...   ♘de5

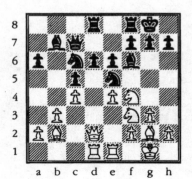

Black gets the maximum benefit out of the e5 square before he blocks it forever on move 21. He instigates the exchange of one knight and the dark-squared bishops to bring his goal of dominating the d4 square one step nearer.

19   ♘xe5

Now, the wrong recapture would leave Black facing a storm on the kingside.

19   ...   ♗xe5

Incorrect was 19...♘xe5 as the reply 20 ♘h5 is highly awkward – White threatens to break up the black kingside with 21 ♘xf6+ and also clears the way for f2-f4 to attack the black knight. The rather hopeful 19...dxe5, which attacks the white knight and uncovers an attack on the white queen, allows the gleeful reply 20 ♘d3, saving both pieces, when all Black has done is split up his own pawns.

Even if White didn't have the attacking response 20 ♘h5 it would have been strategically wrong to capture on e5 with the knight, as Black's whole idea is to exchange off the dark-squared bishops before snapping his jaws shut on the d4 square.

20   ♘e2

This shows the bankruptcy of White's strategy: the knight was doing nothing on f4 and has nothing better than to return to e2.

20   ...   ♝xb2

Meanwhile Adams continues with his clear, methodical plan. The black bishop that would have been obstructed after his next move is wisely swapped off.

21   ♕xb2

For just a second the white queen enjoys a long dark square diagonal aiming at g7 before the door closes with...

his knight on d4 and so prepares to undermine the beast with the advance b3-b4. Unfortunately this plan does do serious damage to the cohesion of the white queenside pawn structure without gaining any counterplay.

22   ...   ♝c8!

Adams responds immediately to the weakness created by White's last move. He reroutes the bishop to e6 to get it out of the way of an attack on the b file by the black rooks.

23   ♘c3

Although the white knight also has a central outpost the d4 and d5 squares will prove a world apart in value.

23   ...   ♝e6

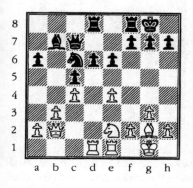

21   ...   e5!

Finally Adams decides the time is right to carry out this pawn advance. Good strategical play is often a question of timing – we all have good ideas, but the problem is playing them at the right time.

22   a3?

The idea is a noble one: White sees that Black is going to put

Black's bishop fits in nicely with the centre pawn structure. It attacks the c4 pawn and can eliminate by exchange the white knight if it ever becomes too annoying on d5. In contrast the white bishop is impeded by its own pawns and cannot return the compliment by getting rid of the black knight if it goes to d4.

24   ♘d5

This centralization is less impressive than it appears at first glance as it is making the d6 pawn safer through blocking the action of the rook on d1 and the black queen is merely being chased where she wants to go.

24 ... ♛b7

The first attack against what will prove a fatal flaw in White's pawn structure: the b3 pawn.

25 ♕c3

The queen steps out of a potential pin on the b file and introduces the idea of b3-b4 to get rid of the sickly backward pawn.

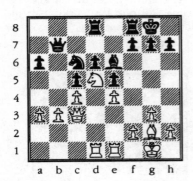

25 ... a5!

Black puts an immediate stop on the attempted break out.

26 ♖b1

McNab persists with the idea of freeing himself with b3-b4.

26 ... ♖b8

...and once again Adams is quick to prevent it.

27 h4

Having been frustrated on the queenside, White turns his attention to the other wing. He hopes he will get the chance to play ♔h2 and ♗h3, exchanging off his feeble bishop; or perhaps the advance of his h pawn to h5 and h6 will cause Black problems. But in reality these ideas are fruitless as the situation becomes desperate far too quickly on the queenside.

27 ... ♞d4

At long last the knight takes up residence on its wonderful outpost. In contrast to the white knight, which looks pretty but does nothing, it can join in a concerted attack on the b3 pawn.

28 ♖e3

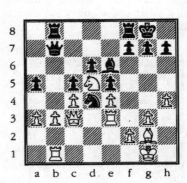

White now has his queen and rooks all tied down to the defence of b3. This is a very bad sign of the health of his position, as the heavy pieces should never just be used to defend pawns.

28 ... ♛a7

The black queen steps deftly aside to let the rooks play the role of assassins on the b file.

29 ♔h2

Even if you have an aversion to calculating variations, I'd like you to try to answer the following question by playing through the moves in your head. Have a go – your tactical ability is probably much better than you think it is!

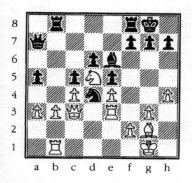

Here is the question. It appears that White can break out with 29 b4 when there are mass exchanges after 29...axb4 30 axb4 ♗xd5 31 cxd5 cxb4 32 ♖xb4 ♖xb4 33 ♕xb4. Now can you see a strong tactical move for Black? Try to visualize where the remaining white pieces are.

As a rule, sequences with captures are much easier to work out than variations with 'quiet' moves. Here there are no sidelines: Black takes, and White recaptures. Play is focused on just one square: b4. Furthermore, there are relatively few pieces on the board.

So did you find the killer move for Black? He can fork the rook and the queen by moving his knight to c2.

Without the aid of his tactical ability, Adams might have failed to keep up the positional pressure with 28...♕a7 as he might have thought that 29 b4 would then equalize.

You cannot hope to play good strategical chess unless you see tactical possibilities.

29 ... ♖b7

All as planned: the doubling of rooks on the b file will spell doom for the weakling on b3.

30 ♕d2

White prepares an ignominious retreat of the knight from d5.

30 ... ♖fb8

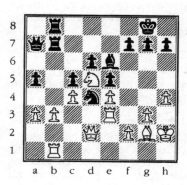

Black's position is a model of harmonious cooperation between the pieces. Every single piece is involved directly or indirectly in putting pressure on the queenside: the two rooks and knight attack b3, whilst the bishop is ready to eliminate the white knight if it tries to aid a break out with b3-b4. Meanwhile the queen supports the advance a5-a4 which would finally put the wretched b3 pawn out of its misery.

31 ♘c3

This move looks like a blunder but there was nothing to be done. If 31 ♕d1 then 31...a4 32 b4 ♗xd5 33 cxd5 cxb4 wins a pawn.

31 ... ♗xc4

Rather surprisingly it is the c4 pawn rather than the weakling on b3 which is the first to succumb to the pressure.

32 bxc4

As every black piece apart from the queen is attacking the b3 pawn this is the only way to avoid losing a second pawn.

32 ... ♖xb1

After the collapse of the barricade on b3 the invaders come crashing through.

33 ♘xb1

It has been a sad journey for the knight from its splendid outpost on d5 to its death on b1.

33 ... ♖xb1

After the multiple exchanges a black rook is left in control of the b file, so White doesn't even gain any respite from the pressure for his pawn.

34 ♖e1

White offers the exchange of rooks before Black has time to seize control of the seventh rank with 34...♕b6 and then 35...♖b2.

34 ... ♖b3!

As at move 17, Adams shows his mastery of the art of not exchanging pieces.

Black would have good winning chances a pawn up with a dominating knight against a bad bishop in the queen ending after 34...♖xe1 35 ♕xe1. However, Black's rook has the only open file on the whole board – so why on earth would he want to exchange it?

35 ♕g5

White finally shows some activity – a threat of mate in one!

35 ... ♕c7

Black deals with the threat and now White has to worry about his hanging pawn on a3.

36 ♖e3

Abject defence, but as long as Black doesn't have a passed pawn there is always a chance for White to fight on.

36 ... a4!

Now Adams is prepared to exchange rooks, but only on his terms: the creation of a gigantic passed pawn on b3.

37 ♕g4

White comes up with a desperate measure to bring his useless bishop into the game. He can't try 37 ♗f3 immediately as 37...♘xf3+ would force him to resign straight away.

37 ... h6!

In a winning position it is all too easy to rush things as the joy of victory is so tantalizingly close.

Here Adams realizes that Black has no need to hurry: his extra pawn and positional advantage isn't suddenly going to vanish if he takes time out for a belts and braces safety move on the kingside.

Therefore he makes an escape hole for his king which frees his queen from defensive duty watching out for back rank mates. He also rules out any white attempt to mate on g7 with the pawn advance h5-h6.

38 ♗f3

Finally the bishop emerges from its bunker, but the main battle has already been fought and lost in its absence.

38 ... ♘c2!

This attacks not only the white rook but also the a3 pawn a second time.

39 ♖xb3

The end is near as White is forced to concede a passed pawn.

39 ... axb3

Here we see that Adams was shrewd to wait a move with 37...h6 and let White carry out his plan of putting the bishop on f3: the bishop is now obstructing the path of the white queen to get back to d1 to fight the passed pawn.

40 ♗d1

The white bishop finally gets to grips with the black knight, but it hops back to total safety on d4 – a square where the bishop can never pursue it, even if the game lasted for another million moves.

40 ... ♘d4

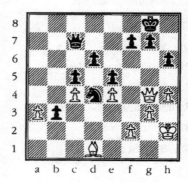

0-1

White resigned as there is no good answer to the threat of 41...b2 when the pawn queens. A fantastic lesson in the art of positional play from Adams.

Index to Openings

Index to Games

THE ART OF COUNTERATTACK: 1 D4 ♘F6

DELAYED DYNAMISM: THE FLANK OPENINGS